THE GLORY OF THEIR TIMES

Crossing the Colour Line in Rugby League

THE GLORY OF THEIR TIMES

Crossing the Colour Line in Rugby League

Editors
Phil Melling and Tony Collins

Vertical Editions

First published in the United Kingdom in 2004 by Vertical Editions, 7 Bell Busk, Skipton North Yorkshire BD23 4DT

Copy Editor, Valerie Rice

ISBN 1-904091-07-5

Jacket design and typeset by HBA, York

Printed and bound by the Cromwell Press, Trowbridge

Contents

Acknowledgements

This book would not have been possible without the work of the contributors and those who also provided photographs, information and inspiration. They include Mark Holden, Graham Morris, Colin Tatz, Alex Givvons jnr, Trevor Givvons, John Blair, Jean Brooks, Brian Walker, Des McKeown, Fred Laughton, Mick Harrop, Roger Halstead, Gerard Platt, Rodney Hinds, Shaun Edwards, David Lawrenson, Doug Laughton, Geoff Strange, Shane Roiser, Ayoola Erinle, Sig Kasatkin, Tony Rea, Marjorie Soloman-Philip, Andy Howard, Stefan Hull, Jonathan Davies, Raymond Fletcher and Trevor Smith.

Foreword by Billy Boston

Rugby League was made for me. I slotted right in. Mind you, if I'd been Joe Taylor I wouldn't have paid £3000 for a nineteen-year-old. I was doing all right but I hadn't played in any big games.

I was one of the first coloured players to come to Wigan and I was scared to death. Coming down Standishgate for my first game I could see this picture inside the bus. It said underneath: 'Billy Boston plays today.' I thought to myself: how the hell do they know who I am?

They obviously did. After that game I knew it was right. Wigan always knew where to play me. After five games I went to Australia. It was there I broke the try-scoring record and I never looked back.

Wiganers have always treated me like royalty. I'd do exactly the same again. I married the right girl and I played at the right club. I don't think life gets any better.

I didn't find rugby league hard but it was more enjoyable than union. Before I signed in 1953 I scored six tries in the Army Cup Final at Aldershot. On other days I could have had a smoke.

Rugby league was different to union. For one thing you had centre play of the highest quality. Lads with vision like Ernie Ashcroft and Jackie Broome. When I was young Jackie brought me on at Wigan. He never gave me a bad ball. He showed me how to take my chances.

If you came from Wales you got looked after. Some of the lads found it tough but as far as I can tell players who were coloured like Johnny Freeman, Colin Dixon and Alec Givvons were treated well. Many a time I stayed with Johnny when we played at Halifax. He'd lived behind me in Tiger Bay and all the girls thought he was something. Johnny was a dancer and could have gone pro, but he had this stutter. During the war the houses got bombed and he came outside and stepped on a body. After that Johnny was timid but rugby league brought him out.

The same was true of Levula and McArthur. I never heard anyone say a bad word about the colour of their skin.

It's no good writing a book about rugby league and talking about the colour bar. In this game there isn't one. If I got insulted on the field, and that was rare, people came up and apologised after. It was heat of the moment.

They'd belt you of course. Mick Sullivan did me once when I was on the floor. Cut me round the mouth. I jumped up and said to Eric Ashton: 'Who the hell was that?'

'Need you ask?' said Eric. And opposite, there's Mick Sullivan looking at the sky and doing his bird impressions, hands behind his back.

'Are we playing you again this season?' I said.

'Away,' replied Sully.

'Well make a note in your diary,' I said. 'I'll be coming to find you.' And I did.

In the bar after, I put my thumb up. 'One all,' I said.

'One all it is,' answered Sully and he bought me a pint. That's how it was. I wouldn't have wanted it any different.

Billy Boston
January 2004

Introduction

In September 1895, just days after the split from rugby union, a supporter of the new Northern Union wrote to the *Yorkshire Post*: 'I say with Mark Twain's bold, bad boy, that we glory in the sentence of outlawry pronounced on us, as freeing us from the tyrannical bondage of the English union, and we breathe pure air in being freed from the stifling atmosphere of deceit in which we previously existed.'

This type of support for the split was widespread across the north of England. But it was the reference to 'Mark Twain's bold, bad boy' that made the letter remarkable. For the bold, bad boy was Huckleberry Finn, Mark Twain's most famous literary character, and the reason for Huck's 'badness' was the fact that he had made friends with Jim, a young runaway black slave. Twain's novel, published in 1885, was the classic anti-slavery, anti-racist book of the age.

Then, as today, many people in rugby league shared Huck's defiance towards authority and his belief in doing the right thing whatever the consequences. And this is one of the reasons why rugby league is almost unique in British sport in having a proud record of black players, captains and coaches at its highest levels for the best part of a century. This book is part biography, part history and part tribute to just some of them and their achievements.

The achievements of black players in rugby league is one of the great untold stories in British sport. Black players first played professional rugby league before the First World War, appeared at international level in the 1930s and from the 1950s were such a common sight on rugby league pitches that it almost ceased to be a matter for comment. Certainly in comparison to soccer, the contrast is striking. Whereas Wales' George Bennett became the first black player to appear in international rugby league in 1935, followed in 1937 by England's Jimmy Cumberbatch, it wasn't until 1979 that Viv Anderson became the first black player to play soccer for England. And although Clive Sullivan first captained the British rugby league side in 1972, it wasn't until 1993 that Paul Ince became the first black player to captain the England soccer team.

Even today no top-flight British soccer club has appointed a black British person to the role of manager, almost half a century after Roy Francis, and many others in his wake, achieved the feat in league. Ellery Hanley's achievement of becoming the national coach of the Great Britain rugby league side in 1994 is even less likely to be emulated in any of the other football codes. Rugby union in England and Wales fares no better than soccer. Aside from the isolated example of James Peters in 1906, no black player appeared in an England rugby union national side until Chris Oti in 1988. Similarly, despite numerous black players appearing in the Welsh national rugby league team, no black player was selected to play for the Welsh rugby union side until Glen Webbe in 1986. Even in boxing, traditionally a sport with a strong black presence, black boxers were banned from competing for British boxing titles from 1909 until 1946.

In contrast, the welcome of dark-skinned players to rugby in the north of England can be traced to before the 1895 split. In 1888 the predominantly Maori New Zealand Native rugby team toured Britain. Unlike in the south, where the welcome was lukewarm to say the least, their popularity in the north meant that many of the clubs which were to join the Northern Union arranged a second tour match with them. The sports journalists of the north were so supportive that the tourists' manager Thomas Eyton, said that they were 'almost members of the Maori Brotherhood'.

But it wasn't until 1912 that rugby league had its first black player, when Hunslet signed Lucius Banks. His story would have been exceptional regardless of the colour of his skin. He was an American soldier who was spotted as an American football quarterback in New York by an ex-member of Hunslet's management committee. The club bought him out of the US Army and he made his debut on 27 January 1912, scoring a try in a match against York. But the transition from gridiron to league was always going to be tough – playing on the wing he scored four tries in his first three games but the strength of Hunslet's back division limited his opportunities. An attempt to develop his skills as a stand-off was unsuccessful and he faded from the scene in 1913.

As Banks' rugby league career faded, Barrow signed the first black Englishman to play the game, James 'Jimmy' Peters, a dock worker from Plymouth. Unlike Banks, Peters had a rugby pedigree. He was the lynchpin of the all-conquering Devon county rugby union side and had played five times at stand-off for England at union between 1906 and 1908. In 1912 he had been one of the players involved in the attempt to establish league in the South-West. In his early thirties when he switched to league, Peters was past his best by the time he moved north and spent most of his time in Barrow's 'A' team before moving in 1914 to St Helens, where his career was ended by the onset of the First World War.

By the 1930s black players had become well established in league. Alec Givvons at Oldham, George Bennett at Wigan, Jimmy Cumberbatch at Broughton Rangers and his brother Val at Barrow were among the stars of the day. Bennett, a Welsh stand-off who signed for Wigan from Weston-super-Mare rugby union, eventually made 237 appearances for the club and joined the elite band of players who have scored over 100 tries in cherry and white. When he made his debut for Wales against France in 1935, he cleared the way for dozens of black players to play league at the highest level.

Two years later, he was followed by the first black England player, Jimmy Cumberbatch, who marked his debut against France with two tries. Liverpool-born Jimmy and his brother Val, who also made a try-scoring England debut against France in 1938, were two of the best wingers of the 1930s. In 1936 Jimmy was on the verge of being selected for that year's Lions' tour down under and even played in two trial matches, but had the misfortune to be playing at the same time as Alan Edwards, Stan Brogden, Jack Morley and Barney Hudson, four players out of the very top drawer of wingers. Both Jimmy and Val played for Lancashire and even today Val is regarded as one of the greatest wingers ever to grace Craven Park. Given the relative lack of research that has been done on the game during this period, it is safe to assume that there were other black players at this time who didn't reach the heights of the Cumberbatch brothers; for example, Dewsbury's Willie Hall, who signed for the club from Coventry rugby union in 1931 but whose career was cut short eighteen months later by injury.

These players helped to establish league's tradition of openness to players from diverse backgrounds which flourished after the Second World War, many of whom are profiled in this book. This inclusivity wasn't restricted to black British players; the game also had a place for numerous Maori players, Australian aboriginal players and Jewish players. And, unlike most British sports at the time, many rugby league supporters understood the importance of racial equality and integration. When Cec Thompson was overlooked by selectors for the Great Britain team in the early 1950s, Eddie Waring warned about the dangers of racism in selection policy. In 1957, in response to RFL secretary Bill Fallowfield's plan to take the Great Britain team to South Africa after that year's World Cup, the *Rugby League Gazette* launched a campaign to stop the sport becoming involved with the racist apartheid regime, possibly the first campaign against sporting links with apartheid.

This isn't to ignore the real problems that have existed with racism in the game. Sadly Fallowfield did take the Lions to South Africa in 1957. Racial abuse on and off the pitch has continued to be a problem, although never remotely on the same scale as in soccer, and there is still a tendency for black players to be stereotyped as being fast or strong and be selected on the wing or in the second-row, rather than in the decision-making positions in the half-backs or as hooker. In 2000 Leeds winger Paul Sterling accused the club of racial discrimination and took his case to a tribunal, where it became clear that there were still some racist attitudes behind the scenes. In the 1980s it also became apparent that the game was doing little, if anything, to attract the Asian communities which had settled in traditional league supporting areas such as Bradford, Halifax and Keighley. To some extent, the game's earlier history of black players had led to complacency when it came to integrating new cultures. Even so, Ikram Butt remains one of the few British Asian athletes to have represented England at any sport.

The players featured here, such as Ikram, are just some of the more colourful players who have contributed to rugby league. Not all of these are stars and celebrities on the rugby field. We remember players like 'Rocket' Ronnie Braithwaite from Wigan, ten years in the 'A' team at Central Park. Or David Nelson from the Queens amateur club in Leeds, who played for Sheffield and Castleford in the 1980s and 90s. Similar players exist at every level of our game from students like Paul Singh, the Sikh prop forward who blazed a trail at Swansea University in the 1970s; to Green Vigo, the fisherman from Saldanha Bay, who thrilled the crowds on the bleakest of days at Central Park. The contribution to rugby league by players of colour, large and small, has been immense. It is over 90 years since Lucius Banks first turned out at Parkside, and today we can see the emergence of yet another new generation of black players, such as Leon Pryce, Waine Pryce, Mark Calderwood and Ryan Bailey.

These players demonstrate how league's tradition of racial integration is continuing. Like the black American culture that created jazz and the eastern European Jewish culture that created Yiddish theatre and music, rugby league is a culture that was born in opposition to the status quo. The game has survived despite continual attempts to undermine or suppress it. And a key strength in that resistance has been its ability to draw in others who also felt a sense of alienation from the established order. Black South Africans, Australians and Welshmen have come to play rugby league because it offered opportunities denied them because of racism in their own countries.

It is impossible to think about the history of rugby league without thinking of black players. Where would wing play be without Boston? What would coaching be like without Francis? How much further behind Australia would the British game be without the consummate professionalism of Hanley? To ask these questions is to underscore the fact that the game's history has been made by black and white players alike.

It is to those players, who have helped to create a game which, despite its problems, points the way towards complete racial equality and a truly human society, that this book is dedicated.

1

ALEX GIVVONS
Michael Turner

Who's Alex Givvons?

Young Alex? He's a scrum-half just come up from't valleys to play for Owdham.

Alex? He's going great guns for the Roughyeds and he's just been picked for Wales.

Alex? You know Alex! Coloured loose forward, just come back to 'sheddings from Fartown.

Alex? He's trainer for the 'A' team. He has been for years. Lives on Watersheddings Street.

Owd Alex? He's kitman for the Roughyeds or Bears or whatever you call 'em now. I've heard he was a cracking player too. Welsh international you know!

There you have it. Condensed and to the point. Rather like the man himself. A minimum of fuss was fine with Alex. A man well known and respected in the local community. Alex was a player for Oldham and Huddersfield. A good player! A Welsh international and a member of the British rugby league teams that toured France in the 1930s. He also served the Oldham club in coaching and backroom capacities and he was coloured – black – Afro-Caribbean, call it what you will but to the people of Oldham, Huddersfield and wherever rugby league was played, Alex was first and foremost a rugby man. His ethnic origins were undeniably there for all to see but it was just another fact about the man and so, in my imaginary questionnaire through the ages, it is included where it deserves to be, as just another fact about this remarkable character.

Alex wasn't one for over-elaboration. Well at least not in my conversations with him. Ever since I began to watch Oldham in the early 1960s, Alex seemed to be always on the scene. A constant presence at his beloved Watersheddings. A staunch traditionalist, he cared little for the modern Australian terminology that now dominates the media reporting of the greatest game. Softly spoken, with just a trace of Lancashire seeping into his Welsh accent, the conversations I shared with him were usually brief but he was always ready to offer a forthright opinion on any facet of Rugby league. One thing I would like to point out from the outset is that to the vast majority of Oldhamers Alex's name was, and still is, always pronounced Alec.

Oldham FC, as the club was known in Alex's days, had long been associated with bringing in players from all over the rugby playing world. Even in the so-called amateur pre-Northern Union days the Roughyeds had managed to lure top calibre Welshmen up to the heartland of 'King Cotton' country. David Gwynne and Bill McCutcheon both won international honours for the principality while at Watersheddings, the latter being a member of the first Welsh team to win the coveted Triple Crown. At the dawn of the professional era Oldham were right up there as one of the premier clubs – and no corner of the British Isles was ignored in their quest to assemble a match-winning combination.

By the time of the momentous split in 1895, in addition to the by now steady flow of Welshmen, there were Scots, Cumbrians, West Countrymen, Midlanders and players from the North East all vying with the best of the domestic talent for the chance to don the red and white hooped jersey. Nor did the talent come only from these shores. (Some Irishmen too would come to try their luck at the professional game, although not until the 1920s.) The legendary New Zealand three-quarter and all-round athlete George (G.W.) Smith signed for Oldham at the conclusion of the 1907 'All Golds' tour, of which he had been vice captain. He was followed by a string of top notch Australian internationals – Tom McCabe, Sid Deane, E.A. Anlezark and last but not least the Farnsworth brothers: Billy and Viv. Those latter siblings being of aboriginal origin, Viv being particularly dark-skinned, probably qualified as the first ethnic players to represent Oldham. Not that it mattered then or any time since to the people here. Maryport or Newport, Waterhead or Wollongong, Royton or the Rhonda, made no difference – if you were good enough, you were good enough! Skin colour? I remember one old supporter telling me once that: 'After they'd been rolling around in't 'sheddings mud for eighty minutes they all looked like Alex.' That was about as much as the colour question mattered.

Alex was born of West Indian parents in Newport, South Wales on 2 November 1913. He began playing rugby at the age of nine at the Holy Cross school and soon so impressed the local selectors that he was picked for and subsequently became the captain of Monmouthshire school boys. His local contemporaries at schoolboy level included the ex-Rochdale Hornets and Oldham favourite, Mick Downey, and no less than the legend of Bradford, Wales and Great Britain, Trevor Foster. At the age of seventeen he was playing for the Pill Harriers (Newport) RUFC, who once boasted the services of the stalwart Oldham full-back, R.L. 'Dickie' Thomas. The usual next step for successful players at that level would be to go to Rodney Parade and play for Newport. However, as Alex himself once stated, 'They were good to me at Rodney Parade, but they always had a lot of college boys back during the holidays. I couldn't afford to socialise with them and Newport were always the most amateur of clubs in terms of what they would give a player in terms of financial help. I went to play for Cross Keys and had some marvellous times there'. Alex would always stress that his decision to leave Newport was in no way due to any race-related discrimination.

The connection with Oldham goes back to January 1933. A deputation from Watersheddings went down to look at, and eventually sign, Tommy Egan, a half-back playing for Aberavon. However, during their stay in Wales the Oldham men also took in a match involving Cross Keys and were immediately impressed by the form of their young scrum-half. On returning to Oldham the full committee were informed of the discovery and when it was learned that Huddersfield were also in the hunt for his signature, a decision was taken to offer terms and endeavour to secure the young Welshman's services without further delay. All went well and Alex duly signed for the Roughyeds on 19 January 1933.

The sporting headlines of the time were dominated by the notorious 'Bodyline' cricket test series being played out in Australia. However the capture of the two Welsh half-backs certainly merited some column inches of their own, which left Douglas Jardine, Harold Larwood and the entire 'leg theory' furore sharing the limelight with Messrs Givvons and Egan, and their eagerly anticipated debuts. So, keen to put a positive slant on the affair and the signing of Alex in particular, the local press included this quote from the old Welsh rugby union international Clem Lewis:

> 'One of the chief reasons I visited Cross Keys the other week was to see the dark skinned scrummage worker, Givvons. Let me say at the outset that on his form against Pontypool, he is the biggest discovery I have seen since the war! Powerfully built he has all the attributes of a great inside half. His service is a delight and he is a terror round the scrummages. I foresee Cross Keys recapturing their old glories and, chiefly, I see the eighteen year old Givvons becoming a much discussed figure in Welsh rugby.'

High praise indeed coming from the former Cambridge University player who was capped eleven times by Wales at stand-off half between 1912 and 1923 and, one would presume, a man who would know a good half-back when he saw one. The path Alex would soon choose to take however, prevented Lewis's prediction from coming to pass in so much as his impact on Welsh Rugby Union was limited to some few such enthusiastic reviews of a talented young player. There was no doubt that he did become a figure much discussed in the world of rugby, albeit in the cotton towns of Lancashire and the industrial centres of Yorkshire rather than in the valleys and coal mining communities of Wales.

Even with his outstanding reputation as a player, the move north must still have been a daunting step for the young man to take. He was still some ten months short of his twentieth birthday when he took the professional ticket and headed north. There was much poverty in South Wales at this time and despite being held in the highest regard at Cross Keys he decided the opportunity and lure of the Roughyed's offer was too good to miss. What an alien environment it must have seemed. A place where the inhabitants spoke in strange accents and for the most part earned their living in the magnificent cotton mills with the accompanying towering chimneys that dominated the East Lancashire skyline. Even the sport that had lured him away was different. Thirteen-a-side! No rushing around the line-outs or charging to be first to the ruck and maul. This was a more structured game, not that a quality half-back would not make an impression, just that the execution of the skills needed to be tailored to fit. The people of Oldham took to

Alex immediately, so much so that when he arrived at his first house on Sharples Hall Street, which was just a matter of yards from Watersheddings, a good number of the local residents were out on the street to greet him and wish him well.

Alex made his Oldham debut at Watersheddings against Barrow on 21 January 1933, just two days after signing for the Roughyeds. That match was lost by eight points to seven and so were the following two: the first at York and the next at home to Broughton Rangers. There was no doubt that the new acquisition was enthusiastic and keen to be involved in the play but it was soon evident that a spell in the 'A' team would not go amiss while the youngster grew more accustomed to the intricacies of the thirteen-a-side code. Five or six weeks in the reserves seemed to do the trick and for the last four matches of the season Alex was back as first choice scrum-half for the Oldham senior side. When asked if he ever thought he was singled out because of his colour, Alex said he thought he was sometimes a target but preferred to think it more because he was a dangerous player rather than any other reason. He particularly recalled receiving something of an aggressive reception on trips to Hull but was quick to add that once the game was over everyone in the East Riding and elsewhere was very friendly.

The following season was the most successful for Oldham during the period between the wars. The Lancashire Cup was won for the first time in nine years and the club reached the semi-final of the Challenge Cup. In the Lancashire Cup semi-final at Wigan, Alex was said to have varied his scrummage tactics judiciously and played a zealous game in the loose. However, a cruel turn of fate befell him when the week before the final Oldham were soundly beaten at Barrow in a match when Alex and his stand-off partner, fellow Welshman, Jack Reynolds, were continuously swapping between the two half-back positions. On the same day Tommy Egan played a blinder in the 'A' team with the end result that a new combination of Egan and Reynolds was preferred for the final against St Helens Recs at Swinton and Alex was in the reserves at Salford. I remember once asking Alex about that disappointment and he just shrugged his shoulders and said, 'Tommy played well in the 'A' team the week before and probably deserved his place. Anyway we won the Cup so everything turned out fine.'

In short, a minimum of fuss. Five months on from the Lancashire Cup triumph and Oldham were back at Station Road. The fine old Swinton stadium, as it was at the time, was chosen as a neutral venue.

This time it was in the Challenge Cup semi-final against Widnes and Alex was in the team. A tough, dour encounter was anticipated and duly came to pass. A hotly disputed try by the Chemics hooker, Ratcliffe, after eighteen minutes was the difference between the sides as Widnes triumphed by seven points to four. The entire second half was scoreless and Alex had to retire briefly from the fray after suffering a leg injury. He returned to the field obviously limping and in some discomfort but nevertheless he soldiered on and almost won the day as the *Oldham Chronicle* reported: 'the defences of both teams held out although the wounded Givvons almost bored his way through in the last minute before being stopped just short of the try line'.

In that 1933–34 season Oldham played an incredible forty-nine first-class fixtures with Alex in the first team for thirty-two of them. For all but one he was at the base of the scrum and a sign of things to come occurred in the match against London Highfield at Watersheddings on 27 January when Alex was selected at loose forward.

Over the next nine years Alex continued to endear himself to the rugby-loving public of Oldham. Initially still at scrum-half but eventually he went into the pack, occasionally in the second row but mostly at loose forward. Reports of his play would often mention his eagerness and agility. Indeed, in a great percentage of my personal collection of Oldham match photos from the 1930s, Alex is seen to be in the thick of the action. Here was a man who got involved. This ever-present enthusiasm combined with his increasing understanding of the thirteen-a-side game eventually caught the eye of the international selectors which resulted in him being capped by Wales – an honour of which Alex was immensely proud. His debut came on 7 November 1936 at Pontypridd when England were defeated by three points to two. This was the first match of the then existing tri-nation European Championship. A month later Wales wrapped up the tournament with a nine points to three victory against the French in Paris. He was partnered in both matches by his Oldham colleague and good friend Norman Pugh. All in all Alex won six Welsh caps finishing on the winning side on every occasion. He also twice toured France with a British Rugby league thirteen and was selected for a 1940 charity representative match that featured a team picked from the 1936 tourists against a side that was thought to represent what would form the basis of the cancelled 1940 tour squad. Alex was a great local celebrity and favourite of the press with the two evening papers the

Oldham Chronicle and the *Oldham Standard* always ready to feature Alex in articles, photographs or especially cartoon features. Notwithstanding the major distractions of the time it still came as something of a shock to all the Oldham supporters when in October 1942 Alex was transferred to Huddersfield for what the press described as a substantial fee considering it was a war-time transfer.

So it was over the hills and into Yorkshire for Alex where, as in Oldham before he became much beloved of the Fartown aficionados. Alex's sons, Alex junior and Trevor, both recall how fondly their father looked back on his time at Huddersfield. Amongst their souvenirs are a batch of letters from grateful Huddersfield fans sent to Alex on his return to Oldham in 1948, in which they thank him for his contribution to the cause of the claret and golds. During his time at Fartown Alex was a member of the team that won the Challenge Cup in 1945: a two-leg affair against Bradford in which Huddersfield prevailed by the staggeringly low aggregate score of thirteen points to nine.

There were opportunities for Alex to move into coaching with offers on the table from both Barrow and the newly formed Workington club. After much deliberation he decided that uprooting to Cumbria was not for him and his family, and so he stuck it out at Huddersfield. Just about the only shadow that was cast on the Huddersfield period of Alex's career was his omission from the team for the 1946 Championship Final against Wigan at Maine Road. He did play twenty-nine games in that season and therefore qualified for his Championship runners-up medal. In spite of that obvious disappointment Alex left Fartown having made 149 senior appearances which yielded him thirty-three tries and an accumulation of happy memories and mutual goodwill with the Huddersfield public.

After five years of sterling service to the Yorkshire outfit Alex came back to Oldham just before the 1948 Challenge Cup signing deadline and almost exactly fifteen years after he first signed for the Roughyeds. He held down the loose forward position for the rest of the season and opened up the next campaign at Keighley in the same position but that would be the last time Alex figured in the Oldham first team as he slotted into his newly appointed post as coach to the 'A' team. When asked about the players he rated as the best he played with or against, he had much regard for Jim Sullivan, Tommy McCue, Arthur Clues and gave particular high praise to Herbie Goodfellow, 'as good as any half-back I've seen in either code'. Alex concluded his Oldham career having scored fifty-four tries in 241 first team appearances.

Alex retired from the playing side of the professional game with the reputation of being a lively, consistent player right from his early days at scrum-half to his later career at loose forward. His six Welsh caps would perhaps have been supplemented by a tour call if it hadn't been for the war. The outbreak of war unfortunately coincided with Alex moving into the prime phase of his playing days. He also left the game having endeared himself to many of those who came his way on a personal level. A good example of the Givvons thoughtfulness and consideration was recently related to me by Gerard Platt, brother of the late Oldham three-quarter Lawrie. Apparently there was a knock at the Platt family home on the evening of Good Friday, 27 March 1948. The door was opened and who should be there but Alex. After the usual courtesies were exchanged Alex was shown into the house to deliver a message for young Lawrie: 'Early night tonight Lawrence! You're in the first team at Rochdale tomorrow.'

This was to be Lawrie's debut match for the Roughyeds and naturally the young centre was a little apprehensive about the game. However, from the moment the team boarded the bus Alex took it upon himself to reassure Lawrie and convey a few of the do's and don'ts of playing in the senior squad. Lawrie would go on to develop into a fine centre or wing three-quarter and be capped by Lancashire County. Gerard recalls that from that opening match, which by the way Oldham won by three points to two before a crowd in excess of 10,000, Lawrie was forever grateful to Alex for his assisted passage into the rigours of senior rugby league. Likewise, I recall a conversation with Ron Meredith, the stand-off half and captain of the crack Higginshaw (Oldham) amateur team of the late 1930s. He mentioned that during the war years Alex took him over to play a few games for Huddersfield and was very much the father figure looking after all the young lads who were guesting at Fartown.

So after his playing days were over Alex was appointed to be in charge of the Oldham 'A' team, a position he would hold on and off for twenty years. Dealing with the young players was something he really enjoyed and would speak of them as his 'stars'. It would seem that they also enjoyed working with him for there are printed accounts of the gratitude and appreciation of Alex's methods from Oldham tourists Terry O'Grady and Frank Pitchford who both came under his wing when joining the club as fresh-faced youngsters. O'Grady in particular related how Alex would stress the need to always give of their best no matter what the perceived importance of the given match. He was soon instrumental in persuading his cousin Trevor Williams to come north and try his luck with the Roughyeds. A centre who also came from Cross Keys he later went to play for Belle Vue Rangers. One thing Alex did not like was when a late withdrawal from the senior side meant one of his reserves was called into the first team. Not that he didn't want one of his lads to get a chance with the seniors. That, after all, was what the 'A' team players were all longing to happen. No, it was when he had to subsequently ask one of the local amateur sides to provide personnel to fill the gap. He didn't like to think he was disrupting another team's plans.

For many hopeful young rugby players in Oldham, Alex was the first contact with the professional club. He ran training and coaching sessions for aspiring teenagers. Des McKeown, the local former Oldham forward, was one such player and he recalls Alex well:

> 'He was a courteous almost fatherly man who nevertheless demanded very high standards. During training sessions he would gently enquire of individuals if they were tired. If there was a negative reply Alex would blast "Then why are you standing around?" The effect was always a dramatic increase in effort and perseverance.'

Des went on to say that Alex would set himself up as a human tackling bag and would only be satisfied when one of his charges had crashed him down with a full-blooded bone cruncher. It would be wrong to give the impression that it was always 'wine and roses' between Alex and the Watersheddings hierarchy. There were occasional rifts and during one such occurrence. when Alex wasn't on the Oldham staff, he intercepted a still teenage Des on the way to a match. He then proceeded to suggest some techniques for breaking away from the scrum using two parked cars as opposing packs of forwards. Des went on to win a Lancashire Cup winners' medal when he played in the 1958 final against St Helens and goes on record to give Alex credit for helping himself and other stars of that fabulous Oldham side of the late 1950s realise their true potential.

In later life Alex went on to be the kit man where he would ensure that everything was done by the book. Woe betide any individual who tried to make off with an item of kit! To Alex the privacy of the dressing room was sacrosanct and many a visiting official or pressman was barred access with a polite but firm. 'Sorry son. You can't come in hee-ur.' Like anything else when given a task to do, he liked to do it right. Yet still he regained a caring attitude. After a string of vehicle break-ins on the Oldham RL car park he advised the video commentator, Fred Laughton, and his camera man, to park in front of his house on Watersheddings Street where their car would have extra security.

Alex had come a long way since that step into the unknown when making the trip north in the cold January of 1933. More than half a century later Alex could be seen in the team group on the pitch at Old Trafford after the club defeated Featherstone in the Second Division Premiership Final in 1988 – a rare occasion when he basked in some of the club's limelight. Five years further on he was still on the back room staff and in 1995 Alex was guest of honour when he performed the opening ceremony at the Oldham RL Hall of Fame. He did express some regret at the way the game he loved had evolved in the Super League era. He admired the fitness levels of the modern players but viewed them more as athletes, even gladiators, rather than the purist skills of the old school. Whether they were half-back, wingman, prop, loose forward or whatever, Alex liked to think that in his day, all positions possessed their own level of expertise.

Until shortly before he died Alex lived on Watersheddings Street (where else?) and as the memory of the old ground fades into the history books it is comforting to know that one of the club's greatest servants will be ever remembered in the area, due to the fact that part of the new housing development that now stands on the Watersheddings site is called Givvons Fold. This honour is usually only bestowed after the death of the person concerned and the fact that Alex lived to see the deed come to pass is a reflection of the affection and esteem in which he was held in the borough of Oldham. I have no doubt that there would have been joy mingled with sorrow at the announcement with Alex having preferred for his old stomping ground still to be in existence.

The death of Alex Givvons on 14 June 2002 took away one of the grand elder statesmen of the Oldham rugby league fraternity and although their number will be much sadder for the loss, he has left behind a legacy of fine example and an extended backlog of rugby memories. In preparing this chapter I interviewed a number of people who knew this remarkable man and if I had to say what was the most common adjective related to him it would be 'Alex Givvons. He was a gentleman.'

2

GEORGE NEPIA
Peter Lush

One of the reasons that it is so difficult to write good fiction about sport is that the truth is so often more interesting. The life of George Nepia, arguably New Zealand's greatest rugby player, and a great sportsman, has more than enough in it to fill a couple of lengthy novels.

Nepia only played rugby league for four years. On my office wall is a photo of him with Jim Sullivan, taken after his debut for Streatham & Mitcham against Wigan on 14 December 1935, in front of a 15,000 crowd. He had arrived in London three days earlier, after a six-week boat journey from New Zealand, and had never played rugby league before. The two great full-backs are pictured shaking hands after an epic clash. The newspaper headlines said that Nepia had performed better on the day, although Wigan had won the match 11-3.

My interest in George Nepia began in 1994 when, with my co-author Dave Farrar, we were doing the research for our first book, *Touch and Go – a history of professional rugby league in London*. We had a copy of Robert Gate's obituary of Nepia, who died in 1986, headed 'A King of all Maoridom' – and from this account we could see what a significant signing he had been for the new Streatham & Mitcham team. Three years later, frustratingly after *Touch and Go* had been published, while browsing in one of the many second-hand bookshops in Hay on Wye, I came across a copy of his autobiography, *I, George Nepia*, which he wrote in 1963 with Terry McLean. It was priced at £4.50; a great bargain as I have seen it on sale for £15 to £20.

I was fascinated by his story, and in 2001, contacted Sir Terry McLean, and with his collaboration, and the support of Oma Nepia, George Nepia's son, we published a new edition of the book, bringing the story up to date. It also meant we could tell the story of his rugby league career in far more detail than in the original book, which understandably focused mainly on his union days.

Relations between the different racial groups in New Zealand, from an outsider's viewpoint, seem to have been far better than in many other parts of the British Empire. Certainly, Nepia's Maori roots and community were clearly very important to him. But Maori players were accepted in both codes of rugby, and, except when the question of playing against, or touring South Africa arose, race does not seem to have been a major issue. Maori league sides had toured Australia in 1908, 1909 and 1922 and the game's roots in the Maori community were underlined with the formation of the Maori Rugby League Board of Control in 1937.

Nepia was born in 1905, and was raised by his grandmother. He had a tough time growing up, and his confidence in playing rugby developed slowly. He worked as a farmhand and building railways to save money to go to college when he was 16. But on the way to Te Aute College he was travelling with a friend who attended the Maori Agricultural College, and on a whim he decided to go with his friend, and attend that college. The college principal accepted him as a student. This was in 1921.

Three years later, having developed his rugby under college coach Elder Moser, he was selected for the All Blacks 1924 tour of Great Britain and France. In another of those 'stranger than fiction' moments, it was Sir Terry McLean's father who selected him for his first representative match. At college, he developed his kicking game, spending many hours practising, and his tackling. Both these were key parts of his game in both codes. He describes in *I, George Nepia* the practice in developing a 'spiral' (spinning) kick with both feet. His handling was top class, as was his positional play. He had every attribute needed by a full-back in either code.

His start in representative rugby union came with Hawke's Bay in the Ranfurly Shield. Hawke's Bay dominated the competition until 1926, a huge achievement against the bigger city teams. With fellow student Lui Paewai, he was selected for a New Zealand Maori team to tour Australia. But the college principal decided he was too young to go and refused him permission. It was in 1923 when he was advised to try the full-back position rather than five-eighth. In 1924, he was chosen for the trial matches for the great tour, and when the team was announced, he was the first one named for the squad.

The record of the 1924-25 New Zealand tourists has been well documented elsewhere. The 'Invincibles' won every match, and Nepia played full-back in every game – as a 19-year-old with little experience in that position. The victories included revenge for the 1905 All Black tourists' defeat in Wales, and a win in the final match in Great Britain at Twickenham against England, despite Cyril Brownlie being sent off after 10 minutes.

Naturally, Nepia's prowess attracted the attention of rugby league scouts. Certainly offers were made, but Nepia had no need to turn professional at that time, and returned to New Zealand to get married in 1926, continue his rugby union career, and develop his life as a farmer. One of the great 'what ifs' on Nepia and rugby league is what would have happened if he had taken one of the offers to stay in England? Given his prowess in the game ten years later, undoubtedly he could have become a leading force in the game for a decade.

In *I, George Nepia*, he recalls his anger when, in 1921, after watching the first South African union tourists to New Zealand narrowly beat a Maori team, a South African journalist reporting home wrote of his disgust at 'Europeans frantically cheering on a band of coloured men to defeat members of our own race'. Nepia wrote that to the Maoris this reference was grossly insulting, and that 'the hurt which was then done has never been forgotten and never quite forgiven'.

In 1927, the issue arose again, when Nepia and fellow Maori, Jimmy Mill, were deliberately left out of the touring party to go to South Africa on racial grounds. This decision was not a great surprise to them, but Nepia wrote that 'Most of all, perhaps, we were saddened, disappointed and humiliated by the attitude of the body, namely the New Zealand Rugby Union, which purported to be our guide, philosopher and friend'. He outlined the role the Maori community had played in rugby union in New Zealand, and that the NZRU Board's 'obligation' to their South African hosts 'overlooked a much older, closer obligation to Maori Rugby and to the Maori race as a whole'.

Nepia recalls how he marched against apartheid in 1960, when the South African tourists were again visiting New Zealand. This issue continued to divide New Zealand until the end of apartheid.

It is indeed ironic that in early 1986, a few months before his death, Nepia was honoured by the South African Rugby Union for his achievements in the game, and made an honorary vice-president. The Board's vote for this was unanimous. Of course, he was the first non-white to receive such an honour. It is a pity their forbears did not allow him and his fellow Maori players to play in their country.

By the early 1930s, Nepia's rugby union career was winding down. He played against the British Lions in 1930, but was more concerned about keeping his farm afloat during the recession. Some people claim he switched to rugby league because he was not selected for the 1935 All Blacks tour to Great Britain. He denies this, saying he had not played representative rugby for five years. But he was selected for the New Zealand Maoris' tour of Australia. Such was the state of his finances and farming business that one of the Maori community leaders lent him money to buy a suit of clothes for the tour. More significantly for rugby league, Nepia was angry that his cousin, Charlie Smith, was not selected for the All Blacks, and instead joined him on the Maori tour.

Ever since 1895, rugby league had been grappling with the problem of how to develop outside its northern heartlands. Before the First World War, a base had been established in Wales, which then collapsed and was briefly revived in the 1920s, and international matches had been taken to various areas to try to encourage interest By the early 1930s, although the game had grown numerically and the Challenge Cup Final was now played at Wembley, sustained development geographically was still absent.

Ironically, it was the growth of another sport, greyhound racing, which gave a temporary boost to geographical expansion in rugby league. Entrepreneurs were building stadiums to accommodate this new sport, which was often opposed by the church and others concerned about the growth of gambling. Using the stadiums for rugby league could attract more income, and help establish a stadium, which could then apply for a greyhound racing licence.

The first attempt in London to establish the game was at the White City, a great bowl of a stadium owned by the Greyhound Racing Association in Shepherd's Bush in west London. The Wigan Highfield club was losing money consistently, overshadowed by their more glamorous neighbours at Central Park, and in 1933–34 moved down to London, and played as London Highfield, staging matches under floodlights on Wednesday evenings. The players were based in Wigan, and after home games got the midnight train from Euston back home to return to their jobs in the mines and factories the next morning.

This venture started well, but the crowds dropped off, and the club returned north after only one season, to have a chequered career in and around Liverpool until suddenly pulling out of the League in the late 1990s.

In 1934, Sydney Parkes, a London entrepreneur, wrote to the Rugby League enquiring about entering two teams in their competition – one in west London in Park Royal: Acton & Willesden and one in south London: Streatham & Mitcham. Both would play at new stadiums, with the prospect of greyhound racing coming on the scene.

Surprisingly, given the parochial nature of some of their officials, the League accepted his proposals. The RFL Secretary, John Wilson, had been a longstanding advocate of expansion, had encouraged development in Wales, and played a role in moving the Challenge Cup Final to Wembley. Unlike London Highfield, the matches were to be played on Saturday afternoons, which meant that they clashed with association football and rugby union.

Inevitably, given the lack of any base for rugby league in the south, most of the players were recruited from elsewhere, a theme that has been common throughout the history of league in the capital up to today. Some were recruited from the north, some, particularly for Acton & Willesden, from Welsh rugby union, and some from overseas.

An agent approached Charlie Smith to join Streatham & Mitcham. Disillusioned after being omitted from the 1935 All Blacks, and supported by Nepia, he signed for £100, and went on to have a distinguished career in league. He was not the first Maori to play in British rugby league though. Burly forward Len Mason signed for Wigan following the 1926 Kiwi tour and picked up a winners' medal for the club at the first Wembley Challenge Cup Final.

Nepia, jokingly, told his cousin to say that he would play league as well. He recalls that he forgot about his flippant comment until a telegraph boy arrived with a telegram offering him the chance to play league in England. He replied that he would come – for £500, a huge sum in those days, and expected not to hear any more. Two days later, he was shocked to find his offer accepted. After two days' discussion with his wife, he decided to take the offer, and solve his financial problems. In *I, George Nepia*, he says that if the Labour government had come to power in 1934, instead of 1935, with their guaranteed price scheme for butterfat, he would not have changed codes, and league would never have experienced Nepia's play at full-back.

I, George Nepia is primarily a rugby union book, written at a time when there was a huge gulf between the two codes. In it, while he stresses the business side of league and the necessity to be professional, he says he found league 'fast and exhilarating' to play. He said the tackling was tough, but the standard of play very high. He found he had to adjust his kicking game, but in open play could take advantage of the greater amount of space available.

However, on his departure from New Zealand in 1935, he had said that 'I am now in the great rugby league game and feel happier for it. My opinion is that it has great possibilities among the Maori people…' He also told the reporter that he hoped to make good in England, both as a Maori and a New Zealander, and had had a desire to play league for several years.

While Nepia said he had no regrets about leaving rugby union, it is probably fair to say that his primary reasons for changing codes were economic, particularly as it meant a two-year period away from his family. He was given a great send-off for the long trip to London.

Nepia was the fourth New Zealander to be signed by Streatham & Mitcham. As well as Charlie Smith, George Harrison and Jack McDonald, both 1935 Maori union tourists to Australia, had signed and 1934 All Black Eddie Holder.

Nowadays, the trip from 'down under to London' can be made in twenty-four hours. In the modern incarnation of league in London, the London Broncos, Australian Dennis Moran scored a hat-trick one Sunday in 2003, flew home for a family funeral, flew back – arriving a few hours before kick-off for the next match the next Sunday – and scored another hat-trick. In Nepia's time, the trip took a more leisurely six weeks by ship.

Streatham's first match in London in September 1935 had attracted 24,000 fans to see Oldham win 10-5. However, the team was improving with the gradual arrival of reinforcements from New Zealand. Nepia, with typical modesty, says he 'acquitted myself tolerably well' against Wigan, although, the newspapers gave him stronger praise. However, one did report that Nepia had not quite grasped the rules of his new game, and the referee pointed out his mistakes on occasions.

After less than a month in south London, Nepia was made captain and manager of the team, a position he held until the following September. The team improved in the second half of the season, winning nine more matches, with Nepia kicking 29 goals. There can be little doubt that he was an attraction – ever the entrepreneur, Sydney

Parkes started asking clubs Streatham visited for 25 per cent of the gate receipts to guarantee Nepia's place in the team.

In the Challenge Cup, after an 18-5 victory at Hull KR, Streatham faced Leeds at Mitcham Stadium. Once again, Nepia faced another legendary full-back, Jim Brough, who he had played against on the 1924–25 tour. Leeds won 13-3, although reports said that both full-backs gave 'a fine exhibition'. Reports of Streatham & Mitcham's matches regularly highlighted Nepia's play and performances.

At the end of the season, Nepia was selected for a Dominions XIII to play France in Jean Galia's last match, and played there for a combined London team.

Parkes' team in west London had been losing money, and for the 1936–37 season, Acton & Willesden withdrew from the Rugby League. Parkes had also been granted a greyhound licence for that stadium, so he did not need League to keep the stadium in use until the dogs started running. But in June and July, the Surrey County Licensing Justices rejected his application for a greyhound licence for Mitcham Stadium despite a vote in a referendum of local residents in favour of greyhound racing. This decision was the first nail in the coffin of professional club rugby league in London. A club official was quoted as saying that the business was 'absolutely hopeless' without greyhound racing.

One activity for Nepia over the summer was playing baseball. The Streatham & Mitcham players had played the game during their training sessions, and Sydney Parkes entered a team in a new baseball league, although it does not seem to have been very successful. Nepia had played the game before in New Zealand, not America as was reported in some papers. Another new experience was playing in a charity Rugby Netball match. This curious hybrid sport was played on Clapham Common, and the Streatham players took part in a match to raise funds for a local hospital.

Ten players from Acton & Willesden joined Streatham & Mitcham for the new season. The other great 'what if' in Nepia's rugby league career is what would have happened if Parkes' greyhound licence application had been successful? He had invested a great deal in rugby league, and with the additional income from greyhound racing, his whole enterprise would have been more viable in the long term.

The reason this is of interest is that for the first few months of the season, Streatham & Mitcham were very successful. Two of the new recruits were Welshmen Dai Jenkins and Con Murphy, who went on to have distinguished careers in the game with Leeds. Both won international honours, and Jenkins was a 1946 British Lions tourist to Australia. Another team mate was George Banks, a prop-forward who played 246 games for Wigan after leaving London. Second-rower Ike Jones also went to Central Park, as did Holder and Harrison. If this team had been able to stay together, the history of league in London, and indeed in Great Britain, could have been very different.

The season started with two victories over Bramley, but then two defeats saw Nepia removed as manager. It was reported that the additional responsibility was affecting his play. He played a few games at centre at this time, and was reported as being 'a great success' against Hull KR, and 'outstanding' against fellow new boys Newcastle – another team based in a greyhound stadium – in a 39-3 victory. He scored all Streatham & Mitcham's points in a 19-12 defeat at Halifax. From early October, the team put together a run of seven consecutive victories, and were being talked of as possible champions.

In November, Rochdale Hornets came to Mitcham Stadium, accompanied by well-known popular singer Gracie Fields, who was from the Lancashire town. She kicked off the game, dressed in rugby kit, and received a great ovation. Her presence and the team's success saw the best attendance of the season, but there was also speculation in the press that the team would leave the league at the end of the season because of financial problems.

The unbeaten run ended at the beginning of December, with defeat at Barrow followed by a home loss against Swinton, when the local paper reported that 'Nepia and his men seemed off form'. Maybe speculation about the club's future was affecting them. Charlie Smith had been transferred to Halifax for a reported £1,250 at the beginning of December – a huge amount, which was bigger than the then world record of £1,200.

Nepia had been the team's driving force during the autumn. But Smith's departure was a sign that the end was in sight. The local paper blamed the public for not supporting the team, saying that 'Streatham play the very best type of rugby league football which would draw crowds of something like 20,000 every week were their headquarters in the north'.

Murphy and Jenkins joined Leeds for £600, and then just after Christmas, Nepia was sold to Halifax for £300. Streatham & Mitcham drifted on for a few more weeks, but in February 1937 withdrew from the league. It was to be 43 years before Harold Genders and Ernie Clay bought club rugby league back to London, when they launched Fulham in 1980.

Sydney Parkes never did get his greyhound licence for Mitcham Stadium. Some amateur rugby league was played there in the late 1940s, but it was demolished in 1956, although the main stand was sold to Leyton Orient FC, where it is still in use.

Nepia made his Halifax debut on New Year's Day 1937, in a 20-5 defeat against Leeds at Thrum Hall. However, a 16,500 crowd, paying £797, came to see Nepia's debut.

It was probably clear to all concerned that Nepia would only see out the rest of the season with Halifax. His rival for the full-back position was Hubert Lockwood, who despite being disappointed at losing his place at times, when interviewed by rugby league historian Robert Gate in 2001, at the age of 92, remembered Nepia fondly, and had found him a delightful companion.

Nepia's form with Halifax was uneven, partly because he played both in the centre and at full-back. Towards the end of the season, alternating with Lockwood, he even played a couple of games in the 'A' team, one of which attracted a 3,000 crowd. He played a couple of representative games before the end of the season: for a Dominions XIII in France, and a Northern Rugby league XIII in a match to raise funds for the struggling Newcastle club. His final game in England was a charity match in Whitehaven, against Barrow. During the second half, Lockwood and Nepia swapped positions, so the crowd could see Nepia play at full-back.

He only played 15 first team games for Halifax, scoring two tries and 14 goals. But by all accounts he had been popular with the club's supporters, and increased attendances when he played certainly covered his transfer fee. Apparently, Newcastle and Leigh were interested in signing him, but it was clear his future lay in New Zealand.

However, it may well have been the case that his success led other Maori players to see their future in England. After the end of the Second World War a number of outstanding Maori came to British clubs, including Kia Rika, and Johnny and Enoka MacDonald at Halifax, Hapi Nepia at Dewsbury and Johnny Wilson at Bramley. And of course, since the 1980s there has been a steady flow of Maori players who have graced the British game, ranging from the mercurial talents of Dave Watson to the blistering power of Dean Bell.

Like all of these players, Nepia seems to have been popular and well received by supporters during his time in England. Certainly he was an attraction and raised the attendances when he played. He does not mention any problems with racism in his book or other writing. Of course, the black community in London and the north would have been fairly small at this time, and it was the Jewish community who bore the brunt of racism in this period of Mosley's Blackshirts and the battle of Cable Street.

On his return to New Zealand, now aged thirty-two, Nepia played a few games of club rugby league, and was then selected for two international fixtures. The first was for the New Zealand Maoris against the Australian tourists, the Maori side winning 16-5; the second was a full international against Australia, which New Zealand won 16-15. In the first game, the New Zealand Herald reported that Nepia 'gave an exhibition of line kicking the equal of which has not been witnessed for some years'. The report also said that not a single attacker passed him during the match. In the second match, Nepia saved four certain tries, and 'his defence and positional play were very sound, his kicking brilliant and his tackling deadly'.

In 1938, Nepia played a few games for Manukau, a predominantly Maori side in the Auckland Rugby league. He was selected for the New Zealand squad to tour Australia, but did not tour, preferring to concentrate on work on his farm. It seemed that he had retired from the game, but in 1939 he returned to play virtually a full season for the club. Although now aged thirty-four, he featured regularly in the reports of the club's matches. He was also selected for trial matches for the forthcoming tour to Great Britain, but despite positive reports of his play, was not selected.

A couple of weeks before the tour party were due to depart, a businessman offered to pay for Nepia to join the party as player-coach, but the New Zealand Rugby League declined the offer. Maybe he was fortunate. With war clouds on the horizon, the tourists arrived in Great Britain, played one match before war was declared, and were given special permission to play another fixture before having to make a hazardous trip home by sea.

After the war, Nepia was reinstated into rugby union, the NZRFU granting an 'amnesty' because of the war to permit league professionals to rejoin the 'amateur' code. He played against his oldest son George in a match, and took up refereeing. *I, George Nepia* ends with him writing movingly about George being killed on active service in Malaya.

He continued to work on his farm, and later worked as a refrigeration engineer. In the mid-1970s, his wife Huinga died of cancer. With a friend, she had been out shopping, and saw a mobile x-ray caravan run by the Cancer Society. They thought they would give it a try; a few days later the hospital summoned her for further tests – within weeks she had died.

George suffered a heart attack, and moved to live on the coast. He died in August 1986. The *New Zealand Herald* reported the news on its front page: 'Tangi for Legendary Nepia'. The report of his funeral was headlined: 'A Giant Kauri has Fallen'. The Minister of Internal Affairs, Mr Tapsell, described him as a 'leader of all Maoridom' and said that all members of the Government were saddened at his passing. In London, *The Times* printed an obituary, recalling him as an 'outstanding' member of the 1924–25 tourists.

Four other events confirm the regard and respect for George Nepia. In 1982, he was the manager of the New Zealand Maori tourists to Great Britain. In their match at Swansea, he was walking along the front of the stand, unannounced, and the crowd recognised him and gave him a spontaneous standing ovation. He was feted everywhere in Wales on the trip. In 1990, he was remembered on a New Zealand stamp, one which supported children's health, something that would have pleased a man to whom his family were very important. And in writing the foreword for the new edition of *I, George Nepia* in November 2001, his son Oma revealed that Nepia had been recommended for a knighthood, but had turned the honour down.

But maybe the greatest tribute was the television programme *This is Your Life*, shown a few weeks before he died in 1986. The programme was scheduled to run for 30 minutes, and went out live. Unprecedentedly, it went on for 42 minutes, was watched by 1.2 million people – a third of the population – and was repeated the following week.

Of course, the producers were not to know that within three months, Nepia would be dead. To start the programme, he was met by presenter Bob Parker, and shocked him by claiming never to have heard of the programme. Parker asked him this again as they entered the studio, and Nepia admitted with a wry smile that he had heard of it.

After introductions of famous All Blacks in the audience, the programme showed wonderful old film of union matches from the 1920s and 1930s, combined with meeting fellow 1924–25 tourist Alan Robilliard and Welsh opponent from 1930 Herbert Bowcott. Sir Terry McLean was another honoured guest, saying that Nepia had 'balance, fabulous hands, a prodigious kick – all the qualities for a great rugby player'.

Just before the commercial break, Bob Parker revealed that Nepia had made a hit record in the early 1930s, *Beneath the Maori Moon*, and played it on an ancient 78rpm record. As Bob Parker recalls: 'As the record began to play it was clear it had a major emotional impact on George. He listened intently to the music and his voice from many years earlier. On the screen the network went into a commercial break, but in the studio all eyes in the audience stayed on George as he stood, at first mouthing, and then his voice growing in strength, fully singing along with the old 78 rpm recording. There were tears in all of our eyes as this great old man sang his heart out.' He later explained to Parker that he had always sung the song for his wife. The director had recorded Nepia singing the song, and it was shown in the repeat of the programme.

The rest of the programme was tributes from family and friends. One was from former neighbour and fellow farmer, Victor Rikard, who said that 'George, you were a good farmer' – from his point of view a greater compliment than anything that could be said about rugby.

Bob Scott, who had played league for Ponsonby before switching to union to become the only All-Black full-back to compare with Nepia, recalled how when he played rugby as a child, the argument was always who would 'be' George Nepia. While Scott was speaking, Nepia quietly whispered to Bob Parker 'this man was greater than I ever was'.

It was a truly moving programme. Unfortunately, rugby league, and being a dual international was not mentioned. Wouldn't it have been nice for Hubert Lockwood, or one of the other stars he played with at Streatham & Mitcham to have been invited as well?

The party after the show went on into the small hours. As Terry McLean put it, 'he displayed in *This is Your Life*, the special qualities which had placed him apart – the modesty, the bearing, the smile… the deeply lined face which was the book of his life. He had delivered, to a Pakeha's game, the outstanding qualities of Maori warriorhood – strength, pride, determination, craft, skill'.

More simply, Bob Scott summed up George Nepia during the programme: 'A great All Black full-back and also a great New Zealander'. And someone who also had the strength and skill to play rugby league at the top level.

3

ROY FRANCIS

Trevor Gibbons

When I was young I dreamed in black and white. The currency of my schoolboy dreams was the feared Hull FC team as the 1950s turned into the swinging 1960s – the team that Roy Francis built. Even now, four decades later, the names come tumbling out Tommy Harris, Mick Scott, the Drake twins and of course Johnny Whiteley.

I didn't even really see that famous team play but I was brought up on its exploits and the name Roy Francis was spoken in the reverential tones reserved for true rugby league heroes.

Then in my teenage years the excitement reached fever pitch, when the messiah returned to coach again at the Boulevard. 'Now we'll see some fireworks' said the older fans. I was there in the Threepenny Stand, jumping up and down with excitement, as the living legend emerged up the wooden steps from the dressing room onto the Boulevard's best stand side. The crowd rose as one in a standing ovation and I looked on in awe. As it happened this second spell at the Boulevard, following a controversial departure from Australia, was actually very short and swift.

Roy Francis was regarded as a god but the real man I saw that day was black, wiry, unassuming and in his fifties. To me he was an old man, how could he have inspired such anticipation and devotion? But I learnt why Roy Francis had burnt himself indelibly into the minds of rugby league supporters.

His later reputation really came from his coaching.

Go on try this test: Ask anyone who remembers Roy Francis what really made him stand out and they will say one of two things. 'Best coach we ever had' or 'He was twenty years ahead of his time'.

Now the constituent parts of a great coach are many: motivator, teacher, scientist, psychologist to name a few. Great coaches do not have to have been great players and great players do not necessarily make great coaches.

However, simply to regard Roy Francis as only a coach is wrong; although many of his playing exploits were over sixty years ago, his on-field skills form part of the story. Roy Francis was that rare commodity, both a great player and a great coach. And he was a valuable commodity, at the pinnacle of his coaching fame he was poached by the Australians as the world's best example of man-management.

It all started a long way from the beaches of Sydney and at some remove from the middens of northern England. Roy Francis was born in Brynmawr, Wales, in 1919 as the memories of the First World War and the fatal influenza pandemic, that killed far more people than the armed conflict, cast a long shadow over the year.

His rugby league career was mercurial, starting barely seventeen years later. It was in late 1936 that Francis signed for Wigan and few could guess his career in the greatest game would extend over forty years. Yet the cherry and whites nearly pulled off a notable double while capturing Roy. As Bradford's own Welsh legend, Trevor Foster, remembers vividly:

> 'My parents ran a pub in Newport called the Church House. There was a rugby league scout in the town and he approached my parents saying "I'd like Trevor to come to Wigan for trials, there's a chap in Brynmawr going up. The pair of them can meet at Newport station and travel together." '

The 'chap in Brynmawr' was of course Francis. Roy duly went up to Lancashire to try his hand at rugby league but Trevor Foster decided not to get on that particular train north and a playing career that could have started alongside Roy Francis eventually took a different turn. Not that Francis's league career got off to a glittering start – Roy was busy learning his trade, in the shade of legendary wingers like Alf Ellaby. Keeping a low profile, he played his early games mostly in Wigan's 'A' team with a sprinkling of first team appearances.

Then in late 1938 the Australian, Harry Sunderland, who was to become a legendary administrator, also joined the club set-up. Within three months of Sunderland being appointed manager Roy Francis had abruptly left Central Park.

For the first, but not last, time in Francis's career it appeared racism had reared its ugly head. Rumours abounded locally that the fact Francis was leaving Wigan was down to prejudice on the part of Sunderland.

At the time of the incident Francis maintained his own counsel and even close friends were not aware of the real background. It was only decades later in 1985 that Roy Francis made plain it was the colour of his skin that had had a bearing on leaving Wigan. The unpalatable, hidden background was finally explained in Francis's *Code 13* obituary written by rugby league historian Robert Gate.

So life was not always plain sailing for Francis, as a black man in his chosen career, and yet he made a virtue of never complaining publicly. In fact in public Roy Francis sometimes maintained that his colour could even be an advantage

In the mid-1970s Roy Francis was asked by journalist Raymond Fletcher if his colour had ever held him back. 'No' said Francis, 'far from it.' He went on to claim that during less racially diverse decades his colour had made him stand out. And as far as Francis was concerned standing out from the majority of players made him into a personality every time he stepped on the field.

So at the time of his surprisingly abrupt move from Wigan, Roy simply shrugged his shoulders in public and got on with the job, moving even further north to join Barrow in January 1939. Now, as the Second World War loomed, world events were about to also interrupt Francis's career.

During the war Roy joined the army physical training corps and as a sergeant instructor put his talents to rebuilding injured soldiers. It was a duty that fitted Roy, a professionally qualified masseur, perfectly. He began to meld physical exercise with an interest in the use of psychology and motivation to improve the men in his care both physically and mentally.

The war of course had a profound effect on millions of people but Francis also experienced a more unusual conversion. During 1943 the proud Welshman became English – at least in the eyes of the Army rugby union team. It might have taken the events of a bloody world war but the imperious rugby union decided conditions were such that it could deign to allow the usually tainted league players to try their hand at Forces rugby union. So it was that Roy Francis was selected at rugby union for both England and Wales!

Trevor Foster, by this time playing league at Bradford Northern, had met up again with his fellow Welshman in the army and he explains, 'A Major Sloane was the officer in charge of rugby union and he picked Roy on the wing for England. When Roy told him he was Welsh Sloane said "never mind" and that was that.'

Roy ended up playing rugby union seven times during the war for his 'adopted' England.

For one war-time England rugby union international against Scotland played at Leicester, Roy found that even gaining entry to the ground could be eventful. In his thesis *Rugby League in Wartime* John Schleppi describes how Roy arrived at the venue early in order to get some rest before kick-off. His entry was barred by two elderly gatemen who informed Francis that the turnstiles did not open until an hour before kick-off. Roy told them that he was going to the dressing room as an England Player. This explanation was met with disbelief and laughter as one jobsworth declared to the other, "Hey Charlie, THIS is playing for England."

It took a further ninety minutes and the assistance of the England manager for the black international player to gain his rightful entry.

In what was to be an eventful sporting war Roy Francis was also a player in both rugby league teams (Northern Command and Combined Services) that beat rugby union teams at their own game in 1943 and 1944.

People who properly understand the essential difference between the two games will not be surprised to learn that the rugby league side – stuffed full of famous players as it was – contained nobody of higher military rank than Sergeant. In comparison the union side contained a majority of officers. But shoulder pips were no defence out on the field and the enlisted men of rugby league were victorious in both tussles.

But it was in West Yorkshire playing rugby league, as a guest with the Dewsbury club, that Roy Francis hit a rich wartime vein of form that he was never to better.

His peacetime Barrow team was in suspension for the duration of the war so Roy, stationed in Halifax, was guesting for the heavy woollen side managed by a relatively unknown young man named Eddie Waring.

The flying Welshman (Roy was the holder of several army sprinting records) was leaving defenders trailing and crossing the whitewash for

Dewsbury regularly – scoring a try a game operating as a winger, centre or even stand-off. Roy posted 58 tries in 57 appearances wearing the red, black and amber. This lethal strike rate was a major feature in the two wartime Championships gained by Dewsbury in this fertile period.

Playing rugby league with such gusto was no easy matter. For one Dewsbury game Roy Francis was now rather further-flung, stationed at a camp on Salisbury Plain. John Schleppi outlined his journey. First he went to a local train station on foot, then a much delayed train took him to suburban London. There he took a motorbike and a lift on a truck to get to a main-line station for the train from London. The trek took almost fifteen hours just to reach Dewsbury.

With the ending of the war in 1945 and the gradual resumption of normal life, rugby league re-emerged and Roy Francis represented the country of his birth. He gained the first of his five Welsh league caps against France in Bordeaux.

A bigger trip than the hop to France was on the cards when the historic decision was taken to restore the war-interrupted Ashes tour to Australia. A Great Britain squad and a small party of journalists – including Eddie Waring in his reporting role – assembled on the aircraft carrier HMS Indomitable for the trip to the other side of the world. It was widely expected that the one man strike-force Francis would take one of the wingers' places available in the tour party. However, it was not to be. Post-war Australia operated a colour bar and it has been suspected that Francis's selection could have led to political repercussions. Roy, for whatever reason, was not selected in the team to make the trip. It was one of his greatest disappointments not to make the tour and his friend Trevor Foster knew he was 'broken hearted' by the decision.

That wrong was righted when in 1947, when safely on home soil, Roy was finally selected for Great Britain. As a Barrow player he was selected in the third and deciding Test match against the Kiwis at Odsal in front of, what was then, a record test crowd of over 42,000. Fittingly Roy showed his pace and scored two tries in the 25-9 victory thereby helping to win the match and the series.

Roy was the first black player to pull on the red, white and blue of Great Britain. Once again rugby league – so often reviled as a backward game – was in the forefront of British social and sporting history. By comparison, another thirty two years were to pass before Viv Anderson became the first black player to represent England at Association

Football. For the game of rugby league, so often the recipient of sporting discrimination, seemed on the surface less bound by racial discrimination than other sports.

At Bradford that day Francis had reached the pinnacle of his playing career. But it was a false dawn. Despite his milestone making the record books; it was Roy's only test appearance. However, there was no way, thankfully, that Roy Francis was to become a one-hit-wonder and fade into obscurity. Such was his status as a player that Roy now joined the reigning rugby league champions, Warrington, in 1948. He was influential playing in the season's Championship Final but he couldn't tip the balance and the game saw the Wire narrowly go down 13-12 to Huddersfield.

Then at the very end of the 1940s and in his fourteenth season as a player Francis moved to Hull. According to Robert Gate, writing about Francis in *Gone North*, some people considered the £1,250 fee paid by Hull was excessive. Some fee, some excess – when his association with Hull finished 14 years later in 1963, Francis had taken a mediocre team and made them a real power in the land. As a player, player-coach and then coach, Francis became a rugby league legend in Hull (or at least the black and white half).

At the Boulevard Francis had a profound and personal effect on another future giant of rugby league, Johnny Whiteley. The renowned loose-forward says Francis was 'light years ahead at the time' as a coach. According to Whiteley, Francis's powers of man management made an impression on more than just the playing style of that Hull team:

> 'The players at Hull, we were from the back streets, with no education. He showed us the other side of the road. He said we could change and move on in life as well as sport. Instead of making do with living in a one-up one-down terrace I finished up in a nice area with a three-bedroomed semi. He was such a man of the world, he was unique. We players looked up to him as a father figure.'

Perhaps Francis's impact was all the greater with the Second World War recently ended. As a child growing up in the conflict Whiteley saw little of his real father who was away in the navy. In fact between the ages of ten and fifteen years old Johnny Whiteley saw his dad just twice. Then a young Johnny went away into the army and thence straight from the forces to sign for Hull. As Whiteley describes it, 'Roy Francis took over the lives of thirty lads and we were like disciples'.

Roy Francis also knew the power of image. He always cut a dash wearing smart, expensive clothing, even to the Boulevard for training and he diligently worked his way up through several different makes of car to finally drive a Jaguar while at Hull. Seeing Roy Francis turning up for training in his smart car left a deep impression on Johnny Whiteley, the boy from nearby Hessle Road, and Francis's power and poise meant he vowed to himself that he would always have his destiny in his own hands when he left the game. When Whiteley left rugby league he was determined to become self-employed because of Roy Francis's insistence on having personal control and responsibility.

Roy Francis was a strong man physically and mentally. Ever aware of his own worth, he made sure his personal contracts were lucrative and that he was the highest paid person on the staff at Hull. But did Francis suffer any discrimination in Hull? Johnny Whiteley was not aware of any racism towards Francis:

> 'I didn't understand racism then. Black, white, yellow it made no difference to me and he never spoke about any problems to me. But then in Hull he had such success. Roy Francis was the unofficial Lord Mayor of Hull. We had won championships, been to Wembley, players had become internationals and the crowd loved the way we played. It was Roy and his coaching that blended us together as that team.'

Francis melded that team with his coaching ability and one of his facets was the strength to stand up to fearsome rugby league forwards and imprint his will on them. He was not afraid to use his strong physique and when he fell out with any of his players there was only ever going to be one apology – from the player to the coach.

At the Boulevard that strength welded together players – Whiteley, Tommy Harris, Mick Scott, Jim and Bill Drake, Harry Markham, Bob Coverdale and Cyril Sykes – that would form one of the most intimidating and feared packs in rugby league. And Francis ensured that pack would go down in history by revolutionising Hull FC's game and inventing a new concept – the 'running forward'. Not only were these guys fierce during the game but they actively looked for the ball, were happy to find the space to run wider out and could exploit an opening with the handling skills to deliver a well-timed pass. Well before the 1970s Dutch soccer side would unleash their orange brand, Francis's total football revolution was scripted and trialled on the fields of northern England.

Another future coach of Hull, David Doyle-Davidson, also trained as a player under the Francis regime. When he signed on in 1960 Francis was already using a camera to film matches, these films would then be shown to the players and Roy would point out mistakes. It was another innovation before its time. Doyle-Davidson is clear 'there was no doubt, in my opinion he was the best coach ever'.

As well as a film camera, a stop watch was a vital part of Francis's training armoury – all the player's speed work in training was done by the watch. Whether it was the 400 yard laps or flying sprints of 50 and 100 yards, everybody was measured against the progress of those sweeping hands. Then in the gymnasium Francis made good use of circuit training. It was this 'technical' side of his coaching that he allied to great effect with his man management. As Doyle-Davidson remembers:

> 'We never trained as hard as we did under Roy Francis and I think that was a great compliment to him. When he later went to Leeds, Alan Smith and John Atkinson thought they were fit guys. Two of the greatest and quickest wingers and they couldn't believe how tough training was under Roy. Both John and Alan said to me "We know now why sometimes a Hull side with lesser players used to beat us at Leeds".'

Under Francis Hull won the Championship in 1956 and 1958 (and were the runners-up in 1957). They also visited Wembley in 1959 and 1960. However, despite the fearsome pack the Boulevarders did not have enough footballing skills in the backs to fully exploit the potential of total football and despite some glories, Hull FC were unable to totally lose their tag as a nearly team.

After almost a decade and a half in Hull, Roy Francis left and made the trip to coach Leeds in 1963. His arrival was to synthesise forwards and backs and unleash the Loiners into a purple patch against which all Leeds teams are still measured. In five years with Francis at the helm Leeds won trophies and admiration for their style of play in equal measure. Success wasn't an instant process at Leeds. Roy Francis found there was a young team to develop and bring together so perhaps it wasn't until 1967-68 when the team really gelled and reached the heights.

Of course in 1968 Leeds took the Challenge Cup by one point from near neighbours Wakefield, wading through the infamous 'watersplash' final. And so after thirty years in the game, Francis had finally grasped one of the great prizes of British rugby league.

Despite the dramatics of the rain-affected Wembley win, including the late conversion miss by Don Fox from in front of the posts that is forever etched in the memory by Eddie Waring's commentary and the grainy black and white TV pictures, for many Loiners fans it was at the semi-final stage of that year's competition that Leeds reached their peak. In that match against Wigan many people feel Leeds had the perfect game. Stuart Duffy, currently Bradford Bulls media manager, has been a life-long Leeds fan:

> 'I remember the semi-final very well – the young guns had finally taken over. I think that match was the epitome of what Roy was trying to do on a football field. His ideas were fantastic, both backs and forwards should be able to contribute to the game equally. And Leeds were as likely to start thinking about attacking from behind their own line. Francis always believed that the opposition were most vulnerable when the ball was in Leeds's own half. He gave the Leeds team licence to do the unexpected.'

One of Francis's nurtured stars at Headingley was impressive half-back Barry Seabourne, Roy moulded him into the team starting very young, just as Francis had once done. Barry Seabourne was just 16 when he started in the successful team:

> 'Roy Francis always said be yourself and do what you think. We talked a lot about things in the game and then we put them into fruition. Roy didn't say what he wanted – rather he saw players and qualities and worked on their weaknesses. He was a man who believed in having all the qualities but in playing off the cuff. He brought four things to Leeds – discipline, enjoyment, speed and fitness. He had vision and knowledge and was able to put his

> ideas into us. His playing motto was "enjoy yourself". Before the game his speech was simple "Let me enjoy the game and if I enjoy it, certainly you will as players".'

However, strangely for a man famed for his coaching skills and motivation Francis could appear almost semi-detached during the actual game. He no doubt had faith that the players he had moulded would have the necessary skills to win the game. It was an approach that was to lead to personal criticism in a later episode when he coached in Australia but it seemed to work at Headingley. Barry Seabourne remembered the coolness:

> 'He didn't shout in the dressing room. If we were having a bad time then he would just come into the dressing room, and this was before substitutions, and say "Look – it's your problem, you sort it out. I'll see you after the game". There were no temper tantrums.'

It would be wrong to construe this attitude as softness, just as at Hull the Leeds players knew that Roy Francis was not to be trifled with. Seabourne remembers 'You only got two rollickings off Roy, the first was bad and the second meant you were on your bike'.

The Leeds fans, and the whole rugby league public, were entertained and just as importantly the Headingley trophy cabinet was put into use. Roy's total football had found its peak. The fondness for Francis that is still felt in Leeds was not only because Roy and his team were winners but also because of the entertaining football that the team were able to play.

Five years in Leeds had seen the team, with players of the calibre of John Atkinson, Alan Smith, Mick Shoebottom, Barry Seabourne, Bev Risman, Bill Ramsey, Ray Batten and John Holmes, reach the heights as one of the best teams in the history of rugby league.

However, Roy Francis' special ability to get the best out of a team had been noticed on the other side of the world. He was now in demand in Sydney.

Hard as it may be to believe, following almost thirty-five years of Australian domination, but there was a time when Britain and her coaches were in the vanguard of international rugby league thinking. Australia, in the sporting shape of North Sydney Bears, was interested in importing British coaching know-how. And that information could come no better than in the guise of master coach Francis.

Australia the country that had, perhaps, declined to accept the colour of his skin for the tour in 1946, was now desperate for the content of his mind in the late 1960s. And in a move that stunned the rugby league world, Francis was invited to put some life into a stuttering North Sydney season during the summer of 1968.

1968 has gone down as a year of turmoil around the globe, student demonstrations and strikes in Paris, riots at the Democratic convention in Chicago, the Prague uprising. In sport the Mexico Olympics of that year was ignited by the actions of sprinters Tommie Smith and John Carlos. The two successful American athletes had given the clenched fist Black Power salute from the podium during the official medal ceremony for the 200 metres. The salute was a last minute decision by the athletes but it was seen as a shocking, militant gesture and the pictures flew around the world. Today it is difficult to comprehend the indignation of the (white) press in America and around the world as politics, race and sport were firmly enmeshed in that summer.

Francis flew out to Sydney to take on the ailing Bears. Norths were bottom of the table with only one win so far that season. Roy Francis had just six weeks to turn the situation around and prove the reputation that had preceded his arrival.

It was a tough situation and Francis almost walked into a player revolt in support of Col Greenwood, North's existing South African coach. The mood at the club was ugly but at a heated players' meeting Greenwood himself said the best thing to do was to accept Francis's appointment and go out and win the remaining football games.

By the end of the season Norths had picked up six further points, as three of the last six games were won with Francis at the helm. The hard-won points only allowed the Bears to move one place up the ladder but the message had been made, Francis had turned the easybeats of the competition into a force to be reckoned with.

Once again Francis was hailed as a messiah, this time in Sydney, and given a new three-year contract at Norths with full control over football matters. His tough methods revolutionised Australian coaching and he started a programme of team training three or four days a week. Francis found to his surprise that neither the playing nor administration of the game was as professional in Australia as back in the UK.

A Norths player at that time, Denis Cubis, remembers that Francis 'was a super salesman and a good communicator. He took the role of leader and was charismatic. He was very refreshing and charming company'.

In an Australian television interview broadcast in May 1969 Roy was able to outline the character he was looking for in a player. It gives a valuable insight into his approach, speaking in the soft Welsh lilt that still accented his speech he explained what made him tick:

> 'I have a basic football knowledge, dedication, honesty and sincerity and I require exactly the same from the players. There must be a high percentage of ability, of course, for a player and they have to be dedicated. A person must also be honest with oneself.'

Many of Francis's imported new ideas sowed the first seeds for the coaching revolution that was to eventually put Australia at the very top of the rugby league pile. Australian coaches like Frank Stanton requested, and were given access to, his training schedules as Australia began to implement Francis's doctrine of intense physical effort allied with man motivation.

Another local coach who is reported to have benefited from an insight into Francis's methods was Jack Gibson. Not yet the coaching guru and icon he was to become but having tasted success with Easts, Gibson was keen to incorporate successful coaching methods into his own growing, unique footballing philosophy.

When after the 1969 season Norths finished half-way up the Premiership ladder it seemed that Francis and his methods had found a welcoming home down-under. However, the storm clouds were gathering and were about to deposit a downpour of tropical proportions straight over the head of Roy Francis.

Rugby league in Australia was more advanced than the UK in one area – fevered media scrutiny – and Roy was about to come under the microscope. The first sign of unease with his methods was from an unlikely quarter. Roy Francis decided that a new jersey would give the Bears a welcome fillip. The players took to the field in 1970 in a new design, wearing a white strip with a single band of red, black and red.

The 'English-style' jersey created disharmony even before the start of the season with much of the media and some important people at Norths against a change. Although the Australian game has always had a healthy regard for tradition, the level of discontent about changing the playing kit from the usual red and black design seems an out-of-proportion reaction but it was a harbinger of worse to follow.

In the first game of that 1970 season Canterbury played North Sydney at Belmore. During the game the Norths players were incensed at apparent bias from the referee after he had sent off two Norths players, John McDonell and club legend Ken Irvine. Irvine then led a walk off the field by the remaining Norths players. Following a touchline conference the players were eventually persuaded to return to the game and play continued. The event caused a media storm and from then on it was a rough ride for the Bears and for Francis.

In his attempt to drag the Australian game into the modern era Francis's insistence on high standards of fitness and training had instigated some player resentment among the Bears. However, Roy had also got on the wrong side of an increasingly influential media as, for whatever reason, some newspapers seemed to take comfort in the gathering problems at Norths.

The search was on to find any cracks to exploit in Norths' facade. Perhaps Francis's two perceived weaknesses in Australia began to count against him; he was a 'pommie' and a black man. North's stalwart Harry McKinnon (quoted in *The Mighty Bears*, Andrew Moore's social history of the club) thought that the press campaign was 'a rude manifestation of Anglophobia or some other phobia'.

As the pressure mounted, and following an on-field thrashing by St George, an unusually emotional Roy is reported as pulling up his shirt sleeves and exclaiming to journalists: 'When you have a black skin like mine you have to accept humiliation, but I was not born with the North Sydney team and I don't have to live with this kind of humiliation.'

In *Rugby League Week* following that outburst Roy was attacked for his 'method acting' and was accused that his speech 'carried a dash of Malcolm X' the controversial black American civil rights activist. It is hard to imagine how coaching a football team could be in any way compared with fiery polemical speeches and militant political action. Yet it seems that the press took every opportunity to exploit the situation and the increasingly influential Sydney tabloid papers led the way.

Eventually the press campaign became so aggressive that Roy Francis's wife Rene, became distraught and had to be sedated for two days. Roy's treatment in Australia, particularly at the hands of the media, was to leave a lasting and painful impression on Rene.

However there were also some doubts expressed as to the actual monetary value of having Francis coaching at Norths. As we have seen, Roy was a capable negotiator and was in Australia on a lucrative three-year contract. He also made sure that moving expenses, accommodation and air fares were covered by the club. It was even claimed that Francis had charged Norths for a briefcase, tracksuit and repairs to his typewriter. The storm continued to grow: he was also criticised by supporters at the Norths' annual meetings for cavalier use of the chequebook on new players.

And the most shocking – his coaching began to be criticised. A Norths committee man, Norm Strong, even felt that the coaching guru was lacking in tactics and knowledge. On a half-time visit to the dressing room Strong felt Francis was lacking in any ideas to help the players correct problems that had been evident in the first half. Remember what Barry Seabourne had to say about how Francis would tell his players '…it's your problem you sort it out.' What had appeared as a faith in the strength of his players was now perceived as a fatal tactical inertia.

Clearly his once sky-high reputation in England was being undermined in Australia. Roy Francis continued to devote most hours of the day to the football club but the number of his supporters could now be at least matched by his detractors and the atmosphere at Norths appeared to be highly charged. At one point the atmosphere got so heated there were even rumours that some players had had their phones tapped.

There was also the small matter of Ken Irvine, the club's figurehead and leading player. He was firmly in the anti-Francis camp. Francis had been critical of Irvine's physical strength on arrival in Australia but had not managed to convince the player of the benefits of his intensive training methods. Irvine's attitude to a disciplinarian like Francis appeared to border on insubordination. The Englishman's request, that the Norths players address club officials as 'Sir', had rankled with the Australian players more used to an easy Antipodean familiarity.

The clash with Francis could not be contained and it led to the hero Irvine leaving Norths for dreaded rivals and near neighbours Manly. Another leading player, Brian Norton, also left the club after a dispute with Francis. The pressure mounted on Francis – press, officials, players and supporters were all wavering over the English coach. Then in March 1971, Roy finally announced that he was leaving Australia and that ended Norths' English experiment. Francis had gone from messiah to misfit in a few short years. Officially, 'business reasons' were cited for the parting but was there more to it than that?

At the time, the strand of racism woven amongst all the other difficulties encountered by Francis in Australia was understated. However eventually by 1985, in a hard-hitting interview in *Rugby League Week*, Francis was to admit that he was 'the man they drove from town'.

But the influence of Francis remained overseas, he had sown some of the coaching seeds that were to flourish into the full-blown Australian dominance of world rugby league. He was among the instigators of game plans and player profiles and was not afraid to go searching with the chequebook for fresh playing talent that fitted into his plans. Roy also took on the wholehearted role of manager-coach. These now commonplace coaching ideas were still viewed with suspicion when introduced to Australia by Francis.

An exhausted Roy Francis moved back to England and took stock. He was away from the game for a few years, before making short-lived returns to Hull, Leeds and Bradford Northern. Even then silverware followed: he coached the title-winning Leeds side of 1974-75 but at the end of that season he was dramatically replaced by his protégé Syd Hynes. The time was finally running out on his involvement with the game.

Roy Francis, rugby league pioneer, died in 1989. For forty years, his charismatic personality had permeated the game. He was a complex man described by Raymond Fletcher as 'larger than life and flamboyant in a quiet way'. In his football career Francis never stopped inventing new ways to do things and one of his favourite sayings was 'Ah well, back to the drawing board!' He had a unique ability to use many and varied influences even from well outside the game to gain a winning edge.

His rugby league epitaph is to be remembered as the man who proved that winning football could be entertaining football. For Roy Lionel Francis rugby league wasn't just the intimidating collision sport of the working man; it was a thinking man's game too.

4

BILLY BOSTON
Phil Melling

If we could visit Wigan in the Autumn of 1953 and join Billy Boston and his brother Herbert on the steps of the London and North Western Station it would be hard to resist the obvious conclusion that the world they looked at was different in kind from the one they had left behind them in Cardiff. More than likely, Billy and Herbert would have gazed on a sea of uniform whiteness: the whiteness of the poor that George Orwell wrote about in *The Road to Wigan Pier*, the lads who drank in The Swan and Railway, the families who lived in Adelaide and Caroline Street and spent their day under the moss-covered arches of Wallgate Bridge listening to the trains.

In the 1950s Tiger Bay was as poor as Wigan but it wasn't the same colour. When Billy lived there, Tiger Bay, not Brixton or Bradford, was the nerve centre of a multiracial Britain. Like a separate country in the heart of the Welsh capital, Tiger Bay was a teeming mix of immigrant chatter and indigenous life. Billy knew this world intimately. He grew up in the company of Greek, Turkish and Ukrainian immigrants; he rubbed shoulders with first and second generation Africans; and when he walked the streets around Loudon Square he did so in the middle of the largest concentration of expatriate Somalis anywhere in the world.

Tiger Bay is often described as Afro-Celtic, but the multi-ethnic and multi-cultural heritage of the community goes far deeper. Even the name originates in the stories of Portuguese seamen who claimed that sailing into the difficult waters of the Severn Estuary was like sailing into 'Una Bahia de los Tigres' – A Bay of Tigers. In the 1950s such was the variety of language, accent and food, that the streets of Tiger Bay had more in common with New York than did New Springs. The area was a labyrinth of intricate colour where, as Neil Sinclair puts it in his book *The Tiger Bay Story*, 'Calabar, Kru, Igbo, Soso and Yoruba seamen met Celtic and Anglo-Saxon brides'.

Billy was the child of one of these relationships. His mother was second generation Irish. His father a Soso from Sierra Leone. The family lived on Old Angelina Street, a hub of activity for local men who gambled outside the Marchioness of Bute on the corner of Sophia Street. Further down, where Sophia Street met Bute Street was Mr Wing's Sam on Yen restaurant. The restaurant was owned by Sam on Yen, an elderly Chinese man who wore a bowler hat and striped trousers, 'the last remnant', says Sinclair, 'of a once thriving Chinese community in Tiger Bay'. Round the corner from the Boston's was Old Christina Street and Khaid Sallah's shop with its Save Palestine box on the shelf. Opposite was Nelson Street, the home of Joe Erskine. Next to him a sweet shop run by Polly Lopes, a black Portuguese woman who kept a parrot behind the counter for the children to stroke, and then Mary Ahmed's, with its incense smells and penny drinks. On the corner of Bute Street and Patrick Street was Frenchies Annex, a dancing school popular with those who liked to hear calypso music, mambo and merengue. At Frenchies, you could learn to dance a West African High Life, courtesy of its owner, a native of Senegal.

Billy grew up amid the smells and sounds of the old world and the new. At weekends, there was conversation with the black GIs from the air force bases at Brize Norton and Birdrop Park, as well as the sounds of rhythm and blues from the gramophones in their girlfriends' houses. In Tiger Bay there was always music for Billy to listen to: gospel music from the Afro-American blues singer, Sister Rosetta Tharp, who sang in Loudon Square in the early 1950s, and the songs of Zola Taylor, female singer with the Platters and a friend of Rohima Ali whose family owned the Bombay Restaurant in West Bute Street. With its music and dancing, Tiger Bay, says Neil Sinclair, 'was the safest haven in Britain' for people of colour to come of age. The willingness of the community to fight for its 'right to be' and its desire to preserve 'a harmonious multi-racial way of life', was 'one of the most endearing aspects' of its culture.

Everything that Billy was familiar with in Tiger Bay seemed to be missing from Victorian Wigan. For those who didn't know it, Wigan in the 50s was little more than a colourless wasteland, a place still saddled with the detritus of the industrial revolution: the mills, mines, bogged-up canals, terraced houses and back-to-backs, the slums of Wallgate, Scholes, Lower Ince. It seemed there was little to distinguish Wigan from the pit of despair that Ellen Wheeton had noted in 1809, when she described the town as 'that place of mental barrenness, where ignorance and vulgarity are their boast, and literature has scarcely dawned, where genius, when it happens to appear, is so often treated with contemptuous neglect'. At first glance, Wigan must have looked severely down-market to Billy. If Tiger Bay had its Arabic language, African music and Oriental cuisine, Wigan had its pie shops, its ballroom dancing at Tommy Moss's, its Lancashire dialect in Lamberhead Green. Maybe there were times when Billy was close to panic: starved of colour, frustrated by the 'mental barrenness' of the town, demoralized by its lack of adventure and surfeited by, what Wheeton calls, the 'ignorance and vulgarity' of the working class.

The problem is, the argument doesn't hold up with Billy. If at one time he did go through a period of doubt and deep uncertainty he doesn't readily admit to it. On the contrary, his memories and opinions have little in common with those who associate the North of England and the game of rugby league with a morbid descent into everlasting hell.

Take, for example, the Swansea journalist, Martin Pitchwell, who, following the decision of Jonathan Davies to sign for Widnes in 1987, warned his readers in the *Evening Post* what lay in store. 'He (Davies) will be hounded, pounded, goaded, insulted, bullied, scorned and, if the northern hard men have their way, humiliated in the next few weeks.' The caricature of Rugby league as a game fit for mercenaries and bullies may owe a lot to David Storey's *This Sporting Life* but, as the cultural historian Martin Wiener tells us, it also incorporates a much deeper level of prejudice against the provincial character of the industrial north. We can see this in the comments that were made by Michael Herd of the London *Evening Standard* on 18 February 1993, when he described rugby league as the sport of 'ape-like creatures watched by gloomy men in cloth caps'. What Herd is doing is to repeat the complaint of Ellen Wheeton, that the North responds to the presence of 'genius' with 'contemptuous neglect'.

This kind of easy prejudice does not find favour with those who have embraced rugby league from inside the coloured communities of Britain. The idea that the game brutalises the sensibilities of those who play it is not, for example, part of the testimony of players like Cec Thompson who went on to become a club director at Barrow, or Frank Wilson, a St Helens and Salford player who became a first-class rugby league coach, or Alex Givvons, who worked for years as an unsung hero with Oldham rugby league club. Roy Francis, who left Wigan in 1938 after a run-in with Harry Sunderland, the club's secretary-manager, was another who had a great career in rugby league. Francis played for Great Britain in 1947, and became the first black person to coach a professional sports team in Britain.

The success of Roy Francis in the 1950s and 1960s and the way he committed his future to the game after a difficult introduction was the start of a period of sustained achievement for black players in rugby league. When Billy signed for Wigan in October 1953, Cec Thompson was in his prime for Hunslet as a second row and had already been selected to play for England. In 1951 Phil Delgardo and Billy Douglas, an ex-Cardiff International Athletic Club's player from Cardiff, had already made the switch to rugby league, while David 'Darkie' Jones had gone from Maesteg to Halifax. These and other players of colour from Wales were following in the footsteps of a family of Italians, the five Corsi brothers, who had left the Fairwater area of Cardiff in the 1920s and 'gone north' to Rochdale and Oldham.

When Billy Boston came to Wigan he joined a long tradition of Welsh players, many of whom, like Johnny Thomas in the pre-First World War era or Jim Sullivan and Tommy Howley in the 1920s, had enjoyed fabulous success. According to Johnny Laurenson, Billy reminded the older fans of Georgie Bennett, a black player who had signed for the club in 1930. A scrum-half and stand-off, Bennett came from Weston-super-Mare and throughout the 1930s was one of the great, attacking half-backs in the game. An irrepressible and charismatic figure, Bennett played rugby league for Wales and made an impact on the Wigan public similar to that of Billy in the 1950s and Henderson Gill in the 1980s. We know this from the number of photos that are taken of him, not just match-day pictures, but the ones that show him in training with the Australian Hector Gee, or socializing with Len Mason, the giant Maori who played for Wigan in the 1930s. According to Laurenson, a winger with Wigan in the late 1940s, Georgie Bennett was every kid's rugby hero, a player who should have walked into the Great Britain side but lacked the political support he needed at the time.

In the early days racial discrimination was never completely absent from rugby league and Bennett may have been a victim of it. But such discrimination did not exist to anything like the same extent in rugby league as it did in other sports, either in Britain or overseas. Georgie Bennett never experienced the problems of Jackie Robinson, the baseball star who blazed a trail for black players with the Brooklyn Dodgers in the 1940s. Nor did Billy Boston or Johnny Freeman, black players who generated phenomenal excitement when they came north in the early fifties but avoided the racism that was often prevalent in other sports.

That's not to say that problems did not exist. They did and Billy experienced them as much as anyone. April 1956 comes to mind, when, in a ridiculous outburst of petulance by the club, he was suspended by Wigan for having played badly in a Challenge Cup game against Halifax. The problem was not racial, and the suspension was only lifted when Billy wrote a letter of apology to the directors. Clearly, Billy was not to blame for what had happened and he was hurt by the club's reaction. It stayed with him for a long time. At the same time, it didn't stop him from topping the league try-scoring list that season with sixty tries; nor did it prevent him from breaking the club record of 478 tries, 100 more than Johnny Ring had scored in the 1920s in a fifteen-year period at Wigan.

In 1957 Billy refused to travel to South Africa with the Great Britain World Cup squad rather than agree to government restrictions that he travel in a blacks-only bus and stay in a blacks-only hotel. Occasionally, Billy was taunted racially – one episode in particular is still talked about in Wigan when he jumped into the crowd at an away game and chased a spectator into the stands. Yet the impression remains that Billy's colour was rarely an issue with rugby league crowds. In 1957, the editor of the *Rugby League Gazette* spoke for everyone involved in the sport when he made his views on the South African debacle abundantly clear:

> 'What the South African government does is its own affair, for its racial discrimination will reap its own whirlwind someday. In the meantime, our game should confine itself to playing Rugby league. We have no colour bar, we judge a man as a man irrespective of colour, and anyone good enough is eligible to play for the country of his birth. That is as it should be, and anyone who tinkers about with this in order to "fit in" with South African standards is dealing a death blow at every civilized concept of sportsmanship… if they (South Africa) are going to lay down the

> law and introduce colour bars and politics into sport then we regret to say that until they learn better manners we prefer to do things our way.'

Billy was sensitive about his colour but rugby league folks tried to reassure him. In the 1950s and 1960s, race was not as much of an issue as it sometimes is today. The feeling of racial harmony that Billy grew up with in Tiger Bay at the South Church Street school was rarely threatened in the north of England by the attitudes of the tabloids. The Wigan folk, furthermore, made an effort with Billy and tried to understand his occasional bouts of insecurity.

Johnny Stopford was one of Billy's closest friends, a Wiganer who played rugby league for Swinton and Great Britain and competed on the wing against him on many occasions. I met Johnny just before his death from lung cancer and talked to him about his friendship. Johnny was effusive about the relationship and proud of the way he had shared many of Billy's closest secrets. 'In the early days we became good pals', said Johnny. 'We had a drink together after a game. It was obvious then he was very conscious about his colour and he wanted to know what I thought of it. "I'll tell you something", I said. "Your colour doesn't bother me. I slept with two coloured lads in the army. And me in the middle. They were boxing champions." Billy asked me who were they. "Joey Jacobs from Manchester", I said, "and 'Joey' Sango from Wales." "Redfers Sango?" said Billy. "Aye", I replied. "Him who got murdered in a doorway in Cardiff." "Well, bloody hell," said Billy, "I went to school with him…" Then he looked at me and I could tell he knew his skin didn't bother me. I remind him of that every time I see him. "You don't look so good mate," I say. "How's that?" says Billy. "You look a bad colour," I say. He laughs and takes it.'

Johnny Stopford's playfulness tells us a lot about Wiganers in general during these years. Colour was not a reason for prejudice. On the contrary, it was the key to understanding the character of the game and the town that had nurtured it. Cherry and white was a bye word for Wigan and the association went back a long way. In Latin, the word *Coccium* – the original Roman name of the town – means red sand and Wigan had been famous not only for its pit sand but its brick-making industry which flourished between the eighteenth and twentieth centuries. The town invoked other associations with the colour red. The River Douglas until recently was a red river – because of the deposits of iron ore and red oxide in the soil. Howard Hawks, the Hollywood film director, as many have attested in the pubs and clubs, received his inspiration for the film *Red River* after visiting Central Park with an American friend who worked at the US Air Force base at Burtonwood during the Second World War.

Another tale has it that the Douglas was coloured red by a vast, rusting, treasure trove of weaponry, which for years, oozed with the blood of warriors from a battle fought in the English Civil War. There is much to commend this story. Wigan's training ground backed on to an area of woodland and forest known as 'The Bloody Mountains'. Here, in the summer of 1651, Lord Derby's Royalist army was engaged by Colonel Robert Lilburne's Roundheads in a set-piece battle. In Derby's ranks were soldiers from the glass-blowing town of St Helens, a windy people who, to this day, find it hard to back a winner! The Roundheads defeated Derby, many of whom were conscripted Wiganers, and the result of that battle was inscribed into the folk memory of south-west Lancashire. The Derby match was a term jokingly referred to by Wiganers whenever the town played St Helens in any subsequent sporting contest. For generations, Wigan versus St Helens rugby league fixtures took place on sacred occasions: Boxing Day and Good Friday, in memory of the blood spilled by Derby and the players of St Helens (the so-called Saints)

For almost one hundred years Central Park was a crucible of colour where different traditions were distilled into a unique blend of flair and finesse. Throughout its history the club was peculiarly receptive to the presence of outsiders, its oral heritage and folk mentality shaped by the comings and goings of exotic people and migrations over time.

Billy highlighted a style of inclusiveness, one that is reflected in the crude but kindly populism of the man who signed him, Joe Taylor: 'If we found an Eskimo who could play rugby league,' Joe once said, 'he'd be living in Wigan.' Joe meant what he said. Over 8,000 people turned out to see Billy play in his 'A' team debut at Central Park on 31 October 1954, the equivalent at the time of an attendance for a first-team match. The speed with which the town responded to news of his arrival has been commented on many times. Billy's arrival was messianic. It generated huge interest, as if people had been expecting him for quite some time. No one knew what he would look like – black or brown they didn't care – or when he would arrive; but they did know that someone like him was on his way, better even than Roy Francis or Johnny Ring or Georgie Bennett. Mike Higham, a friend of Billy's makes the point: 'I was watching Bolton Wanderers in 1952. When Billy arrived, all that changed. There was nothing like it when he hit the touch line.' Billy did the same for everyone. He was a secular messiah. He brought together the devotional energy of a largely Roman Catholic and non-conformist population. Billy explained the need for church worship yet helped overcome the not-inconsiderable, religious divide.

Something similar had happened once before. In October 1923, Wigan signed the brilliant Springbok winger, Adrian Van Heerden. Van Heerden had a powerful effect on Wigan fans in the 1920s and when he defied the dress traditions of the day and refused to wear a hat, the Wigan public decided to copy him. Working-class and middle-class folk alike threw away their bowlers and cloth caps and walked the streets bare-headed. All because a South African winger had said it was cool. Van Heerden became a demi-god in Wigan. Folklore has it that in a Lancashire cup win against Oldham at the Rochdale Athletic Grounds, the stadium was so full that on his way to the try line he had to round a mounted policeman before he could score.

The impact of the flamboyant Van Heerden, who lived and played it close to the line, led Wigan to search for fresh South African talent. Booysten, Van Der Spuy, Burger, Van Rooyen, and Oliver all followed him to Central Park. The effect was mesmeric. People who grew up in Wigan during these years could close their eyes and ignore what the rest of the world thought about the game. Rugby league had successfully turned the middle-class values of English culture into a tissue of lies. The idea of going to a place like Wigan in order to fulfil yourself, in spite of the warnings of John Ruskin and Ellen Wheeton about the perils of living with the working class, was now a fact of life. At Central Park you were able to see how things were done in a stylish and transnational way. Alongside the local lads who plied their trade so brilliantly – Tommy Bradshaw or Joe Egan or Martin Ryan or Ken Gee – were those who came from places you knew you would never get to see: the Johannesburg of Tiny Van Rooyen, the Auckland of Charlie Seeling and Massa Johnston, the Queensland of Hector Gee.

Playing it safe was never the way of doing things at Wigan. At Central Park, colour was the one thing that got you out of trouble. Speculative acquisitions were always preferable to the management equivalent of five drives and a kick.

Paul Wilson's *The Best Years of Our Lives* bears testimony to this.

Wigan's rise from also-rans in the second division in the 1970s to the pre-eminent club in world rugby by the mid-1990s relied on players like Va'aiga Tuigamala, Frano Botica, Ellery Hanley and Henderson Gill. Wigan signed Gill, for example, at the time Maurice Bamford was coach. The club had little money and was being accused by the fans of lacking 'the guts to compete in the transfer market'. Bamford wanted to buy some rough-tough forwards but the new directors, Maurice Lindsay and Jack Robinson, preferred the more unconventional approach. They signed Henderson Gill from Rochdale, a black winger who was unorthodox and unreliable, but with the ball in his hands, almost unstoppable. Bamford was furious when he heard. Wingers weren't costing Wigan games, he argued. The team was short of strength in the pack and experience in the backs. He didn't see what good a quasi-Rastafarian with a reputation for eccentric behaviour was going to do for a club that lacked any pattern to its play. Bamford was a Yorkshireman, profoundly suspicious of erratic wingers with uncertain temperaments who made things up as they went along. Robinson and Lindsay disagreed. They knew exactly what the Wigan public expected of them and trusted their instincts. In 1981 they bought Gill for £23,000, stumping up a lot of the money out of their own pockets. The move paid off spectacularly. Henderson Gill was a bundle of tricks and a landmark signing for the Wigan club. As soon as he arrived attendances doubled and Wigan began to climb up the table. Henderson Gill was in the Wigan tradition; conservatism had been shown the door. As Alex Murphy put it at the time: 'If you think Hendy is elusive on the field, you ought to try catching him on the phone'.

Gill was a cultural icon at Wigan just as Billy had been in the 1950s. He was primarily an entertainer, an epitome of Northern Soul, the black underground music that had begun life with Russ Winstanley in the Riverside Club at Central Park before transferring to Wigan Casino in the early 70s. An athletic performer, Gill's virtuoso style of running, his spins and back flips, were an equivalent of the dance gymnastics and acrobatics of Northern Soul. The connection between rugby player and music fan during these years was uncanny. It signified, as Dave Lancaster, one of the contributors to Russ Winstanley's *Soul Survivors* puts it, a crucial link between Soul music and Soul club. In other words, what Gill was doing at Central Park was just another version of what the dancers and fans were doing in the Wigan Casino on a Saturday night. Here, white kids were simply copying the attitudes of black people and reinventing them in a dance floor setting. Of course, Gill didn't need to re-invent anything. He was black already. And at Central Park he extended that link, recreating one more version of the Motown sound. Sometimes he did it further afield. It was during the Third Test in Sydney in 1988, after he scored a spectacular try, that Darrell Eastlake described him as doing 'a bit of a boogie'.

The importance of black music as a source of inspiration for those who live in an industrial setting like the North of England allows us a point of access to rugby league. 'What the Casino gave us,' says Lancaster, 'were class acts from the United States like the late great Jackie Wilson, Junior Walker and Martha Reeves. The Casino,' he adds, was 'as much a part of Wigan as Uncle Joe's Mint Balls or Wigan Pier.'

Like Henderson Gill, Billy Boston also allows a link to be made with black musicians and aficionados of jazz and soul. And although the restrictions on his movements were far greater, Billy articulated for the fans on the terrace, much the same thing as Henderson Gill did.

Billy arrived in Wigan at a time when the relationship between Wiganers and the big band sound was developing a pace. Billy's style as a rugby player enforced that relationship; it helped it along. What Billy brought with him was the sound of the streets in Tiger Bay and one the fans could easily relate to: a music that suggested the importance of both improvisation and ensemble. Furthermore, Wigan's awareness of the importance of black music made it easy for them to accept the presence of a black genius whose stage was different, but whose performances were just as compelling as those of Count Basie or Louis Armstrong or Duke Ellington. Ted Atherton, a jazz musician who had left Wigan in the 1940s and returned in 1952, the year before Billy arrived, describes the importance that jazz played in the newly-emerging character of the town:

> 'There was the Jazz Club on the market square, big band jazz in The Empress Hall (later to become The Wigan Casino) and small jazz bands like the one I played in at The White Crow. We were all excited by what we heard coming in from the States: the Modern Jazz Quartet, George Shearing, the big band sounds of Miller, Dorsey, Ellington and Basie.'

According to Ted, the Glenn Miller band played its first gig on English soil during the late war years at the Palais de Danse in Millgate, and towns like Wigan were always influenced by the kind of music that arrived courtesy of the US Air Force base at Burtonwood, just down the road.

Billy Boston's interest in jazz and blues is well known and these days he is a keen supporter of the Wigan Youth Jazz Orchestra and a good friend of its leader Ian Darrington. The jazz Billy enjoys fits in with the music that came of age in the local jazz clubs of the 1950s. And Billy's style of play embodied it, not so much the radical bebop of Charlie Parker or Dizzy Gillespie in which, says Atherton, there is no such thing as the unintentional note or riff. But the kind of jazz which Joe Egan, the man who coached Billy, could readily work with.

Wigan paid a fortune for Billy – £3000 – and made an enormous effort to sign him, more than they had for any other player. But once they had signed him Billy was expected to play by the rules. Billy came to a club still dominated by the coaching influence of Jim Sullivan, a Welshman whose leadership style was not dissimilar to that of Duke Ellington and Count Basie. With Sullivan, the band came first. The individual was always given the chance to go solo but within an agreed pattern of play. Primarily, it was team discipline that allowed the individual to show his flair; charisma was crucial, but not at the expense of ensemble harmony and camaraderie. The directors and coaches placed a high priority on style, but playing wrong notes, prima donna behaviour on the field, ignoring your mates, all of this was unacceptable.

Billy understood this from day one. That's the way he'd been brought up by his parents and the way he'd been taught by Bernard Sullivan at the South Church Street school and Bill Barrett at the Cardiff Boys club. Jim Sullivan and Joe Egan reminded him of that. In doing so they allowed Billy to play his rugby the way he lived his life and the way he'd been brought up to behave by his parents. At Central Park, rugby league recreated the community spirit he understood. Big band rugby suited Billy's personality. It allowed him to play like one of the lads. In typical fashion, he put it thus:

> 'During my period Wigan had an absolutely wonderful set of players and I think that this should be made clear. No one man can make a team and I was no exception. You only have to think back and remember some of the names. Brian McTigue, Dave Bolton, Mick Sullivan, Terry O'Grady, Ernie Ashcroft, Jack

> Cunliffe, Norman Cherrington, Eric Ashton: the list is endless. I consider myself very lucky to have played at this time. I am convinced that these were truly great players.'

Billy was a perfect fit for Wigan, a player who danced his way into history and changed the face of rugby league.

5

WALLY McARTHUR

Tony Collins

Wally McArthur was the first Aboriginal Australian rugby league player to play for an English club.

But he should not have been.

That he was the first tells us a lot about the society into which he was born and raised. Although rumours about Oldham's Viv and Billy Farnsworth's Aboriginal background have never been confirmed, the first acknowledged Aboriginal player to come to England should have been Frank Fisher in 1936.

The grandfather of Olympic gold medallist Cathy Freeman, Frank, or 'King Fisher' as he was nicknamed in Queensland, played at stand-off for Wide Bay against the touring British Lions. Gus Risman was so impressed by his performance, and by other reports he heard about the player, he told Frank that when he returned to Salford he would recommend that the club offer him a contract.

When the contract duly arrived a few weeks later, Frank approached the Queensland state authorities for permission to move to Salford. But they refused to allow him to go to Britain, saying that there was already one Queensland Aboriginal sports star, the cricketer Eddie Gilbert, and that they didn't want any more.

Why should an accomplished adult man have to ask permission of his government to work in another country? Because until the late 1960s, Aboriginal Australians were what were known as 'wards' of their state's 'Protector of Aborigines'. In other words they had no civil rights. This meant that they were not allowed to vote or marry whites and were not even included in the national census until 1967. Their lives were controlled in totalitarian fashion from the cradle to the grave by the white government authorities.

One could almost say that they were treated like children, if it wasn't for the fact that many of the children of Aboriginal parents were treated by the government in one of the most horrifying ways imaginable. Since the early 1900s, and in some cases before that, most Australian states had pursued a policy of removing from their mothers the children of inter-racial relationships, disparagingly known as 'half-castes', and placing them in care. Taken at the age of five or six, most never saw their mothers again for decades, if at all. Those boys and girls became known later as the 'children of the stolen generation'.

Wally McArthur, like tens of thousands of others, was one of those children. Born on 1 December 1933 on the banks of the McArthur River across from the tiny township of Borroloola in the Northern Territory of Australia, his mother was an Aboriginal woman and his father was a local white policeman called Langdon. When he was taken from his mother, he was given the name McArthur rather than Langdon because the authorities did not want to acknowledge that his father was white.

In 1998 Wally told John Pilger how he had been kidnapped:

> 'It was a government car, because only the government had cars at that time. The driver put me in the front seat with him and he drove around while I waved at my family. I never seen them since, you know. They were sitting around the camp fire; they didn't understand what was happening.'

His younger cousin John Moriarty was simply taken from school by a government official who did not even inform John's parents; many years later his mother told him what had happened: 'I went to pick you up [from school] on this day and you were gone'. It was to be fifty-five years before Wally saw another member of his family again.

Wally was taken to a Church of England mission in Alice Springs called the Bungalow, where he was supposed to be educated, although in 1937 there were just two teachers for nearly a hundred children. As the Second World War grew in intensity, fear of a Japanese invasion in northern Australia meant that the area became a heavily militarised zone and the Aboriginal children at the Bungalow were evacuated to more southerly regions. The boys at the mission were moved temporarily to Adelaide before being settled in a mission at Mulgoa, near the Blue Mountains to the west of Sydney.

It was here that Wally became noted not only for his incredible athletic talent but also for his leadership qualities and willingness to stand up against injustice. 'People were frightened to call my cousin Wally nicknames,' recalled John Moriarty in his autobiography *Saltwater Fella*, 'because they'd get belted. If anyone picked on me at the home, Wally would stand up for me.'

In 1949 the authorities decided to move the boys at the mission to Adelaide. Wally protested because he and some of the other boys had passed their second year exams at Penrith High School and the move would prevent them from taking their school certificate exams in New South Wales. His complaint was covered by the *Women's Weekly* which ran a feature story on him, and questions were asked in the NSW State Parliament. It was all to no avail and the boys were moved from Mulgoa to the St Francis House at Semaphore, a suburb of Adelaide in South Australia.

In Adelaide Wally's sporting career started to develop rapidly. In 1948 while still at Penrith High School he won twelve of the school's thirteen athletic events and was New South Wales High School champion in the 100 yards, long jump and 440 yards, in which he recorded a time of 52.2 seconds. At the age of fourteen he ran the world's fastest 440 yards for his age group. After he had moved to Adelaide and left school, he became athletics champion of the Le Fevre Boys Technical High School. In 1951 he became the South Australian Under-19 100 and 220 yards champion.

It was at this point that his athletics career came up directly against the racism that had shaped his life. Despite his success, he was left out of the South Australian athletics team to visit Tasmania for the national championships. Wally protested and was told that he could go, but only if he paid his own fare. Fortunately an unknown well-wisher paid for his ticket and Wally was able to compete. Perhaps unsurprisingly given his prodigious talent, he promptly carried off the national Under-19 100 yards championship. This victory against the odds confirmed a growing feeling in South Australian athletics circles that Wally was a good prospect for the 1952 Olympic Games, which were to be held in Helsinki.

Although it was later claimed that he had been excluded from the Australian Olympic team because of his race, it now appears that his times left him just short of having an unarguable case for inclusion in the side that went to Helsinki. Even so, the fact that at that time no Aboriginal athlete had been chosen for an Australian Olympic squad (it wasn't until the 1960s that Aboriginal athletes appeared at the Games) and the way in which he had been treated over the previous two years probably led Wally to conclude that he could go no further in the racist world of amateur athletics. So, in 1953, he became a professional sprinter. He won his first ten races, defeating along the way Frank Banner, the then Australian professional sprint champion. But by the spring of that year, Wally had abandoned athletics to concentrate on his other great sporting love, rugby league.

Wally had learned rugby league at Penrith High School and continued to play when the boys were moved to Adelaide. As it remains today, South Australia was one of the heartlands of Australian Rules football but Wally and some of the other boys retained their love of league. Luckily Semaphore at that time had its own rugby league side, one of five clubs in the small South Australian Rugby League (SARL). He was one of three Aboriginal players in the team, a small testimony to the fact that rugby league, in the words of the leading historian of Aboriginal sport Colin Tatz, 'has always been the most generous of the major sports [that Aboriginal men] play'.

Wally quickly became recognised as one of the state's leading league players, despite his youth. Semaphore went through the 1950 and 1951 seasons unbeaten and in 1952 Wally was voted SARL's fairest and best player. In 1953 he decided to concentrate on professional sprinting but returned to the club part-way through the season and was selected to play for South Australia against Western Australia, where he won the Man of the Match award. In his time at Semaphore he was said to have scored over 900 points.

Given such a record, not to mention his prominence as a sprinter, it was no surprise that rugby league scouts began to take an interest. As early as 1950 Wally had been spotted playing league by Paul Quinn, a former Rochdale Hornets player who was living and working as a moulder in Adelaide. It was Quinn who acted as Rochdale's representative in the negotiations over the contract. Wally's disillusionment with racism in athletics meant that he was now far more amenable to signing for the club because it was clear that in rugby league he would be judged solely on his football ability, not the colour of his skin.

Rochdale were particularly careful about how to proceed with their potential new recruit. International transfers had been banned in 1947 due to fears that the best Australians would all move to the richer

English clubs and Rochdale had been severely criticised in 1950 for trying to get round the ban by persuading league players in Sydney to switch to union for a few matches before moving to England.

Consequently, the press was given the story that Quinn had suggested to Wally that he should finish his engineering apprenticeship in England. It was only when Wally had decided to move to Rochdale for work reasons, so the club claimed, that Quinn had informed Hornets that Wally might be interested in playing for them. As it turned out, the Australian Board of Control (the forerunner of the ARL) didn't pay any attention and the signing went through without incident.

On Thursday 19 November 1953 Wally flew out to Britain from Sydney airport. The news of his imminent arrival was revealed by the *Daily Express*'s Jack Bentley the following day. 'A new Black Flash is on his way to England' declared the headline. Underneath Bentley outlined Wally's athletic achievements and speculated that he could make his debut for Hornets in their match against Leigh the following week.

Leigh's new signing from athletics, MacDonald Bailey, the 1952 Olympic 100 metres bronze medallist and joint 100 metres world record holder, was due to make his first appearance in that match and Bentley suggested that spectators 'may see two black flashes in action – one on each side!' In the end Bailey made just one appearance in a friendly match for Leigh, but Wally was to prove to be made of sterner stuff.

When he arrived in Rochdale a few days later, his signing was described as 'almost unbelievable' by the local press. His athletic records were described with reflected pride by the club and his footballing prowess was recounted by the former Leeds player Jack Lendill who had emigrated to Adelaide. Describing Wally as 'probably the fastest winger in football boots', he went on to predict that:

> 'he will be a sensation in English football. In a league final in Adelaide, the club I played with (Railways) were defeated by Wally's team (Semaphore) thanks to Wally. It was simply impossible to catch him and he turned the heat on that day with a bag of tries. I played centre to Wally for the state team – he certainly doesn't need much room – and as regards tackling, on those granite grounds in Australia he can bowl a man over with terrific strength and power.'

His four-year contract stipulated that he was to receive £200 per year, plus match fees and a return ticket to Australia. The club also arranged for him to continue his engineering apprenticeship at the local Atlas Works of Thomas Holt Ltd.

In general the press paid little attention to the colour of Wally's skin, although it is notable that it was only those players with dark skin whose colour was mentioned; no-one ever called Brian Bevan the 'white flash'. And after a few weeks even the references to the 'Black Flash' disappeared as he became a regular member of the team. Wally was carefully described as 'part-aboriginal' by the few journalists who mentioned it.

The only discussion of his origins appeared in a feature article in the *Rochdale Observer* a few days after his arrival. 'From boyhood, Wally McArthur has been in the midst of one of the greatest Christian and social experiments ever attempted in Australia... Wally appears to be one of many proofs of the success of the experiment,' it claimed, although it pointedly didn't say that this 'experiment' involved him being kidnapped and taken from his mother, never to see her again.

He made his debut for Hornets on 12 December against Salford, playing on the right wing, scoring three goals and creating a very favourable impression among the team's supporters. In thick January fog he appeared from nowhere against Whitehaven to score an outstanding hat-trick. He played another seventeen times that season, mainly on the wing but also starting one game at stand-off in an attempt to get the ball more frequently.

In August 1954 he started the new season with a bang by equalling the club record for most points in a match against Blackpool, when he appeared to be on a different planet to the rest of the players, scoring three tries and kicking eight goals for a total of 25 points. For the first three months of the season, home crowds averaged more than 10,000 per match for the only time in the club's history, no doubt spurred by the hope that Wally's performances brought to the team.

Like many others, supporters' club official Bob Fletcher was stunned by his talent: 'who will ever forget the sight of Wally in full cry? He was probably the fastest runner with the ball ever seen in rugby league football, although he once told me that in his native Australia, where the sun warmed his muscles faster than in Britain, he ran faster.'

The early months of the 1954-55 season proved to be the high point of his Hornets career as he struggled for consistency in a poorly performing side. 'He was given a raw deal on the field of play,' recalled Hornets' supporter John Lang. 'He came to the Hornets direct from junior football in Australia and was immediately put into the first team without a chance of getting used to the conditions over here and adapting himself to the type of play. The crowd expected too much of him. He was given the ball with no room to work in. That again was the fault of those in charge of the team.'

Lang's opinions were obviously shared by a number of other Hornets' supporters. Club officials complained to the local newspaper that some supporters had been telling Wally that he 'would be better off somewhere else' and should move to a club that could make more use of his talent.

It wasn't just on the field where Wally was experiencing problems. A few months after he arrived in Rochdale his fiancée Marlene had joined him and they had been married. Wally had been led to believe that the club would find him and his new wife suitable accommodation but the club backed out of the agreement, claiming that as he had been single when he arrived they had provided appropriate housing for him. This was disingenuous to say the least as all the newspaper reports at the time of his signing mentioned that Marlene would join him as soon as he was settled in the town.

In fact, such sharp practices by club officials were commonplace, especially when it came to offering accommodation and employment to overseas players. Promises of jobs and homes sent by telegram to unsuspecting players often turned out to be quite different when players arrived at their new club; even today examples persist of players going back home or refusing to play until club directors have made good on their promises.

Wally's protests about his treatment led to unnamed club officials complaining that he had 'attitude problems', usually a codeword for someone who refuses to accept their place in the class or racial hierarchy. Unsurprisingly, he became increasingly irritated at the behaviour of the club and in January he decided that enough was enough and asked for a transfer.

On 17 January 1955 the Hornets board of directors agreed to his transfer request and put Wally up for sale for £2,500. 'The idol of thousands of rugby fans in the town, 21-year-old Wally McArthur' reported the *Rochdale Observer*, was set to leave the town and possibly even Britain because he was 'fed up to the teeth' with the way the club had treated him. He even talked about going back to professional sprinting in Australia.

But a fortnight later it looked as if he was about to get the opportunity to play for a leading club when it was announced that he was on the verge of signing for Warrington, the current league leaders and the previous season's Championship and Challenge Cup winners. The prospect of seeing a three-quarter line of Brian Bevan, Stan McCormick, Jim Challinor and Wally McArthur was enough to make even non-Warrington fans salivate. However, negotiations were held up because Wally insisted that Warrington guarantee to pay his passage home when he eventually decided to end his career; no doubt his experience with the Rochdale board made him anxious to ensure that nothing was left to chance.

There then occurred an event which, in hindsight, proved to be crucial to Wally's future but at the time appeared to make sound financial sense. Warrington's former manager, Chris Brockbank, was now the manager of Blackpool Borough and heard of the impasse in the negotiations with Warrington. Seeing an opportunity to capture a star for his new club, he approached Wally with an offer from the Seasiders. Blackpool had only joined the league at the beginning of the season and were looking for a headline name to boost their crowds.

Brockbank agreed to Wally's terms and he signed for the club on 1 February, just a few hours before the deadline to be eligible to play for them in the Challenge Cup. Although Blackpool's contract was undoubtedly attractive, there was just one problem. While Warrington sat imperiously at the top of the league table, Blackpool were rock bottom last, having won just two of their previous twenty-four matches. If Wally had found it difficult to get the service he needed from the Rochdale players, he would find it almost impossible at Blackpool.

Joining the side turned out to be a mistake not just from a playing point of view. Despite Brockbank's assurances, Blackpool were struggling to attract spectators and simply couldn't afford to pay Wally what they had promised. Within twelve months he had again requested a move and the club transfer-listed him at £1,500. Realising that Blackpool's poor form meant that few clubs would be interested in signing him at that price, Wally appealed to the rugby league authorities to reduce the fee.

In December the fee was reduced to £1,000 but there were still no takers. Despite being dogged by niggling injuries and disgruntled at the poor form of the club, which remained locked at the foot of the table, Wally continued to play, scoring twenty tries and thirty-seven goals over his two and a half seasons at the resort. Eventually money matters came to a head again and in May of 1957 Wally complained again to the RFL that Blackpool owed him £750 in unpaid wages for that season.

It is not clear whether Wally ever received his wages because during the summer Salford approached him and he signed for them in June. Although a better side than Blackpool, the Red Devils were at that time a decidedly mid-table team, perhaps marginally better than Rochdale but not by much. But at last it seemed that Wally had finally got the chance to prove himself. He made his Salford debut at Swinton on 10 August 1957 in the annual Red Rose Cup clash, scoring his sides only points with three goals in a 25-6 defeat.

In his first season he scored twenty-two tries and seventy-three goals, finishing as the league's thirteenth highest points-scorer for the season despite the club finishing fifteenth in the thirty-team league. He also played a key role in one of Salford's most memorable victories of the decade, scoring a blistering try and kicking two mighty goals in a heroic 12-7 victory over the all-conquering St Helens side in December 1957.

The rugby league historian and lifelong Salford fan Graham Morris remembers as a young boy the excitement that was created at the Willows by Wally's arrival:

> 'Tall and slim, Wally had the look, grace and speed of an outstanding athlete (which he certainly was) which, combined with a classic side-step, made him a great crowd pleaser at the Willows. Although the Reds were a mid-table team during this period, McArthur still managed 29 tries in 46 matches, a feat aided by the fact that he played outside either John Cheshire or Bob Preece, both robust centres prepared to take punishment and protect the gifted flyer. Wally was undoubtedly, until the arrival of David Watkins in 1967, the most exciting player seen in a Salford jersey in the post-Second World War years.'

In hindsight, his season at Salford was to be the best Wally ever had. But in September 1958 it looked as though he was about to get his chance with a top side when Workington Town, runners-up in both the Championship and Challenge Cup finals the previous season bought him from Salford for £3,000.

Sadly fate let Wally down again. The near misses of 1958 turned out to be the last gasps of the great Town side of the 1950s and in Wally's first season the club crashed to twentieth in the league, just two places above Salford. Even so, he still managed to score fifteen tries and eighteen goals in his twenty-six appearances for the club. Yet again, however, Wally found himself at the wrong end of the sharp practices of club officials. He protested that the club failed to pay him £800 it had promised when he signed on and that it had also reneged on a deal to provide him with a return flight to Australia.

Frustrated, Wally decided that it was time to go back home to Australia and in August 1959 he applied to the RFL for a clearance certificate to allow him to play professionally in Australia. Workington objected, claiming that they had kept their side of the bargain but that he had failed to fulfil his obligations to the club, although what these were was not specified. By October Wally was back in Adelaide; he never received a clearance certificate and he never played professional top-class rugby league again.

But if Wally's career was over, he had helped blaze a trail for dozens of other Aboriginal Australians to come and show their skills in Britain. Indeed, the next player to come was Wally's cousin, Jim Foster, who had grown up with him in the mission homes. Encouraged by Wally, he came over in 1955 and played one senior game for Wigan.

More were to follow in the 1960s. In 1967 future international George Ambrum spent a season at Bradford, where he scored fifteen tries before moving back to North Sydney where he won two Australian caps in 1972. In 1968 Artie Beetson, one of the game's greatest ever forwards and a future captain and coach of Australia, played twelve games for Hull KR before breaking a leg in the last-ever Christmas Day derby game with Hull, leaving behind a legacy which is still remembered by Rovers' fans today.

The lifting of the international transfer ban in 1983 allowed British fans to see some of the greatest Aboriginal footballers of all time. The impact of John Ferguson's single year at Wigan still reverberates and the winger's two tries in the 1985 Challenge Cup final are among the finest to be scored there, while Steve Ella's season at Central Park meant that he probably left Britain with a reputation even higher than the one he had acquired at home.

It is also interesting to note how many of these players captured the imagination of supporters and became cult heroes. What Halifax supporter doesn't remember the full-back of their 1986 championship-winning side 'Smokin' Joe Kilroy, possibly the coolest full-back since Puig Aubert? Ronnie 'Rambo' Gibbs made an even bigger impact at Castleford and became the embodiment of physical intimidation untrammelled by personal fear. And at Leeds, Cliff Lyons, a magician in football boots, demonstrated that the delicate arts of the stand-off had not been crushed under the weight of game-plans and structured sets of six tackles.

But perhaps the man with the biggest impact was Mal Meninga, whose time at St Helens was treated by the club's supporters as a secular second coming. By all accounts the players reciprocated the warmth shown to them by supporters. Certainly Wally and Jim Foster, together with their boyhood friends Charlie Perkins and John Moriarty, who had come to England as soccer players in the late 1950s, found their time in the north of England to be largely free of the overt racism they had experienced at home.

And it is also worth noting that none of these players was treated according to racial stereotypes; they were not simply seen as being fast runners or strong athletes as black players have tended to be in all sports. Tony Currie, whose grandfather had been one of the star Aboriginal league players in the 1930s, playing in a rare victory for NSW Country over Sydney in 1937, and who himself had starred for Leeds in the 1980s, blazed another new trail by coaching the London Broncos from 1996 to 1998, guiding them to their highest ever league position. All of these players, with the possible exception of Smokin' Joe, the ultimate 'laid-back back', were viewed as leaders and examples for other players, whatever the colour of their skin, to follow and emulate.

These masters of the game trod the path that was first walked by Wally McArthur. Today Wally is an old and sick man, suffering from chronic emphysema. Although he never quite achieved the honours his football talents deserved, his memory was imprinted on the minds of British rugby league supporters. When I started writing this article, I wondered whether there would be enough material to make it interesting. I quickly discovered that, despite barely playing seven seasons in Britain, the name Wally McArthur survives strongly in the folk memory of supporters who had seen him play. I rarely had to explain who he was; most of those I spoke to knew the name instantly.

The biggest public acknowledgement of Wally's talent was to be awarded a place in the Aboriginal and Islander Sports Hall of Fame in 1994. But perhaps an even greater tribute is the place he earned in the hearts and minds of those rugby league supporters lucky enough to see him play, 14,000 miles from home in the cold and grey winters of northern England in the 1950s.

6

JOE LEVULA
Harry Edgar

As a boy growing up in the northern county of Cumberland during the late 1950s and early 1960s I had never seen a coloured man until Wigan came to play rugby league in my home town and I first clapped eyes on Billy Boston.

Billy's name and reputation was known by everybody in the community in which I lived, even grandmothers and aunties who had never been to a rugby match in their lives, but only my father had ever seen another black man. In fact he claimed to have seen two in addition to Billy. As a long time follower of rugby league he had watched Cec Thompson many times playing second-row for Workington Town, and he told me of another flying winger called Johnny Freeman who played for Halifax and, like Boston, came from Tiger Bay in Cardiff.

In the innocence of my primary school mind I may have begun to believe that all black men came from a place called Tiger Bay. What was certain at that time, however, was that the only place I would ever see a coloured man in the flesh would be in a visiting rugby league team, and invariably he would be flying down the wing and breaking the hearts of my home town team who not only never had a black player in their ranks, but also never had a flying winger who could conjure a match-winner out of nothing.

Names like Freeman, Boston and Thompson were unmistakably British, but suddenly a new phenomenon hit the game in this country in the early 1960s and it brought something very different and exciting to the rugby communities of the north of England. When Rochdale Hornets announced in the autumn of 1961 that they were recruiting a couple of rugby union players from Fiji, they began exploring an avenue that would bring to rugby league not just a whole new colony of coloured players but also a collection of wonderfully exotic names that immediately became familiar to the game's followers despite their difficulty in pronouncing some of them.

It all started when the Hornets placed an advertisement in the *Fiji Times* newspaper, more in hope than genuine anticipation, seeking rugby players interested in the opportunity to play as professionals in England. Much of rugby league's appeal throughout its history had been based on the English clubs' ability to recruit players from overseas, with many of them becoming star attractions – the charisma of being from a faraway place with a faraway accent adding hugely to their footballing and athletic prowess. And when the primary sources of overseas stars were denied the English clubs by a ban on signing rugby league players from both Australia and New Zealand, those clubs turned their recruiting eyes to nations where rugby union was the only game open to players. South Africa had become a major recruiting ground in the late 1950s and then, in its constant pursuit of the next new thing, rugby league discovered Fiji.

Rochdale's speculative newspaper advert had come a year after their chairman Arthur Walker had first recognised the potential of Fiji's native players when he saw a Fijian rugby union team in action whilst on a visit to Australia. The player who had most attracted the attention of Mr Walker was a big, powerful and fast winger by the name of Josefa (Joe) Levula. Further enquiries by the Hornets chairman revealed that Levula was the most famous rugby player in Fiji as well as being a champion athlete and Fijian sprint record holder.

When approached by Mr Walker, Levula had seemed keen to try his luck in England, but was worried about the possible backlash for his family in Fiji, such was the status and influence of rugby union in his native land. Eventually the message came through that Joe would not be given permission to leave his home country by the tribal chief of Fiji, and that – as far as Rochdale were concerned – must be the end of the matter.

So, Arthur Walker and his Rochdale colleagues consoled themselves with the thought that there might be some other budding Joe Levulas out there, young players without the high status Joe held in his native country, who would be given permission to go overseas, hence their decision to try a newspaper advert.

They got their first response to the advertisement in the *Fiji Times* from a player named Orisi Dawai. Hornets were unaware at that time of the true extent of Dawai's own status in Fijian rugby as the former captain of the national team, but were happy to sign him on after agreeing to his one major request which was that he be able to bring his cousin with him to England to keep him company. Thinking it would be to their own advantage to have their new recruit feeling less isolated in a strange land, Hornets agreed to Dawai's request whilst paying little attention to his additional comment that his cousin had also played a bit of rugby.

Imagine Rochdale Hornets' surprise and delight when they met Dawai at Manchester Airport and discovered that the cousin and travelling partner in question was none other than the famous Joe Levula.

Joe's explanation was that the chief who had denied him permission to leave Fiji over a year earlier had since died, and the change in leadership was adopting a more lenient approach and felt both Levula and Dawai, who had been magnificent sporting ambassadors for Fiji, should have the freedom to go overseas and, hopefully, win more prestige for Fiji in the 'mother country'. It later emerged that Dawai had also been denied a previous opportunity to go and play rugby league in Australia, for the champion St George club, because his request for the necessary emigration permit documentation had been turned down.

The cousins arrived in Rochdale on 13 October 1961 and played their first games of rugby league in the Hornets 'A' team eight days later in front of over 1,500 spectators, some five times the club's usual 'A' team crowd, such was the excitement generated by the presence of these men with strange sounding names who came from a place nobody knew anything about, except that it was thousands of miles away and in the middle of the Pacific Ocean.

And the first impression the people of Rochdale got of their team's new recruits only added to the mystique when the local newspaper pictured them being given their first lesson in the subtleties of rugby league by the Hornets coach Fred Selway, with Dawai and Levula both outfitted identically, wearing their national dress which appeared to be a skirt, along with sandals and their Fijian Rugby Union international blazers. Let me tell you, at that time (still two years before the Beatles kick-started everything and the word swinging became synonymous with sixties) men – especially rugby players – wearing skirts were not commonplace in the Lancashire cotton towns.

The two Fijians' introduction to their new game was impressive enough. In that 'A' team taster they scored all the Hornets' fourteen points in a draw against Liverpool City, both scoring one try apiece and Levula showing his kicking prowess by landing four goals. A few weeks later, on 11 November 1961, both made their debuts in the first team as a left wing-left centre partnership in a 6-6 draw against Whitehaven at the Athletic Grounds, with the whole of Rochdale – to say nothing of the rest of British rugby league – still blissfully unaware of the sheer magnitude of their new recruits although they had huge reputations back in their homeland.

Because Orisi Dawai and Joe Levula weren't just any old rugby players in Fiji, they were legends among their own people, famous names still revered in the annals of Pacific Island rugby a half century since they first came to prominence in their native land – a land where rugby (union) has been the principal sport for almost a century.

It is believed that rugby was first played in Fiji in the 1880s by European and Fijian soldiers of the Native Constabulary at a place called Ba, on Vita Levu island. A club competition began in 1904 in which almost all the players were expatriates. Yet as early as 1907 a well-known New Zealand full-back, AC Holmes, who passed through Suva and played alongside Fijian players, predicted (in a Vancouver newspaper) that Fiji would one day make its mark in rugby football.

The arrival in 1913 of a large group of New Zealanders who went to Fiji to build the Grand Pacific Hotel in the capital Suva, prompted a more serious approach to the organisation of the then casual Fijian rugby, and the following year a so-called 'native competition' began under the leadership of an individual called Ratu Epeli Ganilau. Fiji's first international experience came when they went on tour to Tonga in 1924, with their first overseas match taking place en route as the Fijians stopped in Apia, Samoa. Their match against the Samoans apparently kicked off at 7 am, to allow their hosts time to get to work afterwards, and was played on a pitch with a large tree on the halfway line. Fiji, displaying their New Zealand influences, played in all black and won 6-0.

At their first training session with Rochdale Hornets in 1961, both Levula and Dawai astounded their new team-mates by kicking goals in their bare feet, something that was commonplace in Fijian rugby even then. Actually the Fijians had first played in boots in 1938 in honour of the first New Zealand Maori team to visit Fiji, but there was still a tendency to take boots off during the match and throw them to the touchline, and when Fiji toured New Zealand for the first time in 1939 many players still preferred to play barefoot as one report commented: 'The Fijians played with a carefree spirit, romancing the crowds with their unpredictable running game'.

Incredibly, they also created history by becoming the first team to go through a full rugby union tour of New Zealand unbeaten. In the last of their eight matches on that trip, the tourists 'outclassed' the Maoris 14-4 in Hamilton, and had the *Waikato Times* newspaper running out of superlatives for the Fijian style of rugby, calling it: 'the most brilliant exhibition of football seen for years… almost uncanny in handling the ball, lightening in the pace of their sprinting, relentless in their dive tackling… and all the time pursuing methods of bright, open football… Fiji is destined to play a big part in world rugby'.

It was obvious, already, in 1939 that the Fijian aptitude for playing running rugby meant they really should have been playing the league code which back then would have given free rein to their skills and desires and afforded them much greater joy and success, rather than see their natural instincts and abilities stifled by the set-pieces and technicalities of rugby union. Not surprisingly, but nonetheless sadly, that predicted 'big part in world rugby' for the Fijians has only ever been able to happen in the union code in its abbreviated form of seven-a-side.

Joe Levula's status in Fijian rugby had been immense for fully a decade before he came to England although nobody could ever say with any certainty of being accurate exactly when he was born. Like several other imports to rugby league from rugby union over the years, most notably the Welsh trio of Frank Wilson, Danny Wilson and Gerald Cordle, there was always the suspicion that he was a few years older than was being admitted. When Levula and Dawai arrived in Rochdale in 1961 it was claimed that both were twenty-eight years of age, but Joe had first come to prominence in rugby union as early as 1950 which would have made him only seventeen at the time.

It was none other than the journalist and broadcaster Eddie Waring who first spotted Levula and recognised his potential as a recruit for English rugby league. It was whilst in Sydney, where he was accompanying the 1950 Lions touring team that Eddie claimed to have first seen the young Levula play. A year later, after Joe had made his Test debut for Fiji against the Maori in the New Zealand capital of Wellington, Eddie was hot on his trail, with his enthusiasm only increased when Joe's performances on the Fijians' 1951 tour saw him voted by that year's *New Zealand Rugby Alamanack* as the best winger in the world.

As a former very successful club manager with first Dewsbury and later Leeds, Eddie Waring could claim to have been one of the very first player recruitment agents and played a significant role in bringing many Australians and rugby union players to English clubs, often motivated by the fact that being so closely involved in negotiations gave him the inside information to provide exclusives for his newspaper which no other reporters could get.

With none of the biggest clubs prepared to take a risk on an unknown player from an unknown country, Eddie turned to his old home town club, and sure enough in his *Sunday Pictorial* column on 9 December 1951 appeared the line: 'Dewsbury are negotiating for a Fiji winger Joseph [sic] Levula'. But nothing came of it and Joe stayed at home to continue building his reputation as the greatest rugby player Fiji had seen.

Levula's presence helped the Gaunavou club become recognised as the top club in Suva, with a glamour and prestige no other rugby club in Fiji could match. Joe was one of several former students of the Queen Victoria School in Suva who, in the early 1950s were working as civil servants for the Native Land Trust Board and playing for the Gaunavou club. Translated into English the name Gaunavou means 'new blood,' and one of Joe's team-mates of that time, Eroni Tuisawaqa, explained the philosophy behind the club which came to rely so much on Levula's exploits for its inspiration:

> 'Gaunavou means new blood. When you come in, you change your outlook on things. It's about bringing in new changes and creating new styles of play.'

Joe Levula and his club-mates, one of whom was Orisi Dawai, provided the backbone for the Fijian team's rise to prominence during the 1950s. Their Gaunavou side were described as 'the cream on the cake for rugby clubs in Suva during the 1950s', a decade in which Fiji embarked on ever more high profile tours to both Australia and New Zealand.

Levula and the Fijians were invited to make their first senior tour to Australia in 1952 and their presence helped rescue the Australian Rugby Union from the brink of bankruptcy. The Test series against the

Wallabies was drawn 1-1 in front of big crowds which provided the receipts the Australian Union so urgently needed. Their invitation to the Fijians to tour had come at a time when rugby union in Australia was in danger of being totally usurped by the enormous public interest in international rugby league which had reached spectacular new heights, even by its own immense standards, twelve months earlier when the first French touring team had torn the Aussies apart with spectacular attacking football in two sensational Tests at the Sydney Cricket Ground.

Rugby league in Australia, which already had its long established tradition of four-yearly visits from the tourists from the 'mother country' to do battle for the Ashes, now had an added new dimension brought by the flair and sheer crowd pulling appeal of the colourful Frenchmen inspired by their unorthodox and emotional talisman, the little full-back Puig-Aubert. To save their game Aussie rugby unionists desperately needed to find something similarly new and exciting to put before their public and whilst no sports team in Australia could ever hope to match the exploits and reputation of the 1951 French rugby league tourists, they got the next best thing in the shape of Joe Levula and the Fijians.

With Levula and Orisi Dawai described as being in their pomp, the 1954 team has come to be regarded by many critics as Fiji's best ever. They made their second tour to Australia and attracted record crowds for rugby union in that country as they again drew the series against the Wallabies. But the performances of their 1957 touring team to New Zealand surpassed even that, with a side captained by Orisi Dawai, starring Joe Levula, and containing several other names which were later to become familiar to English rugby league fans like Kaiava Bose, Tomasi Naidole and Josefa Saukuru.

Few people in England had any idea of just how high the status of these players was in their native Fiji, although in later years it became the accepted wisdom that Rochdale and rugby league did not see the best of either Levula and Dawai as both came 'too late' to the game. Had they come a few years younger who knows what an impact they could have made. Nevertheless, their presence in the Hornets team had the whole game talking and within hours of arriving in England they were being interviewed by Eddie Waring on BBC Television's *Sportsview* programme.

Whilst Dawai struggled to come to terms with a new game in a cold climate, Levula had no such problems and he became the centre of attention wherever he played. His long, loping stride seemed to mesmerise opposition defenders and I remember after one game against Workington Town, the international winger Ike Southward describing to the local press in West Cumberland just how difficult it had been to try and tackle big Joe. The same report illustrated a fascination everybody seemed to have with the size of Joe's feet – the word having filtered out that he could kick goals barefoot – when Town's scrum-half Sol Roper, after being accidentally trodden on by Levula, claimed that stud marks on his leg stretched all the way from his knee to his groin. In playing sixteen games in his first season at Rochdale, Joe scored ten tries and kicked nine goals.

It wasn't long before he had more company from home as Rochdale's Fijian colony began to expand rapidly. Arthur Walker had continued his recruitment efforts in Fiji and on 2 February 1962 two more players, this time big forwards rather than flying three-quarters, arrived in the town travelling with the wives of Levula and Dawai. The new boys were the giant second-rower Laitia Ravouvou and a prop-cum-hooker Voate Driu and these two proved to be the most durable of all the Hornets Fijians. Ravouvou, who made his first team debut against Swinton on 24 March 1962, was described by the author of Rochdale's centenary history, the late Bob Fletcher, as 'a mighty man with wonderful potential' and he went on to play seven seasons for the Hornets before moving on to Blackpool Borough. Meanwhile Driu, 'a grafting, courageous player', played five seasons in the cauldron of the front row after making his senior debut against local rivals Oldham on 22 September 1962.

On one occasion around that time I remember being in a throng of young fans collecting the autographs of the Rochdale Fijians and whilst Levula provided a confident and sweeping signature of Joe Levula in my book, I was fascinated that big Ravouvou appeared to struggle to painstakingly print just Laitia.

By Christmas 1962 Arthur Walker had increased Hornets' Fijian colony to six when he introduced two more new recruits, both three-quarters, Litai Burogolevu and Gideon Dolo. The latter was, like Levula, a champion athlete being the Fiji record holder for the triple jump at the time he came to Rochdale. He was also a Church of the Latter Day Saints preacher which helped to continue the media bandwagon surrounding the Fijians off the field because they were perceived as being so 'different' although neither managed to attract any headlines for their performances on it. Neither Burogolevu nor Dolo ever appeared in the Hornets first team and after a handful of 'A' team games they gave up on the idea of making a career in rugby league. They had the misfortune of arriving in the north of England just as the worst winter for 15 years was about to set in. The endless weeks of snow and pitches frozen solid with ice put all rugby league activity on hold and convinced Dolo that this was no place for a man brought up in the warmer climes of his native Fiji, so he headed back to the South Pacific – one of the very few Fijian recruits who ever did go back home.

Rochdale Hornets had now signed six Fijian players in the space of twelve months and despite a strike rate of only three solid successes in the shape of Levula, Ravouvou and Driu, plus Dawai struggling on in the reserves, the venture was regarded as a big enough success for other clubs to want to get in on the act. Having a Fijian player – or at least making a splash in the media to make their supporters think they were trying to get one – became the new trend for English rugby league teams in early 1963 and Rochdale chairman Arthur Walker, who had visited Fiji on the way home from the 1962 Lions tour on which he was Great Britain's assistant manager, was much sought after for advice and contacts by numerous other clubs including local rivals Oldham and Salford, both of whom reports proclaimed would have a Fijian of their own at the start of the following season. They didn't.

But one club who did was Wigan whose signing of a stand-off called Kaiava Qasote Bosenavulagi (known more simply as Kia Bose) made the rugby league world sit up and take notice, and was interpreted as giving a seal of approval to the recruitment of Fijian players to those who, perhaps, had seen Rochdale's efforts as a bit of a gimmick. Wigan's status in the game meant that most of their moves to sign new players caused a stir and one press article at the time suggested that their recruitment of Bose 'really brought home the serious aspect of the Fijian venture to the Doubting Thomases…'

When he joined Wigan in 1963 it was reported that Kia Bose was twenty-four years old. If that were true he would have only been eighteen when he played alongside Dawai and Levula for the Fijian national team on their 1957 tour to New Zealand. He had been recommended to Wigan after their officials had travelled to Catterick army camp to watch several Fijians who were then playing Services rugby union in England. On the strength of Bose's reputation, Wigan had written to him in October 1962 and he agreed to sign for them, leaving his job in the Government printing office in Suva to come to Lancashire. He had been captain of the Lomanate club in Suva for the previous three years and had also toured Australia with the Fijian team in 1961, and came to rugby league with a reputation of being a drop-goal specialist and a magnificent handler and passer of the ball.

I can personally confirm that this pre-billing was fully justified after seeing Bose display all those skills on numerous occasions playing for Blackpool Borough in games where his long loping stride made him appear to glide through defences and his one-handed carrying and passing of the ball mesmerised opponents.

Kia had arrived at Wigan just as the notorious winter of 1963 was at its worst, and there were memorable newspaper pictures of him taking his first look at Central Park skating on the frozen surface as, in the background, workmen with pneumatic drills were trying to break through the ice. Bose settled comfortably into the game in the Wigan 'A' team but, with so many of rugby league's biggest stars at the club, he only ever got to make one first team appearance, against Hull Kingston Rovers on 4 May 1963. Realising he would be better suited to a smaller club where demands and pressures would not be as intense as those at Central Park, Kia made what was a very familiar move for many Wigan wannabees, to the coast and Blackpool where he settled into the full-back role and played for the Borough, on and off, for the next six seasons.

He found a fellow countryman and former international team-mate in the distinctive tangerine, black and white colours of Blackpool in the shape of Johnny Nabou, a loose-forward who had been brought to England by the Borough club chairman Gordon Emery unseen after he had read a magazine article about the 1961 Fijian rugby union tour to Australia in which Nabou was rated their outstanding player. The publicity surrounding his arrival always made great play of the fact that Johnny was a former national wrestling champion of Fiji who could throw men twice his own weight. That great stalwart of the Blackpool club, the late George Lunn, rated Johnny Nabou as the most entertaining of all the many overseas players to play for the Borough, a man who 'excited the crowd whenever he had the ball'.

Nabou had arrived at Blackpool in October 1962 able to speak very little English and was soon desperately uncomfortable in the bitter weather of the winter of 1962–63. According to George Lunn this badly affected his ability to play the game and he languished in the 'A' team throughout that first season. 'On one occasion he was so cold he was on the verge of collapse and had to leave the field in the first half…'

But Johnny was in the first team at the start of the following season when Blackpool opened their new Borough Park stadium and stayed there as a regular for the next two years before cartilage trouble brought a premature end to his career in 1966.

Meanwhile back at Rochdale the Hornets decided it was time for them to boost their own Fijian ranks and in January 1964 they welcomed the man who was to go on to become the most outstanding of all the recruits from the South Pacific, the big forward Apisia Toga. He came on the recommendation of Laitia Ravouvou who, it turned out, was his step-brother. Standing six feet three inches tall and weighing over sixteen stones, Toga made his first team debut against Workington on 15 February 1964 and immediately became a big favourite with the Hornets fans who loved his block-busting style of running. He formed an awesome second-row partnership with his fellow giant Ravouvou and in establishing himself as one of the most effective back-rowers in the British game at that time, Toga inspired Rochdale to reach the 1965 Lancashire Cup final. He also won representative selection for a Rest of the League XIII which played the 1966 Great Britain tourists in a special match at Headingley in November of that year – a match in which Toga scored two tries.

In his four seasons with Hornets Apisia Toga played in 98 first team games and he obviously knew himself he was a good player, so much so that he asked the club to be paid a retainer of £1,800 per season. In those days the only contract payment deemed to be legal in British rugby league was an initial signing-on fee and, whilst there's no doubt this bye-law was widely and habitually broken by many clubs by the provision of under the counter back-handers, such a large amount was way out of the question for a club of Rochdale's standing. Toga's dissatisfaction at not being paid what he thought he was worth simmered until the point where he decided he had had enough of England and headed off to Australia after Rochdale negotiated a £2,000 transfer fee with the St George club. Apisia thrived on living in the warmer climate in an area of Sydney with a growing Fijian population, and he rapidly established himself as an outstanding forward with Australia's most famous club, playing in 103 first-grade games in his four seasons with the Saints between 1968 and 1972.

Toga was at the height of his powers when tragedy struck one balmy summer evening at Kogorah Oval in Sydney during pre-season training early in 1973. He collapsed and died from a heart attack, at the age of just twenty-seven. It wasn't the first time fate had dealt such a cruel hand towards the Fijians who came to Rochdale because the man who started it all, Orisi Dawai, had himself died very suddenly on 25 November 1966 at the reported age of only thirty-three.

Dawai's was ultimately a sad story. His move to England had not produced the new fame and fortune hoped for when he became the first of the Fijians to sign for Rochdale in 1961. In three seasons with the Hornets he managed to play in only ten first team games before his rugby league career petered out in 1963, but he never set foot on his native soil again. A man of such high standing in his home country, still to this day revered as the inspirational captain of the Fijian national rugby union team and the most dignified of sportsmen, Dawai's tragically premature end came as a largely unheralded figure in Rochdale's Birch Hill hospital.

But to his fellow Fijians in England the memory of Orisi Dawai always remained something very special. Almost twenty years after he died I enjoyed a reunion with a group of his fellow countrymen put together by Mike Ratu to enable me to produce a special feature about them in *Open Rugby* magazine, and it was noticeable how overwhelmingly sad their mood became whenever Dawai's name was mentioned. Always described by everybody who knew him as 'an absolute gentleman,' Ratu described Orisi as 'a father figure to all the Fijians who came to Rochdale, and a big help to every one of us'.

Ratu, another winger, had joined Rochdale in September 1965 as one of a second generation of recruits who came to England from Fiji not specifically to play rugby league, but to join the British army. He signed for Hornets along with John Kucuve and whilst Kucuve was another who failed to make the first team, Ratu after making his debut against the 1965 New Zealand tourists, went on to enjoy a successful career over the ensuing four seasons.

Huddersfield had been the first club to recruit Fijians from Services rugby union in England when they signed four players in the lead up to the 1964–65 season – two forwards Josefa Saukuru and John Ravitale, and two wingers Tomasi Naidole and Tom Waqabaca. Both Saukuru and Naidole had been international team-mates of Dawai, Levula and Bose on the 1957 tour to New Zealand and I saw both of them make their rugby league debuts for Huddersfield at Whitehaven in August 1964.

None of the quartet stayed more than a couple of seasons at Fartown and, in truth, they didn't play too many first team games before, in some cases, moving on to Batley and seeing their professional rugby careers fizzle out. Ravitale, however, achieved the honour of being selected to play for a Commonwealth XIII against the New Zealanders in an opener to the 1965 Kiwi tour staged at Crystal Palace, where he played in the pack alongside Voate Drui.

It was John Ravitale who explained to me how so many Fijians had found themselves in the services in England after the British Army went out to the Commonwealth to recruit after National Service came to an end in the UK, and it was Ravitale who also put into perspective other aspects of life the Fijians had encountered when they came to this country. Like all the Fijians I have spoken to, he said he never felt the victim of any racial prejudice or abuse in his time in rugby league, in contrast to what he had experienced whilst serving in the British Army. And the impression I always had as a boy was that the Fijian players were treated with warmth and affection by crowds throughout the game at a time when other players of colour were undoubtedly the victims of attitudes and remarks that today would be deemed, at the very least, desperately politically incorrect if not unashamedly racist.

The only prejudice Fijian players had suffered as rugby players, according to John Ravitale, was from individuals in the rugby union establishment who tried to scare people away from playing the demonised thirteen-a-side game:

> 'The Fijian Rugby Union always put a lot of pressure on their international players. They'd force a lot of this propaganda bullshit on the players, forcing them to sign a paper before they went on overseas tours saying they would not talk to anybody involved in rugby league. That's why Joe Levula never got the chance to go to league until he was way past his best'

Ravitale himself had been a victim of rugby union's apartheid policy after he had been approached to play rugby league whilst serving in the Fijian army based in New Zealand:

> 'I was only approached, I never signed a paper or anything and I never played league. Six weeks later it was all over the

> newspapers in Fiji – I was banned for life because I had links with rugby league. It was the secretary of the Fijian Rugby Union – a Welshman – who set me up. I'll never forget that, even my own family didn't talk to me. The Union was so powerful.'

Mike Ratu, who took a familiar route for retired rugby league players of his era and became a successful publican in Rochdale, gave an insight into how the hugely popular reputations of Joe Levula and Orisi Dawai enabled them to, eventually, override the power of the Rugby Union in Fiji and their attempts to discredit them when they became the trailblazers to rugby league back in 1961:

> 'They were legends with the public and to be leaving the country to go and play professional rugby league in England was a very big thing for the people of Fiji and they were given a big send off.'

Ratu had been a teenager when Levula and Dawai were cementing their reputation as national heroes on the 1957 tour to New Zealand.

> 'We'd gather round the radio and listen to commentaries of Fiji playing in New Zealand and the name that kept coming out was Joe Levula. He was brilliant. Little kids in Fiji are still told the name, Joe was like the Pele of Fijian sport.'

For Mike Ratu the opportunity, a few years later, to be playing in England alongside his boyhood heroes was a magical honour, and it has been Mike who has done most to keep the flame of the Fijian legend still burning in Rochdale. It was a chance meeting I had with him back in 1985 that first made me realise that many of those players who came to England in the sixties were still here, and through him I learnt that Levula, Ravouvou, Ravitale and Kucuve among others were still living in Rochdale and Kia Bose still in Wigan almost twenty years after their playing careers had ended.

They never went back to Fiji. Legends in their native land they stayed, and some have died, in the north of England they arrived in two decades earlier with such high hopes. 'We came to see the bright lights of England, the double-decker buses and the snow,' reflected Mike

Ratu. And as a whole colony of Fijians, some rugby players, some not, came to settle in Rochdale the old Lancashire cotton town became better known back in Fiji than many of the mother country's more traditional tourist attractions.

As for the biggest Fijian legend of them all, Joe Levula, his rugby league career moved on when he left the Hornets after three seasons to join the newly reformed Bradford Northern club. Joe was transferred to Bradford on 20 August 1964 for a £1,000 fee, just in time for him to play in the new Northern's debut match against Hull Kingston Rovers. He left Bradford after one season and wound down his long and eventful rugby career with Batley. The inauspicious end for the man they called 'the Pele of Fijian sport' came on New Year's Day 1966 as a substitute in a badly beaten Batley side at Odsal stadium.

Levula, once a pupil at the prestigious Queen Victoria School in Suva which listed heads of state, governors general and prime ministers among its products, and once probably the most famous man – certainly the most famous sportsman – in Fiji, spent the rest of his working life as a storeman in Rochdale. Joe, like Laitia Ravouvou and his beloved cousin Orisi Dawai, died in Rochdale never ever having been back to Fiji since the day he left on his great rugby league adventure.

Thanks to Mike Ratu the Fijian reunions go on, and family traditions have been maintained with Mike's son Emon being a professional player for both the Hornets and Swinton over twenty years after his own playing days at the Athletic Grounds had finished, and Tomasi Naidole's son Joe enjoying a long playing career with a variety of clubs, a career that is still ongoing with Batley in 2003.

Meanwhile young people in Fiji are still brought up to know the name of Joe Levula and to know that he was somebody very special – it would be nice to think that rugby league could still have enough presence in Rochdale for its young people to know the same.

7

JOHNNY FREEMAN & COLIN DIXON

Robert Gate

When I was about seven I wanted to be either Tarzan or the Household Cavalry. I did not just want to be a member of the Household Cavalry, I wanted to be the whole shebang. Weird. Still, I was only seven. Tarzan was even harder, though. I came from Halifax and did not have an American accent, big muscles or any acquaintance with chimpanzees. Although I was very sporty, shamefully, I did not learn to swim until I was fourteen, by which time I knew I would never be Tarzan.

By the time I was ten, my ambitions were more sensible. I wanted to be Johnny Freeman, or, at a pinch, Garfield Owen. On reflection, I had more chance of winning the football pools, or rather my dad did. Johnny Freeman was Welsh, black, six feet tall, devilishly handsome and death to full-backs and opposing wingers. I was a titch, gingery, freckled, and deaf to my mother's pleas to stop kicking balls about in my school shoes.

Johnny Freeman and Garfield Owen were my heroes from the very birth of my infatuation with rugby league, which took hold at the start of the 1956-57 season. By that time Johnny had been at Thrum Hall for almost two years, while Garfield arrived a couple of months into the season amid a blaze of publicity. He was the current Wales rugby union full-back and reputedly cost Halifax a massive £5,000. He was so newsworthy that his signing took place on live television, on that famous, long lamented programme *Sportsview*, hosted by the imperturbable Peter Dimmock. It was no wonder that I was so besotted by the pair. Garfield kicked all the goals, many of them impossible, and Johnny scored all the tries, many of them improbable.

Johnny, of West Indian ancestry, was born in Cardiff on 17 April

1934. He attended South Church Street School in Tiger Bay, a rare, but unsuspecting, breeding ground for rugby league talent. The fabulous Gus Risman had attended the school almost a quarter of a century before Johnny passed through its portals. Johnny played full-back and centre in the same school team as Billy Boston, while Johnny's cousin Joe Erskine played at stand-off. Joe went on to become British and Empire heavy-weight boxing champion and Johnny maintained a life-long interest in pugilism, although it did not surface too often on the rugby field. A decade later South Church Street School would nurture another pair of future rugby league icons: Clive Sullivan and Colin Dixon.

Freeman, Boston and Erskine eventually graduated to playing for the exotic Cardiff International Athletic Club, a team of many ethnic origins, popularly known as the Kyaks. National Service claimed Billy and Johnny in 1952. Billy, of course, served in the rugby-oriented Royal Signals and on demob was already a professional with Wigan. Johnny was despatched to the Royal Army Service Corps and subsequently returned to playing with the Kyaks. Halifax were soon on his case and he was invited to trial, under the unimaginative alias of 'Smith' on 4 December 1954. Halifax's opponents were Wigan and Billy Boston was on the wing. Johnny was at left-centre partnering another Welshman, Dai Bevan, one of the game's most lethal tackling wingmen, while his co-centre was the great Tommy Lynch, a former All Black. Halifax fielded five Welshmen that afternoon at Thrum Hall and there were a few more on the books, injured or in the reserves. Halifax lost 2-6, Billy failed to score and Halifax decided they had seen enough. They signed Johnny without further trials for £1,050.

Halifax were a superb team in the mid-1950s, always at the top of the league and contesting major finals, which, however, they usually contrived to lose. Johnny was earmarked for the problem left-centre spot but his first season ended after only four games with a bad shoulder injury at Warrington on 5 February 1955. He was fit again for the 1955-56 season, when Halifax came within 160 minutes of lifting all four cups. However, Halifax had in the meantime acquired Geoff Palmer for the left-centre position and he proved a sensational capture. Johnny had to make do with filling in for Palmer or Lynch whenever they were unavailable. The selectors had a real headache, for Johnny was obviously a natural and was scoring some incredible tries, notably when the New Zealanders were beaten 18-17 and against Castleford at

Thrum Hall, when his effort was so scintillating that many old-timers thought it the best try ever scored on the ground. The problem was solved late in the season when it was realised that his best position was left-winger and he replaced Dai Bevan as wearer of the number five jersey.

Johnny played in that role in the Challenge Cup final and the Championship final of 1956, both of which ended in disappointment. At Wembley Halifax and St Helens fought each other to a scoreless standstill for the first 68 minutes before Saints raced away to a 13-2 victory. Johnny had spent the second half hobbling, having crashed into a camera-man shortly before half-time. The following week he scored his twenty-first try of the season – in only twenty-two appearances – in the Championship final at Maine Road only for Hull to snatch a last gasp 10-9 victory with a penalty goal from Colin Hutton.

The 1956–57 season really marked the end of an era for Halifax's great team. They plummeted from top of the league to twelfth and were clearly a spent force. The left wing partnership of Geoff Palmer and Johnny Freeman, however, appeared to be ignorant of the fact. Theirs was a partnership made in heaven. Palmer, well over six feet tall and over fourteen stones, had tremendous pace and balance for such a big man and was the perfect provider for Johnny, who was as fast and elusive as anyone in the game. My own first real memory of Johnny was from a game against Wigan at Thrum Hall on 29 September, which Halifax won 9-3. Alleluia! It was the first time I and 14,808 other spectators saw a direct confrontation between Johnny and Billy Boston as wingers. Johnny kicked a goal but neither scored a try. The most memorable incident, certainly for a junior school kid like me, was when Billy somehow got away on the outside of Johnny on the top side in the shadow of the main stand. Away he went, only to be baulked and driven inside where Johnny recovered fast enough to grab him by the shorts, which came away in his hand. Hilarity and blushes all round. Well, at least among the kids.

Johnny also got the better of Billy later in the season at Central Park, although Halifax were whacked 25-9 on 23 March. Johnny got a hat-trick. Reputedly only Johnny and Swinton test man John Stopford ever scored three tries past Bouncing Billy, when he played on the wing. Johnny's third try equalled the Halifax club record of forty-five tries set by fellow Welsh winger Billy (WJ) Williams back in 1908–09. We all expected Johnny to break the record in the next match two weeks later but Huddersfield won 10-5 at Thrum Hall and there was no try for him. Nor was there any in the next two games, both at Thrum Hall against Workington Town and Warrington. Three home games within the space of a week and not a solitary try! Such a thing had not happened since he joined us. He had never failed to score in more than two successive games. Moreover, Geoff Palmer missed the last seven games of the season, which was not helping. Johnny finally got it right though on 13 April, when he raced over twice in a thrilling 21-20 victory over the French champions Albi in a European Championship fixture. My school cap disappeared when it was thrown into the air along with hundreds of other caps, hats and whatnots after he claimed his first record-breaking touchdown. Two days later he extended his new record to forty-eight with a try in a 33-10 rout of Carcassonne. He also kicked a couple of goals, the last of fifteen he landed in his career. Those forty-eight tries were scored in forty-five games but he was denied his half century, as he missed the last two games of the season.

Even a sprog as green as I recognised brilliance. I also recognised and memorised the spots on the field where bits of players' shorts and jerseys fell to ground after they had been too roughly handled. I built up quite a collection of strips of crumpled, muddy fabric, all of which I could identify. Most of them were from Johnny's kit, retrieved in forays on to the pitch when the final whistle sounded. My mother was mystified at such antics but it was a few years before she finally binned those 'valuable' trophies, by which time even I wondered why I had collected them.

The 1957–58 season saw Johnny Freeman in coruscating form. He was on fire, unstoppable, out of this world. There was no doubt about it. He was the best of the lot and that lot included wingers such as Billy B, Brian Bevan, Ike Southward, Frank Carlton, Frank Castle, Terry O'Grady, Dick Cracknell, John Etty, Alan Snowden, Terry Hollindrake, Malcolm Davies, Wally McArthur and bloody Mick Sullivan. There was a Lions tour scheduled for the summer of 1958 and there was categorically no doubt that Johnny would be on it. All the critics agreed, all the supporters' selections in the newspapers and trade press had the two left wing berths marked down for Johnny and bloody Mick Sullivan. Half way through the season the *Rugby League Gazette* published its world ratings. Top of the list, though oddly as a right winger, was Johnny Freeman, followed by Guy Husson (France), Boston, Raymond Contrastin (France) and the newly arrived South

African, Tom van Vollenhoven (St Helens). The top five wingers on the other flank were Ian Moir (Australia), Carlton, bloody Mick Sullivan, Bill Wookey (Workington Town) and Vincent Cantoni (France).

It appeared that every time Freeman got the ball he scored or at least threatened to score. Certainly the crowds began to expect miracles when he was in possession. Here was a man who could go the length of the field, who could break tackles when apparently held, who could find that extra gear, when seemingly already flat out, who could go past defenders on the inside or the outside, who would be first to any kick forward and who could pluck interception tries out of nothing. He had star quality, good looks and an effortlessness of movement which was captivating. Jack Nott, the *News of the World* rugby league correspondent, later wrote, 'Freeman is fabulous. He seemed to mesmerise the opposition – like the cobra and the rabbit. He would glide gracefully through the defence – like he was in dancing class'. Jack was right, although I hasten to add that we did not get the *News of the World* in our house. It was far too risqué, even in those days. We got the *Sunday Pictorial* and the *Sunday Express* but Eddie Waring and Phil King seemed to pretty much agree with Nott's judgement.

Just how fast Johnny was in his prime is debatable. I certainly never saw anyone catch him from behind and he faced all the very quickest wingers in a period, when they were mostly specialist sprinters. Good judges of athletes, such as Matthew Clamp, a coach to many top sprinters, were at a loss to know why Johnny never took part in professional sprints such as the Powderhall. He had the perfect physique and running style to be a top-notcher. I once interviewed Ken Dean and Stan Kielty, Halifax's famous half-backs of the period. Ken averred that the team's objective became getting the ball to Johnny, as that generally meant three points. Stan recalled sprinting sessions at training in which Johnny would tear clear of everyone else, look back, laugh, stop, run on a bit further, look back, laugh, stop, run on a bit further… and there were some quick men at Thrum Hall.

Anyway, the 1957–58 season was going swimmingly for Halifax, who eventually won the Yorkshire League, and for Johnny. In the first twenty games of the season, he failed to score only three times. His scoring sequence went: 1, 2, 3, 1, 3, 1, 2, 0, 3, 2, 2, 0, 1, 5, 3, 2, 2, 0, 3, 2. Twenty games, thirty-eight tries. That rate of scoring was as good as anything anyone ever achieved – Brian Bevan, Alf Ellaby, Eric Harris, Johnny Ring, Tom Vollenhoven, Martin Offiah, anyone. There was a real threat that Albert Rosenfeld's seemingly unbreakable record of eighty tries in a season, set back in 1913–14, might go. Johnny was getting better as the season progressed and Halifax played another twenty-one matches. Rozzy had scored his eighty in forty-two games so their scoring rates were almost exactly the same.

On 21 December 1957 Halifax went to Batley and won 36-7. Geoff Palmer crashed through for four tries and Johnny and his fellow winger Keith Williams scored two each. Bizarrely, Williams would become Vicar of Batley in later life – no kidding. Johnny could have done with some of Keith's prayers, for in scoring his second try he received a sickening knee injury, which put him out of the game for a year, threatened his career and unquestionably cost him his place on the Lions tour. Still, he was in good company, as his pal Billy Boston was also overlooked, a criminally insane act, if ever there was one. Bloody Mick Sullivan went on to set a Lions record of thirty-eight tries on the tour. That could have been Johnny.

Johnny had scored 109 tries in only ninety-one games for Halifax when his knee was shattered. It would be March 1958 before the chasing pack overtook his thirty-eight try tally. Bloody Mick Sullivan finished top try-scorer with fifty and he had to wait until April to catch Johnny.

When Johnny finally returned to fitness he joined a Halifax team which was in decline, almost all the heroes of the mid-1950s having departed. Mediocrity set in for half a decade. Johnny was never quite the same after his injury, although he was still phenomenally quick and continued to be a match-winner. The standards he had set before his injury meant that the fans expected fireworks when he was in possession. He could still provide the goods, if not quite as often. A whole generation of Halifax fans were accustomed to watching 'Freeman specials'. These usually consisted of Johnny being released somewhere between his own goal-line and 25, whizzing outside the opposing winger, racing towards the full-back and flashing inside or, more often, outside the poor sod, while any defender who was game or daft enough to chase him would soon realise the error of his ways. Most of Johnny's tries at Thrum Hall were scored at the pavilion corner, which was uphill for any covering defender. It always staggered me that Halifax's tacticians did not better utilise Johnny's speed and elusiveness by allowing him to play on the top side of the ground in both halves of a game. The same could be said for Mark Preston in more recent years.

Johnny broke fellow Welshman Arthur Daniels' club record of 215 tries with a hat-trick against York on 5 October 1963 and by the time he retired in 1967 he had rattled up 290 tries in 396 appearances for Halifax. It is doubtful if that record will be beaten. If it is, Halifax fans certainly have something and someone very special to look forward to.

Johnny Freeman was incredibly unlucky not to have won international honours. Basically, it was that bloody Mick Sullivan's fault. Mick had established himself as Britain's left-winger in 1954 and did not vacate the job for almost a decade, establishing a record of forty-six test appearances. There is no doubt that Mick was as suited to international rugby as any player who ever pulled on a Great Britain jersey. That pre-eminence of Sullivan, and Johnny's misfortune at Batley, conspired to prevent the Welshman ever winning a test cap. If he had played in any other era, Johnny would have had a cupboard full. Nor did he ever gain a Welsh cap. Wales as an international side fell into abeyance in 1954 and did not surface again until 1968. Neither Billy B nor Johnny ever got the chance to play for Wales. Johnny did, however, represent a Welsh XIII against France in Toulouse during the Great Freeze of 1963 but no caps were awarded. To add insult to injury, no man has ever scored as many tries as Johnny Freeman and not won international honours. I could certainly name plenty of wingers, infinitely inferior, who have been so honoured... the luck of the draw, I suppose.

The last few years of Johnny's career saw Halifax blossom again. In 1963–64 he picked up Yorkshire Cup and Eastern Division Championship winners' medals. In 1964–65 Halifax finished as Champions, surprising St Helens 15-7 in the final at Swinton. Saints gained revenge in 1966 at the same venue with a resounding 35-12 victory and Johnny was one of the main protagonists in a sensational brawl, which scarred a game simmering at boiling point throughout. It was his last big game.

In his final season at Halifax, 1966–67, Johnny received a benefit which yielded a club record £1,013 19s 0d (£1,013.95). A couple of years earlier, when he should have been eligible for a benefit, Johnny was banned from the game. On 24 September 1964 Halifax were fined £500, three of their directors were severely censured and Johnny was suspended until 1 November, resulting in his missing seven games. His crime dated back to the period of his injury in 1957–58. He had returned to Wales and was contemplating retiring in view of the medical prognosis. Halifax were desperate to get him playing again and gave him £177 for the duration of that season. They also offered him £300 a year for the next three years as an inducement to carry on playing. Six years later this was deemed an illegal payment. The fact that illegal payments, or back-handers in common parlance, were endemic in rugby league and always had been, was common knowledge. No one could recall any other instance of such proceedings being taken by the game's authorities. It was all really a bit rich but just Johnny's luck. The Halifax chairman, Charlie Horsfall, resigned from his position on the Rugby League Council in protest. Ironically, Mr. Horsfall had been Chairman of the Rugby Football League in 1957–58.

When Johnny Freeman fetched up in Halifax in 1954, there was virtually no black presence on the town's streets. He was something exotic, the influx of Asian workers to Halifax's mills and factories being still some years in the future. Once he had got over his injury Johnny settled in the town, living there until very recently when he returned to Wales. In private life he was a painter and decorator and latterly for many years a representative for Refuge Assurance. Once his playing career ended so did his active participation in the game, save for occasional appearances in benefit or charity matches, when he always looked as fit as his successors. One of his daughters, a beauty queen, modelled leisure wear for the Rugby Football League in the 1980s. Needless to say, Johnny was among the first batch of players to be admitted to Halifax's Hall of Fame on its inauguration in 1993.

At the close of the 1960–61 season Johnny Freeman lost his centre partner, when Geoff Palmer retired at the age of twenty-six. Halifax decided that a replacement was needed and quickly. Colin Joseph Dixon turned out to be that replacement and the Dixon–Freeman combination became an unforgettable union for Halifax followers of that era.

Colin Dixon was born in Cardiff on 3 December 1943. His father, a seaman and a former United States serviceman, died when Colin was twelve and he had to grow up quickly to help support his mother and family. His rugby career at South Church Street School had started slowly. When he was seven Colin had been told to report for practice with the older boys but had heard tales of the dreadful things that could happen on a rugby pitch and decided that he would prefer not to get involved! He was soon converted, however, and became enamoured with the sport, graduating from wing to fly-half to scrum-half. He represented Cardiff Schools and played for Cardiff Youth alongside Jim Mills, at whose wedding he would later act as best man. Colin was intent upon winning a Wales Youth cap and was selected for the final trial in 1960, when his half-back partner was David Watkins. Colin was not chosen for the international. In 1993 Watkins told *The Western Mail*, 'He deserved to go on to win a cap. I think it was his colour that worked against him.'

Disappointment at failing to win his cap may have contributed to his decision to accept Halifax's offer of £1,000 in May 1961 but it was of more significance that his mother, Evelyn, actively encouraged him to go north. Tiger Bay was a tough environment, she argued, with plenty of pitfalls for a young black man, so why not take the opportunity to better his prospects. So Colin, training to become an engineer, went to Halifax as a gauche seventeen-year-old with very little idea of what was in store for him. He would, however, spend the remaining thirty-two years of his life in the town of a hundred trades, which clings to the edge of the Pennines, becoming one of Halifax's favourite adopted sons.

In fact Colin Dixon became a genuine legend. The club historian, Andrew Hardcastle, wrote in *Thrum Hall Greats* in 1994:

> 'In Halifax he was a star and a personality. Indeed he will be remembered for his personality almost as much as for his great rugby ability. His huge smile and his friendly, jovial disposition, his eloquence and his ability to laugh at himself – he always seemed to have a humorous line about his colour – contrasted sharply with his hard, physical, aggressive approach to the game, which did not always endear him to opposition supporters.'

In an interview with Pat Farrell in the *Australian Daily Mirror* (17 July 1974) Colin was asked, 'Since you don't seem to mind, my first question has to do with your colour. I imagine the Australians make occasional impolite reference to it in the tests?'

His response was:

> 'Yes, they do, but they can sling as much muck as they like. They're only wasting their tongues and their time… I've been around too long in top league to let it worry me. When I started,

it used to send me mad. Just after I left Tiger Bay to play league with Halifax – I was about seventeen – they'd be saying "you black bastard" and, of course, I'd lash out and get sent off. Then after about a dozen times, my coach reminded me they were just provoking me. And I realised he was right – everybody was collecting his wages bar me.

Actually, it's funny, the way some people are about coloured folk. When I was courting my wife in Yorkshire, there was all hell to pay among her relatives and friends. When they realised we were determined to marry, somebody said to her, "How on earth are you going to feed this fellow?" And she said, "Well, he eats fish and chips like everyone else does." I think they imagined I was a bloody cannibal or something.'

As always with Colin, some of what he said was tongue in cheek. For example, he was not always being sent off. In seven years at Halifax, he was sent off just twice in 245 matches and the first was a few months into his career. It was the day before his eighteenth birthday, in a 9-3 home victory over Bradford Northern – his thirteenth first team game. For a man who played the game with such relentless but controlled and legal aggression, Colin's disciplinary record was an object of wonder.

Colin made his debut at left-centre to Freeman on 12 August 1961, when Halifax won 18-13 at Huddersfield in the annual Charity Cup fixture, although the last thing that abounded in such encounters was charity. He came through with flying colours, Johnny's hat-trick being eloquent testimony to the youngster's success. Influenza kept Colin out of the team for several weeks but by the time he turned eighteen he had established himself in the first team, had played for a combined Halifax–Huddersfield XIII against the New Zealanders, had received that dismissal against Bradford and was enough of a local celebrity to be invited to judge beauty competitions.

As a boy Colin had admired Cliff Morgan as a union player but his real idols were fellow Cardiffians, Billy Boston and Johnny Freeman. He was now playing with the latter and for the first time opposed Billy on 16 December 1961. It had been an interesting and unusual ritual for the last seven years for Johnny and Billy to greet each other and shake hands before the kick-off in their clashes at Thrum Hall and Central Park. Now the crowd were to become accustomed to another six years of the ritual but with the addition of a third black Welsh bloke. Billy soon forgot the pleasantries, however, laying Colin out with one of his dramatic crash tackles as he tried to send Johnny away on the outside. After the game Billy assured Colin it wasn't personal!

Colin had joined Halifax at a period when they were in the doldrums but he was clearly a star in the making. Halifax had no intention of playing him at scrum-half. He was almost six feet tall and over thirteen stones when he arrived at Thrum Hall, much too big for a rugby league scrum-half and he was going to get a lot heavier and stronger. Colin was certainly raw but his enthusiasm and enjoyment of the game were boundless and his bold dashes and inter-passing with Johnny Freeman had the fans spellbound. By the turn of 1963 he was good enough to be selected as partner to Johnny in the Welsh XIII which met France at Toulouse on 17 February, just a couple of months past his nineteenth birthday. Remarkably, he would still be playing international rugby eighteen years later, one of the longest representative careers on record.

The 1963–64 season marked a change at Halifax, where a successful team suddenly emerged under skipper and scrum-half Alan Marchant, ably abetted by two key signings, stand-off Alan Kellett from Oldham and second-rower Ken Roberts from Swinton. On 2 November 1963 Colin was at centre in the team which beat Featherstone Rovers 10-0 at Wakefield to win the Yorkshire Cup, Rovers for once being favourites in a final. It was the first of a dozen major domestic finals for Colin. Six weeks later Halifax travelled to St Helens for a televised game and on the bus it was found that loose-forward Charlie Renilson was unfit. Coach Albert Fearnley decided that Colin should take his place, despite the fact that he was untried as a forward. Saints were a great side and, moreover, had Alex Murphy at scrum-half. Colin's instructions were 'to knock Murphy into the stands' every time he got near him. Easier said than done – Murph scored one try but Colin did pretty well as Halifax won 13-12, a result they have never subsequently achieved in a league match at Knowsley Road.

The die had been cast. Although Colin would still play plenty of games at centre, his future lay in the pack, specifically in the second row. He finished the season playing in the second row, forming a brilliant back three with Terry Fogerty and Charlie Renilson, arguably as fine a combination as ever graced the Halifax pack. A second winners' medal was his when Halifax beat Castleford 20-12 at Fartown in the Eastern Division Championship final.

As a centre Colin was hard-driving, strong and had a good understanding with Freeman but he lacked finesse and was not quite fast enough to be a top-rater. As a forward he had more than enough pace, relished the physicality and had the stamina, guts and bellicosity required. He was a natural. His move certainly paid dividends for in 1965 he played a major part in Halifax's tremendous victory over St Helens in the Championship final, the club's first title triumph since 1906–07. Necessity had him back at centre the following year when Halifax lost heavily to Saints in a repeat Championship final and the advent of limited tackles in 1966–67 accelerated Halifax's eventual fall from grace as the Championship-winning side broke up.

Colin, player of the year in 1964–65 and 1966–67, was given the captaincy in 1967–68. In 1968–69 he was the finished article, a great second-rower and an inspirational leader. At Thrum Hall that season he gave the lie to the assertion that one player does not make a team. Under his leadership Halifax had attained a top four position by December and Colin had made try-scoring debuts for Wales and Great Britain in November. He was the hottest property in rugby league but he was happy at Halifax. The club, however, was in a parlous financial state and when Salford offered a world record £15,000 (including winger Mike Kelly, valued at £3,000), Halifax bit off their hand. Colin was mortified. He had settled well in employment as an engineer at the local Churchill Redman firm, married Anne, a local girl, and was part of the Thrum Hall furniture. He never would leave Halifax, becoming a publican for six years and ultimately a housing officer for the local authority. His popularity was such that a street, Dixon Close, was named after him in Greetland, one of Halifax's outlying districts.

His value to Halifax was reflected in their free fall from the top four to a final position of eighteenth. The heart of the side had been ripped out. His time at Salford, however, was successful and no one could ever accuse Colin Dixon of offering less than his very best. Within a few months he was appearing at Wembley in a 6-11 defeat by Castleford. Many good judges thought he should have won the Lance Todd Trophy, so outstanding was his performance in a well beaten team. Salford were on the verge of great things. They recruited many wonderful players over the succeeding years, already having signed union icons David Watkins and Mike Coulman. Massive league signings included winger Bill Burgess, full-back Paul Charlton, back-rower Eric Prescott and scrum-half Steve Nash, while two superb union wingers, Keith Fielding and Maurice Richards, added glamour, pace and excitement to the three-quarters.

Colin was just as popular at Salford as he had been at Halifax. Salford won the Championship in 1973–74 and 1975–76 and also appeared in eight major finals in Colin's time as a Red Devil, although only two of them were won – the Lancashire Cup final of 1972 and the BBC Floodlit Trophy final in 1974–75. He played in three losing Lancashire Cup finals in 1973 (as a second-rower), 1974 (centre and captain) and 1975 (blind-side prop), while he was loose-forward when Salford lost to Leeds in the Players Trophy final of 1973 and in the second row when St Helens beat them in the 1976 Premiership final.

In 418 games for Salford he claimed 91 tries to add to his 73 for Halifax. He landed a solitary goal for Salford, when his drop goal crept over the bar at Hull KR to give Salford a 15-13 victory in a Players Trophy semi-final in 1972. In 1979 he shared a testimonial with Mike Coulman and played his last game for Salford against Leeds on 27 April 1980. His career ended with 24 games for Hull KR in 1980-81, a season in which Rovers won the Premiership and were runners-up in the Yorkshire Cup and Challenge Cup, although he did not appear in any of the finals.

Colin played the game as hard as it was legally possible to play it. He was perpetual motion. He gave everything in attack and defence and ultimately he became very adept with the ball. He was spectacular in the extreme, often scoring sensational tries over long distances, leaving even fleet-footed backs in his slipstream. He seemed to be omnipresent, indestructible and indefatigable. He was probably even more noticeable simply because he was black and black forwards were as rare as hens' teeth in those days.

I was present at Headingley on 1 May 1971, when Leeds met Salford in a quarter-final Championship play-off match. Salford–Leeds encounters in this period were must-see affairs and I was usually there, as Halifax played on Sundays while Headingley still staged Saturday games. This was another epic, Leeds winning 37-22, but cursed by tragedy. Leeds's test stand-off Mick Shoebottom, every bit as competitive and combative as Colin, dived for a try and copped Colin's boot in the head in the process. It was an accident. Of that, I have no doubt. Nor, it appeared had the crowd, for there was no booing or demonstrations of wrath, just the normal courtesy of a rugby league crowd clapping an injured player being carried from the field.

Unfortunately, this was no ordinary injury. The lion-hearted Shoebottom, the idol of the Leeds crowd, nearly died, never played again and was never the same man.

The clubs' next encounter at Headingley saw Colin subjected to disgraceful provocation both on and off the pitch and for several years his visits to Leeds saw him the object of constant booing and vitriol. Colin rose above it all and simply played as he had always played. Ironically, Colin died on 21 June 1993, aged forty-nine, from a stroke, while playing dominoes. The unfortunate Mick Shoebottom outlived him by almost a decade. Both men would have thrived in the modern game and were exactly the types of player required to restore British dominance to the game. After his death Halifax and Salford decided to commemorate one of their greatest players by playing an annual match for the Colin Dixon Memorial Trophy.

Colin played 738 first class games (177 tries), an achievement bettered only by five other men. He won fifteen Welsh caps (1968-81) and fourteen test caps (1968-74). He was a Lion in 1974, a member of Great Britain's World Cup-winning squad in France in 1972 and toured with the Wales World Championship squad in 1975. It beggared belief that in 2003 he was omitted from the Wales all-time XIII, the members of which were all admitted to the Welsh Sports Hall of Fame.

In 1977 Colin became player-coach at Salford but gave up the coaching responsibilities after ten months. After retiring from playing he did coach again at his beloved Halifax (1982–84) and at Keighley (1986–89). After taking Halifax to promotion in 1983-84, he was making a good fist of the resulting First Division season, when Halifax again poked him in the eye and replaced him with the Australian player-coach Chris Anderson. The fans were outraged – Halifax could certainly have handled it better – but he left the scene with dignity and was coach to the Halifax Academy at the time of his death. That was typical of Colin. He always came back, no matter how hard they put him down.

8

DAVID BARENDS

Mike Rylance

The final of rugby union's World Cup between South Africa and New Zealand in 1995 was overshadowed by the man who wore the Springbok jersey but did not play. When President Nelson Mandela appeared wearing the most potent symbol of South African sport, the unthinkable had become reality. As if it weren't enough that the black freedom fighter should emerge from twenty-eight years' imprisonment to become head of a state once based on white domination, here he was embracing the finest expression of the very culture he had sought to overthrow – and, with the gold number six on his back, raising both fists in triumph when the hosts carried off the trophy with a late drop goal.

While old-time Afrikaners clenched their teeth, a new generation of blacks accused the hero of selling out and booed him when he urged them to support 'rugby'. Mandela's policy of exploiting the situation for the greater good was intended to help remove a set mentality, but in sport attitudes have long roots. Particularly in the reactionary world of South African rugby union, for so long the preserve of white supremacists who clung to the belief that the 15-a-side game was for their exclusive enjoyment. Only a year before Mandela embraced rugby union on behalf of the new South Africa, a renowned ex-Springbok was widely quoted as saying that the game was not part of black culture. Intentionally or not, he was defending union's segregationist stance by voicing a long-held white view that, as in most other forms of organised sport, blacks had shown little interest in rugby union.

Those who would have been happy to see Mandela rot in his Robben Island gaol probably imagined the leisure activities of black South Africans to be either tribal or illegal. Or possibly involved the kicking of a round ball. In this abnormal society, rugby was the preserve of the white man. And yet, in certain areas of South Africa, black rugby was not only very popular but had a long history, going back to the British colonial days of the nineteenth century. At that time Africa's southernmost tip was home to numerous non-white clubs, with a good deal of activity taking place in and around Cape Town. A more liberal attitude to race originally prevailed there and participation in British culture and recreation could be a step up the social ladder for the indigenous population. Despite the social segregation which followed later, rugby remained a favourite pastime of the black and coloured inhabitants, who organised their own clubs and competitions. Clubs often became the focal point of the community, drawing fervent support, and beyond that level provincial and national sides played representative matches. Large crowds turned out to watch the clashes between the Coloured XV, made up of mixed race players, and the Bantus, a generic term for black South Africans. Matches against white representative teams were strictly off limits.

It was from this background that 21-year-old winger David Barends arrived in England in December 1970 to attempt, like other South Africans before him, to make the transition from union to rugby league. Barends had been recommended to Wakefield Trinity by an ex-player, Ivor Dorrington, who had returned home ten years earlier 'too old and too cold' to make a successful switch between codes. Dorrington had watched Barends in action for the South African Coloured team and had been impressed. The Leeds sporting promoter, Jim Windsor, who had connections in the Cape and had brought other players over, did the rest.

Among a spate of South Africans who arrived in England during the late 1950s and 1960s, players such as Tom van Vollenhoven and Len Killeen at St Helens, Fred Griffiths at Wigan, Alan Skene, Colin Greenwood and Gert Coetzer at Wakefield, Wilf Rosenberg at Leeds and Hull and Jan Prinsloo at both St Helens and Wakefield made a big impact on rugby league. Some went on to have an influence on the game in Australia. A number of them had been Springboks, most wore jerseys numbered between one and five and all of them were white. Less well-known were the Leeds forward, Louie Neumann, who had been selected for the Coloured Springboks, and Ghulam Abed Hussein, who, like Neumann, had represented Western Province and the Coloured South Africans before signing for Bradford Northern. In an interview Hussein, a product of the surprisingly intense Muslim rugby competition in the Western Cape, said that his aim in coming to

England was to prove himself 'and at the same time enhance the status of the Coloured South African'. Hussein also made the crucial point about his one-time team-mate Neumann: 'No South African forward has ever made a greater impression than Louie in England and yet he could never play for his own country on account of his colour.'

Like Neumann and Hussein, Barends was also selected for the Coloured XV, being of mixed race – one grandparent was a Boer, another of Portuguese origin. It was when he played against the Bantus in front of a huge crowd at Cape Town that he was spotted by Dorrington, who noted the young winger's try-scoring ability. Barends had first played rugby at his private school, where he also gained a reputation as a sprinter before joining the Roslyn club in Cape Town's District Six. 'In Cape Town everybody played rugby,' he said. 'They also played football, but predominantly rugby.'

The style of play practised by Africans was particularly physical and Barends was a typical product of that school. The stocky, powerfully-built South African looked as if he could provide the answer to the left-wing problem at Wakefield Trinity, who were then lying second in the league behind St Helens. When he arrived in Yorkshire in December 1970 for a reported £1,000 signing-on fee, Barends was predicted by Jim Windsor to become 'another Billy Boston type of player'. There was a certain irony in that comparison. The former Wigan star, so as not to fall foul of apartheid restrictions, was obliged to fly straight home from Ashes duty in Australia in 1962 when the rest of the Great Britain squad went on to play a number of promotional matches in Barends's homeland.

Barends moved into a house which the club owned close to the ground, sharing it with the black winger, Mick Hunte, father of Alan, and made his debut a week before Christmas in the 44-10 defeat of struggling Blackpool Borough, who were fourth from bottom. Raw and unprimed, he nevertheless scored his first try after just half an hour when his centre and captain–coach Neil Fox carefully supplied the pass which sent him over. He crossed the Blackpool line again in the second half, beating two defenders to contribute to Wakefield's ten-try victory. The Belle Vue crowd sensed the newcomer's promise. 'They readily forgave his first-half handling errors and defensive lapses, rose to his tries and gave him a resounding reception at the end,' wrote the *Wakefield Express* reporter.

That initial burst of promise could not disguise, however, the fact that the rugby that held sway in the north of England was far removed, both in character and geography, from the code which predominated in South Africa. 'It was very different, very strange,' a much older and wiser Barends reflected. 'Rugby league is hard work and if you don't work hard, you don't get anywhere.' Articulate and analytical, he maintained that:

> 'Rugby league shows you about real life. When you've got the ball, you have to take responsibilities. It's also about decision-making. If you put your team-mate under stress, if you pass the ball and he gets taken out, it may mean that you've made the wrong decision. The decisions you make have to be achievable, so they have to be made simple.
>
> I think it took me several years to get to grips with the game. I remember playing against Salford in a Player's No 6 tie. I received the ball and the next thing I remember was that I had loads of stitches in my mouth. That brought home to me the simplicity of the game! You also have to remember that when you have the ball, the opposition want it back at any cost. No matter how good you think you are, somebody's always likely to take you out.'

Barends's progress in rugby league was not as smooth as either he or Wakefield Trinity had hoped and after three seasons at Belle Vue he moved to York. 'For me as an individual to make an impression I needed to move somewhere where I could show people what I was capable of doing and relaunch my career,' he said. On the reintroduction of two divisions in 1973, York found themselves shuttling up and down, but Barends appears to have been happy there. 'People in York love rugby and we had some of the best supporters,' he commented.

It was during his time at York that Barends won his first representative honours in rugby league when he was selected for the Other Nationalities team which took part in the County Championship in 1975. He scored two tries in the defeat by Lancashire and touched down again in the 16-all draw against Yorkshire at Odsal. Barends was partnered in the Other Nationalities three-quarter line by another black South African who was beginning to make a name for himself. Green Vigo had joined Wigan two years earlier from Saldanha Bay, situated about 100 kilometres from Cape Town on South Africa's western coastline. A centre in rugby union, Vigo was becoming known as an exciting winger with Wigan, though he reverted to the inside position in two of the three county championship matches. Vigo would be remembered by Wigan fans for two exceptional feats. In a Lancashire Cup tie against St Helens he equalled the club try-scoring record, crossing Saints' line no fewer than seven times, while a hat-trick at Leeds forced his opposite number, the international winger John Atkinson, then nearing the end of his career, into believing it was time to pack the game in. 'Those were three of the greatest tries I've ever seen,' said Wigan's test second-rower Bill Ashurst. 'He had so much talent.'

But although Vigo made his mark on the Wigan public, he found the transition from life as a fisherman in the Cape to that of a semi-professional rugby league player in the north of England less straightforward. The segregation laws of his native country had not equipped him to deal with the freedoms of his new environment. Soon after arriving in Wigan, Vigo went into a pub not far from Central Park. As he stepped inside, he saw one door leading to the lounge and another to the vaults. Confused, he enquired at the outsales window which room he was allowed to enter.

'He was a great athlete who always wanted to do his best. He was a terrific trainer and scored some memorable tries,' said another former playing colleague, international hooker Colin Clarke. 'But he was brought over from the outback in South Africa, dropped in the middle of Wigan and just left there. At the time there was no procedure to integrate him into society. He didn't even know how to get back to his lodgings after training. He was a class winger and a great entertainer, but he couldn't come to grips with the culture.'

After seven seasons at Wigan, Vigo moved on to Swinton and then Oldham, but once he gave up playing rugby league, in 1984, no one was really sure what became of him. An erroneous obituary even appeared in one Lancashire newspaper. Stories of Green Vigo abound, most of them probably apocryphal, many telling of brushes with the law, all of them expressing sadness at the precarious situation a once-great player had got into.

In contrast Barends had settled easily into his new way of life. Within two years of arriving in England he had married a local girl, had set up home at Hemsworth, just south of Wakefield, and was working as a financial adviser. Towards the end of his career he joined the probation service, in which he still works as a court officer, with special responsibility for ethnic minorities.

> 'For any black or coloured person to come and live in an English environment, without a support structure, it would be very difficult. I think I was lucky that I was very strong-willed and disciplined and of course I met my wife not long after I came to England. She came from a mining community and they had the support network. Joining Janet's family was like being with my own family.
>
> I was virtually the first black person to come to Hemsworth, but as a sportsperson people recognise you. However you also set an example and I think especially for young people it's important that they see that you conduct yourself respectfully and they know that you're also accessible as part of the community, you're not somebody that stands aside. You're somebody that engages, somebody that communicates.'

Fundamentally, Barends insisted, his adopted home town is no different from the village of Elim, a three-hour drive south of Cape Town, where he grew up. 'Monday to Friday was work, but on Saturday the community watched the game. And of course church on Sunday. I would say that the most important thing for me was my belief and the way I was brought up,' he said, acknowledging the influence of the Moravian church.

> 'One thing that came out of that was the respect you have to earn and the trust that you have to establish and show and to believe that everybody can improve. Just because somebody is down doesn't mean that you should walk on. You should help them, talk to them, because we can all be criminals. The difference is that we have a belief, which is also a discipline, because without having a strong belief when things are down, you will not succeed.'

Barends's personal messiah, in rugby league, came in the uncompromising form of Peter Fox. The Bradford coach, whose brother Neil had been Barends's first coach and was also to move to

Odsal, went to visit the winger at his home with a view to signing him and knocked at the front door. Thinking no one could hear him, Fox went to the back of the house, while Barends in the meantime was opening the front door. When they finally met at the side of the house, Barends threw his hands in the air and exclaimed, 'Ah! You're the man I've been waiting for! I want you to help me win some trophies.'

Fox was as good as his word. With his blockbusting, all-action style, Barends became a key player in Bradford's back-to-back championship-winning team in 1979–80 and 1980–81. 'He had that combination of speed and strength. He was very quick and on the ball,' said the Bradford coach, who also saw his recruit finish third in the list of top try-scorers in the 1978–79 season. Barends returned the compliment, calling Fox 'the best man-manager I ever met'. The move paid off in another sense when international selection beckoned. He was one of the top wingers in the game, but Barends didn't think at first that he would be eligible to play for Great Britain. He was married to an English woman and had lived in England for almost ten years but did not hold a British passport.

The question of whether to allow foreign players to represent Great Britain had been raised before. In the twenties, the possibility of selecting Wigan's South African stars Attie van Heerden and George van Rooyen had been a talking point, just as van Vollenhoven and company had enticed selectors in the sixties. But the definition of nationality was narrower then and the temptation was always resisted on patriotic grounds. But in the 1968–69 season the Rugby Football League bye-laws were amended to allow any player who had first played rugby league in Britain to become eligible. A decade elapsed before the new ruling was invoked. When the Lions squad was selected to tour down under in 1979, only two wingers, Stuart Wright and John Bevan, were picked. Both eventually dropped out through injury. Leeds's John Atkinson was called up but also declined, citing family and work commitments. So it was that Bradford Northern's South African wingman joined three of his team-mates and chairman Harry Womersley, the manager, on Great Britain's tour of Australia and New Zealand. Eyebrows were raised, including Atkinson's, but the chauvinistic critics could hardly complain if a foreigner valued the Great Britain jersey more than the British.

The 1979 tour however was an undistinguished one. The Lions won the series against New Zealand 2-1 and lost only one club match, but in those where it mattered most – the tests against Australia – Great Britain was humbled. Barends's personal pride in being selected for the first test at Lang Park would have been all the greater if his touchdown had not been disallowed, but in the end the Aussies nilled the British for the first time ever and ran up a record 35-0 score on home soil. The Lions went on to lose the next two as well and came home with the unenviable and unprecedented record of having lost all three tests in Australia. But Barends, who played in the first and second, felt no less satisfaction in wearing the red, white and blue.

'That day in Brisbane, when they played the national anthem, I remembered the people that helped me, the village I was from and of course my family,' he said. 'The credit belonged to everybody.' He admitted, though, that as far as the match was concerned, it was as if Australia and Great Britain 'were playing two different games'.

Barends returned to the game he knew best, at Odsal, where he spent the next three seasons virtually ever-present in the Bradford side that dominated the championship. After more than twelve years in rugby league, however, he decided to have one final season at Featherstone, where he teamed up again with assistant coach Keith Goulding, whom he had played under at York. Featherstone had beaten Hull in the Challenge Cup final at the end of the previous season and the two teams met again in a John Player Special second round tie, which Barends had cause to recall.

'That's one game that I always remember,' he said, though it was not because of the victory or the try he scored. 'There was an occasion in the match when three players took me and one of them hit me in the eye. Well, there was a time when I would have knocked one or two of them out, but that day I realised that my career had come to an end. I'd lost my aggressiveness. I looked at my wife who was in the stand and she knew. I didn't have to say anything.'

He went on to reflect:

> 'I always had my best games against Hull. You see, Hull is a unique place. For me Hull should always be one of the top teams, because they have the support of the people. They were always very vocal. They always used a lot of taunting, but when I scored I would go to them and they enjoyed that. I wouldn't say there was a lot of racism because as a sportsman it's your job to deal with whatever is necessary, and at the same time not to create any

> more problems. Sometimes people may use a gesture or whatever, but that can happen in anything.'

Barends could only recall one example of racial abuse elsewhere. His wife Janet took up the story: 'Dave was going to a game at Wakefield and the bus we were on was extremely full. He stood up at the front and I went to sit at the back. Because of it being a small village, thirty-one, thirty-two years ago, it was quite a new thing [to have a coloured person there] and someone was saying things about him – not terrible things, but it was rude. I tapped this man on the shoulder and said, "Why don't you go and tell him what you think? I'm sure he'd be interested."' Barends went on: 'So this man came up to me and said, "I'm sorry" and I said, "No problem" because he was man enough to apologise.'

Some years after he had last laced a boot, Barends was presented with an opportunity to help establish rugby league in his native country. It was the latest in a series of initiatives, going back to the 1950s, which had seen South Africa targeted as a country where the game had a good chance of taking root. Unlike previous attempts, the efforts made in the early 1990s were aimed at setting up rugby league at both amateur and professional level. At the lower level the work which had gone on in black townships was welcomed by the National and Olympic Sports Congress of South Africa, which was closely linked to the coming political party, the African National Congress. As a result rugby league received the NOSC's approval ahead of rugby union. Among those involved in the project was the ex-Wigan winger Trevor Lake, originally from Rhodesia, but Barends turned down the proposal.

> 'They asked me if I would consider going to South Africa to develop rugby league. The unfortunate thing was that for me to have done that I'd have had to leave the probation service. If you were to establish rugby league there you'd need to take it into the villages, to develop the grassroots. You'd need to spend considerable time and you'd need to have the capital to do so, unless of course it was a government initiative. It was the British and Australians who initiated the idea but you need to have a South African infrastructure to develop it. But you need also to understand that rugby [union] is a way of life.'

Volunteers did indeed go into the townships and did good work in

Soweto, where rugby union, even if it had been inclined to do so, did not dare tread. But, sport and politics being closely intertwined in South Africa, the rugby league developments were to be upstaged by the establishment sport. When Mandela's ANC came to power in 1994, rugby union was seen as an important element in binding the nation together. Barends commented:

> 'I think Mandela is a conciliator. As president, he needed to take ownership of that jersey so that people outside South Africa could feel confident that there would be no bloodshed, that the transition that needed to take place would be done respectfully.'

In return rugby union began to reach parts of the nation it barely knew existed. Once its propaganda machine cranked into action, stories of how the 15-a-side game had saved the souls of black township youngsters began to proliferate worldwide.

One of the many advantages, big and small, of the downfall of the old regime was that in 1996 the Barends family were able for the first time to go back to Cape Town as a family. Mr and Mrs Barends, married for almost twenty-five years in England, had never previously been able to stay together under South Africa's apartheid system. Nor had they seen much of the folks David had left behind. 'My family would never leave Cape Town to go to another country because we are South Africans and to us South Africa is the best place,' he explained. 'Not many of my family come and see me because they say it's too cold. The point I'm making is that I personally made a decision [to come to England]. Once you make a decision you have to achieve something, because if you don't become successful, then you've wasted your time to come across here because there are so many people already living here that you could have deprived of a position.'

The Great Britain cap he won was so important to him because it was the ultimate recognition that he had made the right decision and been successful in an alien land. More was to follow in 1999, when Barends received a call from South Africa, asking him to go to Pretoria to receive an honour from the president. The new government had organised an event to salute the unsung heroes of South African sport, those who might well have represented the country if politics had not got in the way. Green Vigo had also been invited but despite much effort could not be traced. Not only black sportspeople were feted, but also those white players who had refused on principle to play for the Springboks. 'They were my heroes of the time,' said Barends, 'players who stood up for their beliefs, because what man would not want to play for his country?

'It was a most amazing day because there were thousands of people in the hall there. You got that electric feeling. I've met royalty and I've met prime ministers, but meeting Mandela was just very, very special.'

Barends was one of those who were presented with the Springbok blazer and tie, a gesture which indicated the inclusivity of the new South Africa. It's worth remembering that back in 1961, in a reverse situation, Colin Greenwood, who had signed for Wakefield Trinity as Barends was to do a decade later, was asked by the South African Rugby Union to return his Springbok gear. The state's attitude to non-whites had been mirrored by rugby union's paranoia towards rugby league. In the new era Barends the honorary Springbok became practically a dual international, straddling not only two codes but two nationalities. Unable to represent the land of his birth, Barends was deeply honoured to play for his country of adoption, becoming the first foreign player – and so far the only one – to represent Great Britain in a test match. Still a proud South African, he called it the greatest moment of his sporting career.

9

BAK DIABIRA
Dave Hadfield

It is a statement of the obvious to say that the players who make the most lasting impression on you are those you encounter when you are at your most impressionable.

For many people, that means childhood. Even those who have seen thousands of games since can cherish an early glimpse of a Brian Bevan or a Billy Boston. Well, my rugby league childhood came late. I was in my mid-20s when I began truly to immerse myself in the game and it was then that I met a player who remains so uniquely vivid to me that even now, when I am asked to name my favourite scrum-half – not the best, you understand, but my favourite – I bypass Alex Murphy and Andy Gregory, Peter Sterling and Andrew Johns with barely a regret.

I do so in order to select a largely forgotten performer, whose career and origins are sufficiently obscure that someone with a pretty encyclopedic knowledge of the game to whom I mentioned this project objected on the grounds that someone else was already covering the Fijians. Bakary Diabira is not Fijian, although they would surely appreciate his range of skills. He was often described during his playing days, when anybody looked into it at all, as 'North African.' But he is not quite that either. He was born in Bordeaux, to an English mother and a father from Nouakchott in Mauritania, via Dakar in Senegal, brought up in Hull and now living in Bradford. He is whatever that makes him. But when he played, he was magic.

Diabira's parents first lived in Hull, but moved to France before he was born. 'My two sisters were born in Hull, but it was a mixed marriage – probably the only one in that area at the time – and things sometimes got a bit naughty.'

The family remembered Bordeaux as a more multi-racial city and Bak spent his first four years there, speaking nothing but French.

> 'We'd probably still be living there if my grandma in Hull hadn't been ill. I started primary school in Hull and the headmistress was the only person there who spoke French. She told my parents that I had to speak English at home and I lost all my French. I can't speak a word of it now, even when I've been there.'

Two other major changes came about during his schooldays. The first was when a new sports teacher arrived and switched the school from football to rugby – much to Diabira's annoyance at the time. He took to the new game sufficiently, however, to make another decision. Although he lived east of the River Hull, deep in Hull Kingston Rovers territory, he became a Hull FC supporter, first attracted to the Boulevard by complementary tickets doled out by a teacher.

> 'Hull were playing Leeds and that was the day I saw my first great player. Lewis Jones was at the back end of his career, but he did some things with the ball that day that stuck with me right through my own career.'

That career began to take shape as Diabira, a stand-off or left centre for his school, played scrum-half for the Hull Schoolboys team and for Constable Youth Club.

'That must be just about the most successful amateur side Hull has ever seen. In four years, only one Hull team beat us and we used to churn out players to professional clubs.' Diabira had trials with and offers from Huddersfield and Halifax, as well as both Humberside clubs. Under normal circumstances, Hull would have been his obvious choice, but he says he was never made to feel particularly welcome at the Boulevard.

> 'The attitude was "Here's another one after your place". It was very dog-eat-dog. At Bradford Northern, it was totally different. The club had gone bust and been re-formed. There was a feeling of all being in it together, of wanting to get better players in and improve.'

In 1966, at the age of 18 and having sampled the atmosphere at Odsal, Diabira was persuaded by Northern's long-serving director, Harry

Womersley, to join Bradford.

The following Saturday, the club's coach, the great Gus Risman, threw him straight in for his first team debut against Doncaster. Just to make it slightly more disorientating, he recalls, it was the first weekend of the short-lived four tackle rule, and nobody had a clue what to do on the last tackle.

> 'I thought I was fit, but the pace of the game was unbelievable. After a quarter of an hour I thought I was choking. It was a good job it was only Doncaster; if it had been Wigan or Saints I would have died.'

He survived – and held his first team place for the best part of the next 18 months. By that time, Risman had retired and the ebullient Albert Fearnley, who was to have a lasting influence on Bak's career, had crossed over from running the club's pools operation to coaching the side. Although he was reasonably well established, Diabira became uncomfortably aware of a couple of deficiencies. He wasn't big enough and he wasn't fast enough. After the fashion of the time, he was advised against weights, but worked hard on a general exercise programme to gain a bit of bulk. The lack of pace was a more intractable problem. 'These days, they would have put me with a sprint coach, but that never happened.'

Nor was he helped by knee problems that began to plague him early in his career. The worse of them, his left, has now been operated on six times and is classified as twenty per cent disabled. His other vulnerable area, his nose, was broken sixteen times. 'Once for every year I played. When six foot players hit someone who's five foot six, that's where they hit them.'

Neither his mum or dad would ever watch him, for fear of what the game was doing to him, but at least he had his hands – and what a pair of hands.

> 'My hands used to get me out of trouble. Albert used to tell me "Don't try and take on the big lads, because they'll kill you. But you can sicken them with your bag of tricks."
>
> I always felt comfortable with the ball in my hands, but sometimes I over-did it and even I didn't know what I was doing.'

That unpredictability could make him an infuriating team-mate to play with, as well as a wonderful one – sometimes both in the same match. His bag of tricks contained the full repertoire of dummies, feints and deceits, back-handed flicks, deliberate juggles and passes arrowed to colleagues having a rest on the blind-side.

There is a picture among those he has dug out of his scrapbooks for me. It is too crumpled and scratched to be used in this book, but it is one of his favourites and I can immediately see why. On the right of the frame, he is racing away as fast as his knees will carry him, ball tucked under left arm. To the left, the entire Leeds three-quarter line is running in the wrong direction, away from him. Even the crowd gives the impression of looking the wrong way. Diabira has just sold the mere and pere of a dummy to the whole of Headingley and if the Aboriginal winger, George Ambrum, emerges out of the background in time he will score under the sticks.

When it worked like that it was dazzling, but he was often classified as a Fancy Dan or a Show Pony – neither of them a compliment in rugby league – and Bradford seemed to spend most of his time there trying to replace him with somebody more orthodox. 'I would just think "Here's another one to see off" but it was the 1973 Cup Final that really convinced me I had to get away.'

Barry Seabourne had played all the previous rounds, but had been seriously injured in the semi-final and Diabira had come in for all the subsequent league games, playing the best rugby of his Bradford career.

> 'I was playing out of my skin, because I was playing for my Wembley place. But the week before the final Albert decided he would play Barry. He'd strap him up and send him out there. He did that and it backfired.'

Northern lost 33-14, with one of the most one-sided of finals effectively won and lost after twenty minutes, and Diabira knew it was time to think about moving on. 'I wanted a free transfer, but it took me until 1975 to get it. I played 126 first-team games for Bradford and I'm proud of that, but it was time to get away.'

Although his place had never been entirely secure, he had, in his nine years at Northern, become a recognisable figure on the rugby league circuit; recognisable enough, at any rate, to cop more than his share of abuse.

> 'The worst place was always the team I'd supported – Hull FC. Some of the stuff they used to shout was terrible – bringing your wife and family into it. I could see some of the people that I knew, who I'd had a drink with and regarded as friends – and they were giving it to me, calling me a black bastard and everything!
>
> In the middle of one game, I shouted back at one guy in the Threepenny Stand: "What about Sully? Haven't you noticed he's black?" He shouted back: "Sully's not black, he's black and white".'

Diabira and the late Clive Sullivan – one of his heroes when he watched Hull as a teenager – had a good chuckle about that.

> 'Sully was "it" as far as I was concerned, but my big regret was that I never got to play against Billy Boston. He was in his last season at Wigan when I was in my first and it was the one match I was dropped for.'

If that was a disappointment, then playing for the revived Other Nationalities side was a career highlight, turning out with players like John Bevan and Keith Fielding – Southerners were foreign enough to qualify – in the County Championship in the mid-70s. It was easier to hold down a place in that team than at Northern.

One of the scrum-halves with whom he had been in competition for a place at Odsal, Paul Daley, stepped in to take Diabira to what was then known as New Hunslet, where he had taken over as coach. The club was in its rebuilding phase at the Elland Road greyhound track, with its infamous 'tuning fork' goalposts. It was not to be a happy hunting ground for Bak. 'I'd started to have really bad problems with my knee and I didn't play many games in my two seasons there.'

At 31, he had decided to retire – a plan changed by a phone call from Fearnley, who despite little disagreements like leaving him out of cup finals, had always jokingly referred to himself as Diabira's dad as well as his rugby mentor. 'Dab, it's your dad,' he said, giving Diabira the chance to utter the immortal line: 'My dad's in Timbuktu.' Fearnley had taken over at Blackpool Borough and wanted Bak to join him as assistant coach and scrum-half.

Once he'd established which dad he was talking to, he told him it would have to be made well worthwhile for him, because he would be taking a risk with his dodgy knee. In the end, he agreed to play on a match-by-match basis and found that a five month break since he had played, or even trained seriously, had worked wonders. When he joined Blackpool, mid-way through the 1977–78 season, he was waiting for the knee to let him down, but found, to his pleasant surprise, that he could get through matches without too much trouble.

This was when I first met Bakary Diabira. I knew the name, of course – it wasn't the sort of name you forgot – but the way he played the game was a revelation. Blackpool had brought in star names before (both Billy Boston and Brian Bevan finished their careers at the seaside with the club and Tommy Bishop had a formative stint there) but no one had quite taken it by the scruff of the neck and transformed its approach like he did. I was pretty much obsessed with Blackpool Borough at the time, writing about them for the *West Lancashire Evening Gazette* and anyone else who would take it, training with them twice a week and playing the odd game for the 'A' team.

I still remember the shock when Diabira turned up at a session at Borough Park for the first time and we saw the things he could do with a ball. It wasn't just a novice like me whom was impressed; I saw a few seasoned professionals' jaws drop. Not only could he throw a dummy that convinced you, never mind the defence, that you had the ball, you were sometimes running around and found it in your hands when you were equally convinced he still had it.

It was as though retiring from the game and taking half a season off had given him a new freedom to do what the hell he felt like doing. He'd had his career and this was all a bonus. He had the special relationship with a rugby ball that was denied the rest of us. It started in the changing rooms and, although I have described this elsewhere, it bears repeating, because I have now had the opportunity to check with him that it is actually what he did.

Whilst other players might get used to handling the ball by bouncing it off the floor or the wall or simply throwing it up and catching it, Diabira's idea of getting re-acquainted was to sit there, casually spinning the ball on the raised index finger of one hand. He would then roll it down his arm, across the back of his neck, along the other arm and – don't try this at home – finish with it spinning merrily on his other hand. More often than not, he would be lighting a fag or adjusting his boots at the same time.

You don't actually get any league points for that sort of thing – perhaps you should – but by the end of the 1977–78 season, Fearnley and Diabira were on their way to transforming Borough, who had spent most of their professional existence as a bit of a joke, into a thoroughly difficult team to play against.

> 'After a couple of matches, I told Albert that we were going to do all right, because we had a good, tough pack. We also had a lot of players, like me, with something to prove, because we had been put out to grass.'

The 1978–79 season turned out to be the most memorable of his career. It started with a fixture which, on the face of it, sounds like a mis-match of historic proportions – Blackpool Borough versus Australia. The whole concept sounds unlikely, but these were the days when the Blackpool director, Reg Parker, was an influential voice at the Rugby League and starting Kangaroo tours beside the seaside seemed like a good idea. It wasn't a bad Australian squad either. The team that ran out at Borough Park included Bob Fulton, Steve Rogers, Les Boyd, Craig Young and the like.

They should not really have faced Diabira.

> 'I'd dislocated my elbow and there was no way I was playing. I was in my local in Bradford having a few pints when Albert came on with another of his "It's your dad" phone calls. I told him I was no good, but he's going "Dab, Dab, we need you. Have as many pints as you want, but help us out tomorrow".'

Strapped up and injected, he did so and put over a drop goal – by then a Diabira and Blackpool speciality – to put Borough in the lead. All right, they eventually lost 39-1, with Allan MacMahon scoring three tries from full-back, 'but we had them worried!' Even playing injured, Bak made an impression on people who had never seen him before. Australian journalists sent reports home marvelling at his trickery. Ian Heads, the most authoritative Australian league writer of his generation, says in his book *The Kangaroos: The Saga of Rugby League's Great Tours* that 'Bak Diabira, a black half-back with a cracked shoulder and a wonky knee, produced some magic for the locals'. Whenever Ian and I get to reminiscing over a glass or two of wine, he will ask what Bak Diabira is up to these days.

The serious business of the season, however, was an utterly unexpected promotion campaign. With a little extra quality from players like Tony Redford and the still developing Alan Fairhurst and Norman Turley, plus the tough, nasty streak represented by the likes of Peter Clarke and John Corcoran, Diabira had a proper band to conduct and Borough were on the fringes of the top four.

There was one major setback. It came back at the Boulevard, where Blackpool were denied a victory by some atrocious refereeing. It would have been Hull's only defeat of the season. 'They were like the Real Madrid of rugby league. They were probably the best side in Britain, never mind the Second Division, so it was heartbreaking. I was crying after the game. I can't ever recall doing that, but I was distraught. Harry Hunt was the referee,' he says, almost spitting out the name.

Despite that setback, Borough were still in the race for one of the four promotion spots as the season neared its climax. But then Fearnley went to Keighley and the Blackpool board asked Diabira to take over for the rest of the season. Despite worsening problems with his old injuries, plus a few new ones, Bak guided the side through the ups and downs of the last eight games. At the death, they needed to beat Whitehaven at Borough Park to go up.

'I couldn't play. My shoulder had gone, Alan Fairhurst was playing great at scrum-half and there was no way I was bringing myself back for the glory.' Borough won and Diabira was carried shoulder-high, but the seeds of his departure had been sown. 'I'd been offered £1000 to take them up, but they denied it. I didn't want to leave, I just wanted them to make me an offer to stay, but I went to Keighley with Albert as player-coach.'

The first edition of the *Rothmans Rugby League Yearbook* shows the two men jointly winning one of the first Sereena Coach of the Month awards, but in playing terms, it was always a mistake. 'I said I'd have another season, but I used to dread match day coming around. I'd had enough.' The one game that revived his appetite was a John Player cup tie against Northern.

> 'I had so much painkiller in my knee that I was told I wouldn't feel it if I broke my leg. Then I did something stupid. I threatened to knock them through the window if they didn't give me another jab at half time.'

Keighley didn't win, but Diabira rolled back the years and reckons that he had his best-ever write-up in the *Bradford Telegraph and Argus*. Again, he took over as head coach at Keighley from the departing Fearnley. His body was no longer up to the rigours of first team football, but he would still help out the 'A' team when they were short.

> 'I remember my last game. It was the semi-final of the Yorkshire Senior Competition against Hull KR and I was given the run-around by Paul Harkin. He'd been a young kid at Bradford when I was there and went on to have a very good career, but I thought to myself: "Diabira, it's time to call it a day".'

His coaching career did not last much longer. A disagreement with the new chairman over the way things should be done at Lawkholme Lane saw him resign and a stint coaching his local amateur side, Victoria Rangers, was short-lived. Not surprisingly, they lacked the commitment of professionals and he could not come to terms with that.

Since then, Diabira's involvement with rugby league has been at arms-length. He still gets to some past players' events, but, although he lives less than two miles from Odsal, in the house he moved into with his wife, Brenda, 32 years ago, he doesn't go to matches. Nor does he have a Sky dish, so he relies on a mate to video games for him. Not that he is disparaging about the game these days, like so many ex-players. 'I envy them these days. Not so much for the money, but for the conditions they play in. I'd have loved summer rugby – and you get protected by referees these days. You get a chance to show your skills.'

It is rugby league's loss that it did not get to see more of the skills of Bakary Diabira. Sitting in the lounge of his immaculate house, he's starting to get a little wistful now. 'I'd love to have played with Henry Paul,' he says. 'At his peak, I thought he was the complete footballer. We could have done a bit of damage together. And I like Jimmy Lowes as a hooker.' Modern Bradford supporters would not immediately think of bracketing his with names like those.

Now working in the warehouse of a local supermarket – he was sacked from his old job, along with the only other black manager, and won his case for racial discrimination – he comes across plenty of the type of Johnny-come-lately Bulls fans for whom rugby league before

1996 is a foreign country. A few months ago, he was getting teased over his own, supposedly modest career and having it compared – inevitably unfavourably – to the glory days enjoyed by Lowes, the Paul brothers and the rest of this lucky generation.

'Show them the book,' urged his workmates. He didn't want to, but eventually he showed them the book. That book was *XIII Winters*, in which he looms large in the chapter devoted to Blackpool's promotion season, a chapter in which, like this, I hoped to capture something of the magic and the mystery of the way he played the game. 'We take it all back,' they told him. 'Please accept our apologies. You must have been one hell of a player.' It is the best review I've ever had and the best I ever hope for.

Diabira remains one of the very few black men to have made the grade in this country as a scrum-half, which has always been arguably the most important position in the game. Jason Robinson started there but was soon shifted; apart from him, it is largely a matter of imported players from the southern hemisphere, a tradition continued by Adrian Lam and Dennis Moran.

'There was one other lad, who played for Leeds and Batley. He wasn't a bad player, but I can't remember his name.' He has his theory over why home-grown black scrum-halves should have been so thin on the ground. 'The majority of black lads who come into rugby league are either big lads who play in the forwards, or they have pace, so they gravitate to other positions, wings and centres. But, as I said, I'd got no pace.'

Except between the ears and from the wrists down, that is, but Bak also thinks there might be something in the theory that coaches have traditionally been reluctant to visualise black players in decision-making positions. It took a long time, after all, for black quarter-backs to start to emerge in the top echelons of American football. It's a point of view that should have been fatally undermined by the very mention of another player who began his career at Bradford and, from stand-off and loose forward, called the shots for every team he played for subsequently – Ellery Hanley.

Diabira achieved a fraction of what Hanley did in the game and earned a smaller fraction from it, but he seems at peace with what he did and who he is. 'I'm proud to have been a black man who played the game, but I feel 100 per cent British. I don't regard myself as French at all, although I was born there. In fact, I can't stand them.'

That stems back in part to the French authorities' attempts to call him up for national service, something that put an end to any idea that he might play for France. Feelers were put out during his Blackpool days, but he feared being apprehended for a stint in the army if he set foot on French soil.

And what about Africa? Does he feel any sense of belonging there?

> 'I'd never had any contact with my family there and one of the biggest mistakes I ever made in my life was getting in touch with some relatives shortly before my dad died in 1986. From knowing nobody in Africa, I suddenly seemed to be related to all of them and they were all coming to stay with me in Bradford. I think they saw me as a bit of an opportunity.'

Just occasionally, someone comes into his local in Wyke – although never anyone from Mauritania – and recognises him from his playing days. 'Eee... you had a few tricks up your sleeve,' they'll say and, almost always, go into an elaborate and contorted little mime that looks like a man with rubber arms wrestling with a cocktail-shaker. If it's done right, people should go running the wrong way across the pub.

Not everybody in rugby league remembers Bak Diabira, but, for those of us who do, that is the sort of effect he has. There aren't many players, of any background or any era, who can say that.

Jimmy Cumberbatch

Wigan half-backs Hector Gee and George Bennett (with ball) in training

Jimmy Peters of Barrow, St Helens and England and Devon rugby union

Alex Givvons in his Welsh RL cap and shirt

George Nepia

Wigan's pioneering Maori forward Len Mason

Roy Francis

Billy Boston, his sister and mother on one of their first visits to Central Park

Wally McArthur

Joe Levula in support as his Bradford colleague Lord dives over for a try in Northern's comeback game against Hull KR at Odsal in August 1964

Kia Bose arrives in Wigan in 1963 to discover the Central Park pitch completely frozen

Four great Fijian players: John Kucuve, John Ravitale, Mike Ratu and Laitia Ravouvou

Halifax's Johnny Freeman being shadowed by Wigan's Billy Boston

Colin Dixon looks to off-load the ball

David Barends

Bak Diabira works his magic direct from the scrum

Clive Sullivan in action at the Boulevard

Frank Wilson for St Helens escapes the clutches of a York pursuer

Des Drummond

Wigan winger Green Vigo tackles Roy Mathias

Henderson Gill tries to throw off the St Helens' defence

Mark Calderwood and Anthony Farrell in action for Yorkshire against Lancashire

Phil Ford uses his trademark sidestep for Great Britain against New Zealand

A classic Martin Offiah try for Widnes

Malcolm Reilly, Ellery Hanley and Martin Offiah line up before a Great Britain match

Gerald Cordle cuts outside of the French defence for Great Britain

Ikram Butt makes a break for Featherstone Rovers

Ellery Hanley powers through three former Balmain team-mates at Wembley in 1990

Carl Gibson, Paul Dixon, Roy Powell and Gary Schofield celebrate victory over the Australians in 1990

Anthony Sullivan on the attack for St Helens

Wigan's Jason Robinson prepares to scoot through the Leeds defence

Cec Thompson outpaces Hull's Johnny Whiteley to score in the corner

10

CLIVE SULLIVAN

Bev Risman

The greatest accolade a player can receive is knowing that his name strikes fear into that of his opponent. As full-back for Leigh and Leeds my first thought when we played against Hull was always the same: 'Is Clive Sullivan on the team sheet?' Hull had an awesome pack in those days, led by the great Johnny Whiteley, but we were always confident that our forwards could handle them. Sullivan was different because he was always capable of producing a moment of magic. The fear factor focuses your attention and you have to make special plans to counter the danger.

My main concern was to prevent Clive getting into a one-on-one situation against me because, as Eddie Waring used to say, 'That Risman, he is deceptively slow!' and I would have had no chance.

Sully, as he was affectionately known by his friends and fans; was the ideal attacking winger. He had scorching pace, he was quick and elusive and difficult to pin down and – despite his comparatively slim and spindly frame – he was deceptively strong out of the tackle. Given room, he was always a danger, and, once in the clear, he would never be caught, as he proved in the 406 times he put the ball over the try-line. He was in the top six of all-time try scorers, and for more recent rugby league followers, was very much in the style of Martin Offiah.

My team-mates at Leeds in the late 1960s included Great Britain wingers John Atkinson (twenty-six caps) and Alan Smith (ten caps), and stand-off Mick Shoebottom (ten caps), who all played against Sully many more times than me. John usually played opposite Clive and, according to his great mate Smithy, used to have real problems defending against him. With his tremendous pace, John preferred to show his opponent the touchline and then take him out from the side, and few players ever got round him. But he could not afford to give Clive more than half-a-yard because he was equally quick and he had this superb ability to stop the defender with his elusive footwork and then accelerate away before they could recover.

The plan for Leeds, and no doubt other clubs, was always to cut off the ball supply to Sullivan, or try to take him out, man and ball at the same time. Smithy, possibly due to his relative lack of real pace, had developed a fearsome crash-tackling technique, taking the man out just as the ball arrived. Sometimes, as the story goes from Smithy, John and he swapped wings to counteract the danger. Mick Shoebottom, one of the most ferocious and hungry tacklers in the game, was instructed to cover when the ball went Sullivan's way to provide an extra line of defence.

I do not think the battle was ever completely won or lost over the years, but it speaks volumes for Clive Sullivan's ability that teams and quality players had to go to such lengths to counteract his lethal attacking skills. Imagine the number of urgent discussions that went on in changing rooms and on the training grounds throughout the world as Sullivan plied his trade in rugby league for over twenty years.

Clive Sullivan's glittering career and life-story has been well-documented over the years. Joe Latus, in his book *Hard Road To The Top – The Clive Sullivan Story*, presents a moving and emotional account of his life as a Hull player, encapsulating the highs and lows in his life and his continuous battle to overcome the horrific catalogue of injuries he received, both on and off the field. Richard Tingle and Alex Service combine the story of father Clive and son Anthony in *The Flying Sullivans*, with an absorbing history of their lives. There is also an excellent account of Clive's career in the second volume of Robert Gate's book *Gone North*. The over-riding theme that seems to come through in all these accounts is the passion and determination to succeed and the will to overcome what might appear to normal mortals as insurmountable odds.

The word legend should never be used lightly, but Clive Sullivan established his place in the hearts and minds of the people of Hull – a hotbed of rugby league with a host of heroes – in which he stands supreme. Everyone who enters Hull – rugby league followers or not – is made fully aware of this when they see the name of the main arterial route into the city from the west: Clive Sullivan Way. Clive received national recognition for his services to rugby league when he was awarded the MBE while still at the height of his career and he was the first rugby league player to have his truly remarkable and unique career recorded on television's *This Is Your Life*.

The story of Clive Sullivan's early life in a happy but poor home in the Welsh villages of Splott and Ely, brought up by a single mother, an elder brother and two younger sisters, gives a clue to the development of his character. He was born in 1943 into a close-knit family, who worked together and supported each other and, although as a coloured family, the Sullivans were in the minority, they were well-respected in the community. The boys had to shoulder a lot of responsibility from an early age. With a working mother they had to fend for themselves and look after their young sisters. They also had to think for themselves and work hard for everything they got. Clive's brother, Brian, was talented, academically and athletically, and Clive became totally consumed with matching up to his brother. This must have contributed to his passion to be successful, which hardly wavered throughout his life, despite all the setbacks. If it did, there were always family and friends to give him a helping hand.

Much of the life in the village communities in South Wales revolved around sport and massive encouragement was given to any youngster who showed enthusiasm and ability. Clive had these characteristics in abundance and, driven by his determination to rival Brian, he found the key to his future success.

Athletics and rugby became his life and, fuelled by sporting success at school, his future looked rosy. The story of his first serious injury – which threatened his whole future – and Clive's miraculous recovery, seems hardly credible. The diagnosis, treatment and medical advice for what appeared to be either a severe over-use injury or a growth problem in the thigh muscle, led Clive to spend over two years as a virtual cripple, under the impression that he would never be able to fully participate in sport again. But for the care and support of his family and friends, and his own unquenchable desire to recover, Clive could have been lost to sport forever. It was probably a case of mind over matter that eventually enabled him to resume his sporting life.

After this, his career was a roller-coaster ride, involving a multitude of magnificent triumphs and career-threatening disasters, both on and off the field. The legacies of his early life stayed with him and his desire for success burned as strongly as ever, as he overcame one crisis after another on his way to the ultimate triumph.

Did Clive Sullivan always have a secret ambition to play rugby league? One of his heroes in his younger days was the incomparable Billy Boston from Cardiff's Tiger Bay. But Clive had no opportunity to shine in rugby union in Wales and his introduction was not typical of the majority of Welsh imports into rugby league. However, when he joined the Army and was posted to the Royal Signals at Catterick, he was very close to the heartlands of rugby league.

Perhaps his thoughts turned to Billy Boston as he gradually recovered from the injury to his leg. He tentatively resumed playing rugby and eventually started turning out for the regiment's rugby union team. Once he realized that he was back to fitness again, he may have thought about the possibility of playing rugby league. Clive had not played rugby union at any standard and could only have dreamed of being good enough to play professionally. But rugby league scouts were everywhere, his potential was spotted and he was offered a trial at Bradford Northern. For whatever reason, after one trial match, Bradford did not pursue the matter, but he impressed one of the match officials, Jim Harker, who recommended him to Hull. Clive did not know about this development and when Hull tried to contact him he had been posted to Farnborough in the south of England. Luckily, despite losing contact with him initially, Hull persevered and invited him for a trial.

Surprisingly, he was picked for the first team against Bramley and his debut, as a trialist is now part of Hull's folklore. Advised by coaching guru, Roy Francis, and protected by Johnny Whiteley, Clive played in the centre and scored a magnificent hat-trick of tries, one of which was the first of a trade-mark of wonder Sullivan tries. He was offered a contract immediately and had no hesitation in signing on the dotted line. The year was 1961.

Toughened by experience, Clive now embarked on a brand-new phase in his life. He had to try and combine two careers, a challenge that life in the Army enabled him to overcome. Discipline and organization were a great help to Clive while he tried to establish himself in rugby league.

For three years he was only able to play for his team when he had leave from the Army and despite a series of injuries he matured into a complete footballer. He had a natural feel for the game as well as being an exciting runner. He was tactically aware, always alive and involved and he became a superb defender. A natural try scorer, he could make something out of nothing from almost any area of the field.

It is amazing that Clive played for twenty-three years, during which time he overcame serious injury on numerous occasions, including life-threatening injuries which he sustained in a car crash prior to his release from the Army. His powers of recovery, both physically and mentally, were to become as legendary as his playing career.

Clive Sullivan's first international appearance was for Great Britain U24s against France in 1966. He played for his country thirty-seven times between 1966 and 1979 and, while recognizing that all players have injuries from time to time, there is little doubt he would have made many more but for his injury setbacks. All his Great Britain appearances came as a Hull player at a time when Hull were not a particularly successful side despite the presence of such quality players as Johnny Whiteley and Arthur Keegan. Clive could easily have moved on to one of the great clubs at the time like Leeds, Castleford or Wakefield, but remained a faithful team-man at Hull for thirteen years.

Even before his international career commenced he had become an idol of the supporters, both for his electrifying try-scoring feats, and his magnificent defensive qualities. According to full-back, Arthur Keegan, 'Clive was the best defensive winger I have played with or against, not only for his one-on-one tackling, but also for his crossfield covering. He made my life easy playing almost as an extra full-back'. It may have been that his phenomenal work-rate and his willingness to cover for his team-mates contributed to the frequency of his injuries. His frame was not as powerful as that of Billy Boston and Ellery Hanley and was subjected to tremendous pressure week after week. However, he came through his injuries time after time and eventually played 346 matches for Hull, before moving on to a second career at Hull Kingston Rovers. When he left Hull in 1974 he had won only one medal – as a member of the winning team in the Yorkshire Cup Final.

He had a wonderful time with the Airlie Birds' fans. He became their adopted son and established himself and his family as part of the community. His colour was never an issue and, in fact, there were numerous stories of light-hearted and harmless banter about his colour. Clive took no offence when jokes were made by comedians in the Threepenny Stand at the Boulevard. Friends I have spoken to tell these stories and swear they are true. Hull's traditional black and white horizontal striped kit and Clive's glistening black legs and face produced a striking picture and led to him being affectionately christened 'the liquorice all-sorts man'. Floodlit matches were often a great source of amusement at Clive's expense. On one occasion Clive lost the ball in the lights and it hit him on top of the head and rocketed into the crowd and a supporter yelled out 'Bad luck Sully, in off the black!' Another time, on a particularly wet and miserable night with all the players caked in mud, a comedian shouted out 'Keep your mouth closed Sully and they will never see you!' Clive gave the crowd a dazzling white-toothed smile. An unfortunate supporter, arriving late for a match at Widnes, rushed into the ground just in time to see a black and white clad figure with a black face and shiny black legs popping the ball down for a try and shouted 'Well done Sully, great try!' He was immediately howled down by all around him because the try scorer turned out to be Dennis Brown, the Widnes black winger, playing in the black and white stripes of Widnes.

One of the most interesting situations arose when Hull brought over three black American football players for trials. When they saw Clive, they greeted him with big bear hugs and, 'How are you brother?' Clive was nonplussed and did not understand the significance of these gestures. Here is an indication of the extent of Clive's integration into the Hull community. His colour had become a complete irrelevance.

Clive loved playing for Hull, although he was one of few players in the club who represented Great Britain over a long period. Since Tommy Harris (1954–60) and Johnny Whiteley (1957–62) only Arthur Keegan (1966–69) was capped during his era. There was a shortage of quality international wingers after the great days of Billy Boston, Mick Sullivan (no relation) and Ike Southward and but for his injuries he could have easily been selected long before his first full cap in 1967. Only John Stopford and Bill Burgess were carrying the mantle of the classic wingers and rugby league was crying out for a new wing sensation. There had been no black players in the team since Billy Boston and a new hero was long overdue.

Sullivan must have been an enigma to the international selectors. It was obvious he had talent to burn, but he was playing in a moderate team and always seemed to be struggling with injuries. The risk involved in choosing him must have been great, even though quality wingers were thin on the ground.

He did not make the 1966 Australasian tour, although he played in a warm-up match against the chosen Great Britain squad. Stopford and Burgess were selected, along with Geoff Wrigglesworth and Berwyn Jones, the Welsh and Great Britain athletics star. Clive must have been disappointed not to have been chosen ahead of Wrigglesworth and Jones. They were both good players, but Arthur Keegan, whom he had formed such a great partnership with at Hull, was in the squad at full-back. Amazingly, Keegan and Sullivan never played together in the same international team, neither was there a black player in the tour party.

Injury and selectorial whims kept him out of the test series against France in 1968 and the World Cup in 1970 in England, but prior to 1970 he made his big breakthrough when selected for the 1968 World Cup in Australasia. I had played in the matches against France earlier in the season, and then had the great honour, just like Clive in 1972, of being chosen as captain of the squad in the absence, due to injury, of the great Neil Fox.

Like Clive, the selection as captain came out of the blue because, although having captained teams in the past, I had never been a regular captain at my clubs Leigh and Leeds. I know exactly the feelings of shock, surprise, elation and joy that Clive must have experienced in 1972 at receiving the highest honour the game can give.

Unfortunately, unlike Clive's triumph in 1972, we had to endure the agonies of failure. We lost 25-10 against Australia in the first match when referee John Percival awarded penalty after penalty against us for obscure technical scrum offences and Australian full-back, Eric Simms, kicked eight goals. Sullivan scored a typical try, but in the next match he hardly touched the ball in a match that should never have been played. In atrocious conditions of rain and mud we were surprisingly beaten 7-2 by France. The dressing room after the match was like a morgue and Clive had to share our distress at losing to a team that we had twice beaten in 1968. All our dreams had been shattered, but we came back and played like we knew we could against New Zealand to win 38-14 and Clive showed his pedigree with a hat-trick of tries.

When you are on tour with a representative team you are confronted with a series of new challenges, both on and off the field, particularly with regard to personal relationships. Players you previously knew only as opponents or even enemies now become your colleagues and team-mates. People with contrasting personalities are thrown together and you have to learn to get on with each other immediately. You will never become bosom pals with everyone, but most rugby players tend to have similar interests and learn to adapt. Often though, new and lasting friendships are made and respect for each other grows within a new peer group.

Clive was the only black player in the party and amongst people he did not know, and tensions could have emerged. There were none and Clive earned respect by his actions on the field and a quiet, confident and friendly manner that gained him many new friends. John Atkinson, who was also on his first tour, and who had only known Clive as a deadly enemy in the past, became a close friend. They went on to occupy the Great Britain wing positions on numerous occasions. They often shared a room together especially in the magnificent World Cup triumph of 1972, when both played in all four matches.

Clive was hitting his peak prior to 1972 and he was chosen for the 1970 tour to Australia and New Zealand along with Alan Smith and John Atkinson, the dynamic Leeds duo. He did not quite hit top form due to niggling, rather than serious, injuries and the two Leeds wingers took their chance and kept him out of the test teams throughout the tour. Agonizingly for Clive, they retained their places for the 1970 World Cup in England and the test matches against France in 1971. Altogether, Clive missed eleven test matches. This was one of the most frustrating periods of his career because he was playing at the top of his form.

Clive continued to turn in great performances for his club and in 1971 was finally rewarded with selection for the test match series against New Zealand in England. In Australia in 1970 things had gone against him, but he knew that if he persevered the tide would turn. Clive played well against New Zealand, although the series was lost. Frank Myler, who had captained Great Britain brilliantly in 1970, had left the scene and the selectors tried Syd Hynes, Doug Laughton, and Roger Millward as captains. For various reasons none of these made the squad in 1972 for the test matches against France, so the selectors had to choose a new captain. There was no obvious candidate and the selectors, in their wisdom, decided Sullivan had the required qualities.

It was an inspired choice. Despite having no previous experience, and the fact that there was some comment that the wing position was not the best from which to captain a side, Clive proved to be a natural leader. He was already greatly respected as a team player, and always set a good example on the field, but he showed a quiet, but firm authority which created a positive response from his team-mates. He led the team to two victories against France and then came the crowning glory in the World Cup in France. The team won all its matches en route to the final and won the trophy in the now famous 10-10 draw against Australia. Clive scored in every match – a test record – and his length of the field try in the final is still one of rugby league's most talked about incidents. He made a critical contribution to the Mike Stephenson try which saved the day for Great Britain but his greatest moment was when he received the winners' trophy.

Sullivan was now a living legend, not only within his sport, but across the whole country. He had become the first black person to captain Great Britain in any sport, he had appeared on *This Is Your Life* and been awarded the MBE. He went on to captain his country again in the 1973 test series against Australia and, having returned to his club an even greater hero, played through the 1973–74 season.

The city of Hull was subsequently rocked to its foundations when, at the age of thirty-one, and at the peak of his popularity, Clive Sullivan was transferred to Hull's deadly rival, Hull Kingston Rovers. Who knows what persuaded Clive to interrupt such a magnificent career? The real story has never been published but the challenge was one he both relished and needed. His thirst for success remained strong.

The rivalry between the two Hull clubs has always been bitter and they have fought for supremacy of this rugby league city. It is a tribute to Sullivan that he was able to overcome the fans' prejudices and be eventually forgiven by most of the fanatical Hull supporters. For some time afterwards he was subjected to some abuse, not so much because he had left Hull, but because he had crossed 'the great divide' to Hull KR. It took a while for him to be accepted at Hull KR, because at first people were suspicious of his motives, but gradually his personality and his performances on the field gained their respect and support.

He had now matured into a tough, battle-hardened character with a happy family life. Settled in Hull he went on to play, almost injury-free for six full seasons. He helped to wake up a sleeping giant, playing an average of thirty-six matches a season, scoring 118 tries and, most satisfying of all, winning the trophies that had always eluded him at Hull FC. He continued his international career with appearances for

Wales and won a host of medals with Rovers, including a championship medal when they topped the league table in the season 1978–79. However, he had still never fulfilled the dream of appearing in the RL Cup Final at Wembley until in the next season Hull KR made it to the final. It must have been fate that his opponents were Hull FC and, although it was probably fitting that there was no sensational Sullivan try against his old club, he finally received a coveted winners' medal as Hull KR triumphed 10-5.

At the age of thirty-seven, and with this last personal achievement, it was time to call it a day and bring the curtain down on an amazing career – or so everyone thought! But Sully, was not one to be happy finishing at the top. He was still full of enthusiasm for the game and was determined to carry on playing as long as he was wanted. He was released by Hull KR and had a short flirtation with Oldham, before, fittingly, returning to Hull FC in 1981 for one final throw of the dice. But there was yet another twist in the tail. He was coaching the reserve team, but was available to play if required. Hull had a powerful team that season and reached the cup final. Clive was simply looking forward to supporting his club from the touchline. He watched a tense, hard-fought struggle against cup favourites, Widnes, which ended in a draw, with the replay to be held at Elland Road, Leeds. Out of the blue, he found himself in the team due to an injury to star New Zealand winger, Dane O'Hara. As a result, the coach, Arthur Bunting, brought him back to add his vast experience to an emerging side. In an inspired performance, led by Dave Topliss, Hull won convincingly and Clive now had two winners' medals in the space of three years after waiting nineteen years for the first! He thus became the first player to receive a Challenge Cup Final medal for both Hull clubs to add yet another record to his incredible list of achievements.

Clive continued to test himself with new challenges in the game when he took on the impossible coaching job at Doncaster – a club that had struggled in the very basement of rugby league for years. It was the one time that he had to admit defeat, but there is no doubt that if he had had the opportunity he would have been back again to continue his love story with rugby league.

Tragically, Clive's life was cruelly cut short when he died of cancer at the age of only forty-two, after playing in his last match only a few months earlier. His early death deprived the sporting world of a truly great person and sportsman, who may have gone on to even greater glories in the game. He did not have the opportunity to reflect on his life or to tell his own personal story. Much of our information about his life is made up of recollections from friends, colleagues, family and the media. What an experience it would have been to sit down with him now and hear his own thoughts and reflections, both on his life and his wonderful, eventful and inspiring rugby league career.

11

FRANK WILSON AND FRIENDS

Clive Griffiths

In 1979, in the space of six months, my life and my outlook on it changed considerably. First there was the realization of a boyhood dream when I ran out on to Cardiff Arms Park pitch to gain my Welsh rugby union cap. Then, months later, I made my debut at Knowsley Road after I had done the unthinkable and become a semi-professional rugby league player with St Helens RLFC. Sandwiched in between was a tour to South Africa with Llanelli Rugby Union Club where I witnessed for myself apartheid at its worst.

An eventful six months, to say the least, during which I had gone from a national name in Wales – successor to JPR Williams and Triple Crown winner – to an outcast in Welsh society! I was struck off the WRU's coaches register and the Barbarians players honours list, asked to leave the committee box at Stradey Park, banned from entering rugby union club houses and finally ignored by people who months earlier had wanted my autograph. It was an interesting time but after I left Wales, another kind of welcome awaited me and my wife up North.

In the Saints changing room I received a mixed reception. I leant on the broad shoulders of fellow Welshmen, Roy Mathias and Mel James, but even they were powerless to prevent the scepticism and jealousy, over the financial package I had received, and the silent treatment as well as the hatred that surfaced from time to time both on and off the field. It was not long before we went ex-directory and certain people made it obvious that we weren't going to be on their Christmas card list. A member of the local press did a real character assassination and made it his business to stir things up even though I had only played a few games.

We had to tread carefully both in our new home and when we took the trip back to Wales to see our families. It didn't make you feel good I can tell you. So you can see why my outlook on life changed at that time and why the phrase 'black bastard' was a term I came to despise, as much as I did the people who mouthed it. In rugby union, I only played against one black player. Carl Smith, a second row forward for Cardiff and Pontypool. At Llanelli, we went on tour to South Africa and it was there I began to realise how bad things were for black and coloured people. We had been advised not to discuss the political situation; I remember Peter Morgan and myself going for a drink in a local bar in Cape Town and we got into a conversation with a white South African who described black players as 'kaffirs' and 'vermin'. The conversation got quite heated. Both Peter and myself were dead against what he was saying but we kept our cool and left.

When I came home I thought about the stories I had heard and why players like Billy Boston and Colin Dixon had gone north relatively early in their careers, even though they were good enough to play for Wales. Frank Wilson was another who had left rugby union. During my time in rugby league, I became very friendly with Frank, and he told me a lot about the time he'd had with Cardiff Rugby Club in the mid to late 1960s. Cardiff had gone on tour to South Africa in 1967 but they hadn't taken Frank with them. At the time Frank was an outstanding player. In the 1967–68 season he was Cardiff's top try scorer with 22 tries in 37 games, not a bad strike rate. In December 1967 he represented East Wales against the All Blacks and scored the only try in a 3-3 draw. He also played in the Probables v Possibles Trial in 1968 and would have been the first black player to represent Wales had he been selected for the tour to South Africa the following summer. Frank wasn't selected, the argument being that Wales already had three top class wingers. It was felt that Frank wasn't up to the job. People can make up their own mind up that one! All I know is that Frank never got over the disappointment so in the summer of 1968 he signed for St Helens. The rest is history. He had a great career in rugby league.

Frank is the nicest man you could wish to meet. He is now very ill with cancer and I want to record my feelings toward him. He is a good friend of mine and I have fond memories of the time we ran the rugby league coaching courses all over the north: Manchester, Leigh, Wigan, St Helens. Frank and I worked well together and we used to have a laugh. 'If you don't shut up', he'd say to the lads, 'I'll put the lips on you and we'll be here for weeks.' Frank could always make a joke about his colour. He was well respected.

If we're talking about respect then in my experience the person who commanded it as much as anyone on the rugby field, was Des Drummond. I'd watched Des play in the BBC's RL Floodlit Trophy back home in Wales. When I went north, I played against him at St Helens and Salford and I coached him as well during my time at Warrington. Des was a world-class player who gained twenty-four Great Britain caps. During his career he played mainly for Leigh and Warrington, finally hanging his boots up at Workington Town. I always got on well with him, we played opposite each other on a number of occasions, and even though he achieved far more than I did in the game he treated me with respect, which tells you something about the man. He was a great player to coach, on the field he was a fierce competitor, small in stature compared with some other wingmen but pound for pound, he was the hardest hitter of them all. It was x-rated stuff when he came in off the wing to make his trade mark 'spot tackle' which often left the attacker pole-axed. This was often accomplished using his head!

With his great pace Des scored over 250 career tries. That is why I always used to stand outside him in both attack and defence. He was an awesome player and an awesome bloke who enjoyed competing at the highest level. He also took part in four BBC Superstars programmes in the 1980s, winning the 100-metre sprint and the overall runner-up prize. He now lives in Bolton, Lancashire.

Coaching has been a big part of my life in rugby league. When I became coach of the Wales rugby league team, our first match was in October 1991 at the Vetch Field, Swansea, against the touring Papua New Guineans. We were seen as the ideal opponents to kick start their UK tour but two members of 'the family' had different ideas, namely Philip 'Mad Dog' Ford and Anthony Sullivan. Sully arrived in camp accompanied by an infected lump on his forehead (which signalled a mass obsession to squeeze it), but that didn't stop him from scoring a hat trick. Fordie, not to be outdone, matched him all the way. It was a memorable night for Welsh rugby league as we posted a record 68 points to nil victory. After the game David Howes of the RFL Executive paid us a visit. Fordie, seizing the moment, shouted across the changing room: 'Hey, Howsie, ruined your tour, haven't we?'

Anthony Sullivan was born in Hull and started playing rugby league as a youngster. When he was 16 years old he gave it up and decided to play different sports: football in the winter and athletics in the summer. In late adolescence he was invited to play for a local rugby league team in Hull. From that moment he was destined for great things in the game at both club and international level. He began his professional career at Hull Kingston Rovers in 1987 and won the second division championship with them the following season. He then moved on to St Helens where he enjoyed a decade of success, as they won the Premiership title in 1993, the Challenge Cup in 1996, 1997 and 2000, the Super League Championship in 1996, 1999 and 2000, plus the World Club Championship in 2001. He then changed codes and for two seasons, 2001–2003, and played for Cardiff.

On the international stage, Anthony represented Great Britain at U19 (Colts), U21 and Senior level. He gained seven caps, including three Lions tours in 1990, 1996 and 2000. He won seventeen Welsh RL caps and played with distinction in the 1995 and 2000 RL World Cups. Whilst playing rugby union he also gained two senior Welsh caps and thus joined that elite band of Welshmen who have represented Wales in both codes.

'In the early part of my career', he says, 'I was compared to my father, Clive, but I guess that was inevitable, playing for the same club, in the same position and in the same city where my dad was held in such high esteem. I think this comparison diminished somewhat when I left Hull for St Helens.' Sully is extremely proud of his father's achievements both on and off the field. He describes his father as 'an ordinary man who played rugby but had a lot of time for people'.

As one of the few black people in Hull, Clive was easily recognizable, yet he did not let this affect him. For the major part of his life, he lived, worked and took an active part in the Hull community. These were all valuable lessons for Sullivan junior. Anthony says that he can recall only one incident of racism on the field, while incidents involving spectators were few and far between. On the odd occasion it happened the culprits were quickly rebuked by other spectators. He continues, 'It says a lot about the game for it to be a sport that has achieved so many milestones and firsts in black sporting history. Most players, regardless of their ethnic background, came from the working classes and, up to the early 1990s, held jobs within the local community. These lads would play league on the weekend and then go to work on a Monday, rubbing shoulders with the same people who had been cheering them on from the terraces.'

According to Anthony, this served to forge a great sense of belonging and community spirit, with players and fans mixing together in the workplace and socially. People identified with their players, irrespective of colour or ethnic background and this attitude helped break down any barriers that colour may have presented.

Anthony Sullivan is a family man who has been a model professional since his Hull KR days. He is extremely proud of his father and the fact that he was seen as an ambassador for the game. Sullivan II needn't worry; he has done his father and his family proud in that respect as well. He is now retired after shoulder surgery, works as an independent financial consultant in Warrington, Cheshire, where he lives, and has recently taken on a coaching role at St Helens.

Sully has touched upon the subject of racism which was quite a common subject within the Wales rugby league team. An outsider would probably gasp in horror at some of the things that were said, until they realized that what happened was little other than honest fun. Imagine the scene: you are at breakfast in a hotel restaurant and a black person (Welsh player) walks in. As he pours himself an orange juice you hear this white person (Welsh player and team mate), already seated, shout out: 'Hey boy, black boy, coffee for us white men now!' Minutes later you might see the same black player with a white table napkin, shaped like a Ku Klux Klan hood over his head serving the 'white' table, whilst muttering the words, 'Is this black coffee ok for you honkies?'

The main actors in the scene would be Gerald Cordle, David Young, Mark Jones and Kevin Ellis and, of course, Phil Ford. Add a certain David 'The Bish' Bishop and you have a rogues' gallery of players. This lot would endlessly taunt and abuse each other in a knockabout way. But out on the field they would die for each other and any opponent who dared cross the colour line was singled out for some 'extra treatment'.

Gerald Cordle didn't start many games for Wales but he was a real team man who put selection issues to one side and was absolutely brilliant around the rest of the boys. His two tries against New Zealand at Swansea in 1993 nearly gave us a deserved victory and I will always remember him rounding Martin Offiah at Widnes when he played for Bradford and the little smile he gave Martin as he walked back after he had touched down. Gerald went on to represent Great Britain against France at Headingley and everyone was delighted for him. I'd have Gerald in my squad every day of the week. He was a real 'we' not 'me' man, who had the total respect of his team mates.

I can also remember Gerald running into the crowd at Aberavon Quins in a Welsh rugby union cup tie in December 1987, after he had scored his try. Remarks were made in a section of the crowd that Gerald didn't take kindly to and obviously he decided to do something about it. Representations were made between the two clubs and John Billot, in the *Western Mail*, described it as one of the ugliest incidents he could remember in Welsh rugby. Gerald has told me he didn't experience anything like that in rugby league.

Gerald's compadre was Philip Ford, leader of the 'rogues gallery'. Born in Tiger Bay, Cardiff, he represented Great Britain RL thirteen times and Wales RL ten times while his club career took him to Warrington, Leeds, Wigan, Bradford and Salford. Phil returned to rugby union in 1996 to play for Pontypridd where, believe it or not, he won his first club honour, the Welsh Club Championship title. From there, he went on to play union for Pontypool, Rhumney and Fairwater where he eventually hung up his boots at the end of the 2002–03 season, aged 42 years young. During his Wales career Fordie's specialist subject was rubbing me up the wrong way and enjoying himself in the process.

Fordie scored over 250 career tries and on his day was a world class game-breaker and match-winner. He had skill, exceptional speed and a superb side step. Rugby league supporters will remember his individual try for Great Britain in the victorious test against the Aussies at the Sydney Football Stadium in 1988 and the famous, 'he's a stepper Ford', quote from the Aussie commentator Darryl Eastlake.

'That win and the try has to be one of the best moments of my career', says Phil. 'Beating the Aussies in their own backyard was a magic experience, as was my first game for Wales in 1991 playing with the likes of Jonathan Davies, Dai Young, John Devereux and Kevin Ellis. And,' he adds, 'there is one other highlight. My one and only career goal, up in Cairns, on the 1988 tour.'

What sticks in my mind was his try-saving tackle in the corner against France in Perpignan in 1992. This helped Wales record their first victory (19-18) on French soil for thirty years.

However, against the same country on a wet Cardiff evening, in 1994, Fordie had a bit of a shocker. Playing at full-back he dropped everything and in the end I had to substitute him, knowing full well that he would be none too pleased with the decision, but we went on to win the game thanks to a late Richard Webster try. After the game, all was rosy in the garden again as the boys gave Fordie a new nickname: 'Teflon'.

In 1995 Wales RL embarked on a first ever tour to the USA to play a two match Test series against the American Patriots in Philadelphia. In the first game Fordie broke new ground by becoming an international touch judge when one of the officials was taken ill. He did a marvellous job for us! On the same tour he also led a mass exodus from the training field when we were ambushed by what must have been the worst thunderstorm and cloudburst in American history. As the lightning hit the ground around me I turned to find that I was alone in the middle of the pitch as all the players had quickly sought the sanctuary of the grandstand. It was like Custer's last stand except that the Indians were laughing at the Lone Ranger out on the pitch. 'One in, all in', said Phil slyly as I reached the jokers under the stand.

Knowing how proud he was about playing for Wales, I had to make one of the toughest decisions of my coaching career when I left Phil out of the 1995 World Cup team. It was a difficult meeting between us but to his credit he still showed commitment during training and would have been ready physically and mentally if called upon. He bears few grudges today and it is always good to be in his company again. His motto: 'No friends before the game, all friends after the game,' sends out a clear message. Fordie became a publican on his return to Wales in 1996 and is now landlord of the Robin Hood public house in Canton, Cardiff. Watch out sheriff!

Anthony Farrell, Paul Sterling and Wes Davies were also magnificent people to work with. Each made a major contribution to Wales's successful run in the 2000 World Cup. Before the tournament, we went to South Africa for our pre-World Cup training camp and Test against the Rhinos rugby league team. Faz and Sterlo had a few reservations about going but in the end, they got on the plane and saw the country for what it was. It turned out to be an historic and successful trip that bonded the team and management together, especially on the night when we were returning to our hotel after a function. We were told to be very careful as there had been cases of rogue taxi drivers turning off the main road and robbing people at gun point. That night both Mike Nicholas and myself sat between Faz and Sterlo in the back of our taxi on the trip to the hotel. No one mugged us. We were well looked after!

Let me finish my reflections with a Chinese proverb: 'A problem is a mountain filled with treasure'. Both mountains and problems can be daunting and difficult to overcome but we also know that the challenge of the mountain is enlightening and very rewarding. That is how I would sum up my association and relationship with the black Welsh players I have worked with over the years. Like all players, they caused me one or two problems along the way, but the truth of it was that they were always the jewels in the crown of Welsh rugby league.

12

MARTIN OFFIAH
Franka Philip

On Sunday 1 July 2001, an enthusiastic crowd at the Valley in London held their breaths and watched in awe as Martin Offiah collected Michael Hancock's pass to cross under the posts and score a try.

Though it was not a try of particular brilliance, it was one with great historical resonance. For with that try in the thirty-fifth minute of that game for the Salford Reds against his old club London Broncos, Martin Offiah became the first Englishman to score 500 career tries in rugby league.

This feat put him behind Australian Brian Bevan and Welsh legend Billy Boston in the list of rugby league's top try scorers. It prompted a wave of congratulatory newspaper articles as well as widespread debate on radio call-ins, television programmes and on message boards across the internet. Yet surprisingly, Offiah didn't initially place too much importance on such a great milestone:

> 'I didn't put that much significance on it. In fact it was the media that put more significance on it than me because only two men in the history had scored over 500 tries, no other Englishman had scored 500 tries in the history of the game.'

In fact, it was the media hype and the excitement created among rugby league fans that helped him to appreciate the meaning of such a major milestone:

> 'The more that people said it, the more I thought, "Yes it is important, you're going to die and people will be talking about you after". I started to think about it, because when you're coming to the end of your career, you start wondering what kind

> of legacy you're going to leave in the game. You know there are not too many people who can say they've achieved something that so many people had gone into the game to try to achieve and that no other Englishman has. I started to think about that.'

When he finally scored the try, he felt it was a weight off his shoulders.

> 'In the 15 years since I was playing, going back to 11, I never went for three games without scoring a try. Then when I was on try 499, I went for seven games without scoring a try. It was unheard of for me. Each game I started thinking, what if I got injured? What if I don't play again for the year and I don't get signed again? I don't want to come back and play for a lower division club just for the record's sake.'

His fears were allayed on that summer's day, and no one could doubt that they were witnessing a historic moment created by a true rugby league legend, one of the greatest wingers of all time.

This view was endorsed by David Lawrenson, Offiah's biographer. 'People always like to compare current players to players of the past and he was always compared with all the great wingers before he came,' he said. 'But there was never anyone like Martin Offiah before he came, and there never will be again, he's unique.'

Martin Offiah was indeed different from most other rugby league players. Offiah wasn't a Northerner. He was born in Hackney, London in 1965. And unlike many of the great black players who preceded him, Offiah was of Nigerian descent. Legends like Clive Sullivan and Ellery Hanley came from West Indian backgrounds.

Most young black men from Hackney knew very little – if anything at all – about rugby league and could not relate to rugby union, a sport seen as the domain of the white middle classes.

Instead, they dreamed of playing football for one of the glamorous London football clubs like Arsenal or West Ham and for a long time, Offiah was just like them. He was always good at sports. Initially, he was motivated to better his older brother Chike, the star of the Offiah family:

> 'Things happen that shape your character and it was difficult to live up to having an older brother who was better than me at

> everything. No matter how well I did, I was always compared to Chike… I knew I wasn't going to change anyone's opinion, so I just tried as hard as I possibly could. I wanted to provide proof that I was at least as good as him – by scoring more tries than he did, for example.'

His mother was a teacher and like most West Africans, she valued education above everything else and sought the best education for her children. She sent them to Woolverstone Hall in Suffolk. This boys' grammar school was known as the 'poor man's Eton' and provided young Offiah with the impetus to grow as a sportsman.

Offiah tried his hand at everything, including cricket and fencing. He was an avid fencer and represented his school in competitions in France. Offiah the fast bowler played for the school's first team and was feared for his lethal bouncers. He did pretty well in his cricket career, as he eventually became the captain of his school's team, the Suffolk Schools team and represented the county at U25 level.

Rugby might not have had the benefit of Offiah's genius and instead of wearing the chevrons of Great Britain rugby league, he might have been decked in the white flannels of the England cricket team. He played county cricket for Essex Cricket Club's second XI and at one game in Eastbourne he roomed with the future England test captain Nasser Hussain. Luckily for rugby, he didn't enjoy the long days in the sun bowling and fielding and very quickly packed up his cricket gear.

Offiah came upon rugby by accident at school, when he found an oval ball as he rummaged through a storage cupboard. Initially, he wasn't keen on playing and neither was his mother who was afraid that her slightly built son might get hurt. In his final year when he broke his jaw, she thought he would give up, but on realising that he wouldn't she gave in and bought him a gumshield.

Offiah played on the wing in his first year at Woolverstone – something he felt was in keeping with the stereotype of fast black players – but his abilities lay beyond running fast and he also played fly-half and centre for much of his time at school. The game also provided Offiah with the spur to succeed with his education. As he was dyslexic, he found it somewhat difficult and wasn't particularly interested in academic work. He still managed to get four 'O' Levels but to play first team rugby and get into the sixth form he needed five 'O' levels. The next year, he took another five subjects and passed four, ending up with eight subjects – not bad for a kid with dyslexia.

A major turning point came for Offiah when he was 15, when he decided that he wanted a career in sport, to play rugby and wear the red rose of England – all this before rugby union was a professional sport. It was not just the love of rugby that motivated Offiah but the high profile of the sport at Woolverstone appealed to his personality. It was to be a template for his later career:

> 'I enjoyed rugby the most because it had the highest profile. The whole school used to come out and watch a match, whereas you'd only get a handful of spectators for a fencing match. And I responded to a crowd – I've always been exuberant and a bit of a showoff – and I've always tended to play better in front of a good one… having an audience really made a difference to me.'

By now Offiah was consumed by his desire to succeed as a rugby player but he realised that he couldn't achieve his goals at Woolverstone Hall, for although the school had a great rugby tradition, with a population of 380, they were the minnows among the schools in Suffolk. The school's rugby master Kevin Young arranged for him to play for Ipswich Rugby Club where he would launch his attempt to play for England Students. Unfortunately, the broken jaw would curtail his effort, but his ambition never diminished. Showing an uncanny knack for clarity and perspective, Offiah worked out how he would get ahead. He surveyed the London rugby scene, which was dominated by Harlequins and Wasps and opted to join the smaller, less fashionable Rosslyn Park:

> 'If I went somewhere like Wasps, I'd just get lost in the system because the top clubs have loads of good young players, and some never get a chance at playing in the first team. I reckoned if I went somewhere I could get into the first team, I'd be competing against the top players in other teams anyway.'

His rise through the ranks at Rosslyn Park was rapid and in November 1985, he made his first team debut against Loughborough College. Even though they lost, Offiah kept his place and eventually played against the top teams like Harlequins and Wasps. A prolific scorer, he topped the try count for those two seasons. His feats got noticed, and he was picked for London division and the Penguins International.

That led him to the Hong Kong Sevens and a place on the prestigious Barbarians team. It was at this point that Martin got the call that would change the trajectory of his career.

When Offiah got that call from Widnes coach Eddie McDonald, he knew very little about rugby league. In fact, he once thought the game so unattractive, he didn't think he would ever play it. He didn't know who Widnes was and thought they were 'the team that played in red and white'. Maybe that was a sign of things to come, as that team was Wigan.

In fact, the Widnes manager Doug Laughton had never actually seen Offiah play. He got wind of a young winger who was 'running rings around them at Rosslyn Park,' and saw him on a video of highlights from the Middlesex Sevens. 'On the video he didn't do very much in the games but it was clear he was really quick,' recounts Laughton, 'his talent was beyond doubt.'

Offiah was stunned by Laughton's initial offer of £65,000 but he wisely decided to turn it down and hold out for more. When Laughton came back with a second offer of £85,000, the 21-year-old with £250 in his account could not refuse. This wasn't simply an opportunity to make a lot of money, it was Offiah's chance to realise his dream of becoming a professional athlete.

Laughton recalled that during the discussions, Offiah expressed his desire for an England rugby union cap, something the Widnes manager knew he couldn't put a price on. He did however make a very important point to Offiah: no black man had ever played for England, and it was not likely to happen any time soon. 'What I had to show him was that there were more prospects for black players in rugby league.' He drew a parallel with another great winger, Billy Boston who initially turned down the chance to play rugby league in anticipation of a Wales rugby union cap. Boston was advised that he should seriously consider the rugby league offer as a black man was unlikely to play for Wales. Boston went on to become a rugby league legend.

Laughton knew he was taking a risk with the untested young winger but he liked what he saw. 'He believed he had the bottle for rugby league, and he was young so I felt I could mould him.' Offiah's first games were not spectacular, and frustratingly, he hadn't scored any tries. Laughton sensed his new charge was losing a bit of confidence. 'I had a chat with him and told him "remember Dougie loves a winner", but I wasn't worried, because he was sensational in training and he had exceptional pace.'

That first season was quite impressive with one of the highlights being a hat-trick against St Helens that helped Widnes to their first championship in a decade. Offiah would also guide them to the Premiership final, top the League's try scoring table and win the Man of Steel Award. His performances caught the eye of the GB selectors and he scored a try in Great Britain's win against Australia, the first in ten years.

When Laughton signed Offiah, he did it knowing he needed someone who would bring a new dimension to the team but even he didn't know what a gem he had uncovered. 'I knew he was going to be good, but I didn't know he was going to be as good as he was. He did a job for me and in many ways, he felt I did a job for him too.'

One of Offiah's team-mates at Widnes was Welsh rugby union convert Jonathan Davies who said that Offiah was a great character in a lively dressing room that boasted a range of nationalities. 'Martin was a true professional, I think he had everything. He was popular, read the game well and was one of the best supporting players in the team. That's something that people don't give him enough credit for.'

In four seasons at Widnes, Offiah finished as the league's top scorer, he helped them to win the Championship twice, the World Club Challenge and three Premiership finals. It must have been a shock for fans when he handed in a transfer request.

> 'Despite the success I'd had at Widnes, I still hadn't managed to get to Wembley and I was beginning to think I never would with the club. By 1991, I felt I'd gone as far as I could with Widnes, so I asked for a transfer.'

His transfer request coincided with Laughton's departure to Leeds and the most obvious step would be for him to follow his mentor. He met with Laughton and worked out a contract with Leeds who offered Widnes £370,000 but it was not to be. In a scenario reminiscent of a football transfer saga, Wigan, the team that played in red and white put in a world record bid of £440,000 that was accepted.

What would Offiah's career been like if he had joined Leeds? We can only assume he wouldn't have hit the heights he did with Wigan. Wigan was the best club in the league, full of stars like Shaun Edwards, Kevin Iro and Henderson Gill and young guns like Jason Robinson,

Henry Paul and Kris Radlinski. When Offiah arrived, he knew he had to live up to the expectation and the hype of being the most expensive player in the league.

His achievements at Wigan speak for themselves: five Championship medals, four Challenge Cup winners medals and numerous other medals and honours. It was also for Wigan that he scored his best ever try, and most fittingly, he would score it at Wembley in the 1994 Challenge Cup.

Offiah collected the ball from Frano Botica deep in his own half, and looked to make as many yards as possible. He stepped outside Leeds prop Neil Harmon, and broke through the Leeds defensive line. He spotted a gap and soon found himself in space and approaching the halfway line. With no one to catch him from behind in open space, the only obstacle between him and the try line was his former Widnes team mate Alan Tait, who was certainly no slowpoke. Knowing Tait's tactics, Offiah decided to keep the Leeds man guessing about which way he would go, so he took him left, then right before hurtling to the line to score that try.

'I knew he couldn't catch me,' Offiah recalled. 'After I scored, I sank down on my knees and thought: "God, I just picked up the ball from near my own line and scored at the other end." '

That try was named as the second best try of either code by the *Daily Telegraph*, behind Gareth Edwards' try for Wales against the Barbarians in 1973. It is still used on sports quiz shows like *A Question of Sport* and is quoted by rugby league writers as one of the best ever. 'The try was something fairly special,' he mused. 'As a winger, you dream about getting the ball under your own posts and running the length of the field to score. But to do it in front of 80,000 people in the Challenge Cup Final with millions of people watching on television around the world, well, it doesn't get any better than that for a rugby league player.'

Despite his success, it wasn't always easy, as Offiah set extremely high standards for himself that he sometimes felt he wasn't meeting. Team-mate and friend Shaun Edwards described Offiah as a 'real worrier'. He recalls having to reassure him during a patchy period after a shoulder reconstruction. 'Basically, he was worrying himself to death,' said Edwards. 'I think by the time he got to the game, he was absolutely drained, he just worried too much.'

Offiah's worrying was probably a consequence of being in a high performing team like Wigan. 'Of course, everyone knew that Wigan's incredible success wasn't going to last forever: there would be one year in which Wigan didn't go to Wembley and win the Challenge Cup, but none of the players wanted to be part of the team that brought this great era to an end. The fear of failure together with the desire to create a bit of history, was a powerful motivating force to win.'

A scoring touch in a dominant team like Wigan was sure to make Offiah a hero among the fans, but his popularity went beyond Wigan and even rugby league. If Wigan was to rugby league what Manchester United is to football, Martin Offiah was to rugby league what David Beckham is to football.

Offiah himself has admitted that he had a bizarre relationship with rugby league fans. He has even been called the most hated man in rugby league: 'I am probably more revered outside rugby league circles because the things I did before are the things that people who have no affiliation to the either code or to the game as a whole could look at and say, "look what he's done, that's fantastic".'

Even though his friend and Great Britain team-mate Ellery Hanley was something of a household name, he was never as widely popular as Offiah. Offiah's great talent and flamboyant personality were etched in the minds of the general public, many of whom still think of him when they think of rugby league.

His pace and speed even caught the eye of former Prime Minister John Major who apparently described Offiah as 'faster than a camera shutter' after seeing him score two tries in the 1992 Challenge Cup final victory over Castleford at Wembley.

Offiah's personality and wider knowledge of sport meant he was media-friendly, and naturally, he was always in demand as a pundit and for sports quiz shows like *A Question of Sport* and *They Think It's All Over*. And with his good looks and striking physique it's not surprising that he has modeled for the likes of Armani, but his more memorable moments came when he appeared on the soap operas *Emmerdale* and *Hollyoaks*.

Even the RFL appreciated that Offiah's high profile could work in their favour when they used him as the poster boy for the 1992 First Test against Australia at Wembley. The poster featured him with ball in hand and trails of fire coming from his boots with the bold slogan, 'Will the Aussies catch Offiah at Wembley?'

After four successful seasons at Wigan, Offiah felt the time was right to move on, 'I would have been happy to stay at Wigan a bit longer, but I'm a realist: I'd had my time and it was the moment to move on,' he said. 'I realised that wherever I went, it was not going to be the same as playing for Wigan during those glory days.'

After spending nine years up north, it was time to go home to London. For him, a move to London meant more opportunities to develop his off-the-pitch interests as well as having the chance to play rugby union once again. Always one to relish a challenge, Offiah signed up for the London Broncos and Bedford Rugby Union club in the summer of 1996. He was taking on something most players would run from: playing league and union at the same time.

This would turn out to be one of the least enjoyable times of his career. 'The short interlude at Bedford was probably one of the worst years in my career.' When he joined Bedford, there was talk of a possible England cap, but that didn't materialise. Instead, Offiah found himself in a set-up that was way below the standards to which he had become accustomed:

> 'When I first went to Bedford, I felt like a professional in a very amateur environment… but I was prepared for that. Because rugby union had only recently become a fully professional sport the club was very much going into uncharted territory and I knew there would be teething problems.'

So why did Offiah go to Bedford?

> 'It was a financial decision, I was 30 and thinking I'm not going to play this game forever… at the age of 30, I'd say money was important. And I thought that if I could bring some of the dynamism of rugby league to union, people might sit up and take notice, but it was much tougher to make an impact than I thought.'

It was difficult for him at Bedford because he was expected to lead the way as the 'guiding light professional' but he wasn't given a special role in the team.

He tried to carve out a place for himself by taking over sprint sessions but that did not last very long. He was up against a totally different culture where openness was not as common as in rugby league. His openness didn't sit well with the Bedford management and soon enough he was labelled a trouble-maker.

> 'There's a different etiquette in rugby union. I sometimes had problems keeping quiet and if something is really bugging me, I'm the type of person who tries to get it out rather than suffer in silence.'

Although it was a season that seemed to have more lows than highs, Offiah had found some positives to reflect on. Undoubtedly, the high point of his season of playing two codes of rugby at the same time was the weekend he received his MBE at Buckingham Palace. It was a weekend he describes as a 'Mad Weekend'.

Although Offiah was only playing 12 games for the Broncos, it was inevitable there would be some fixture clashes. But on this weekend in March 1997, he was due to play a league game at Warrington on the Friday and a union game at Rotherham on the next day. This seemed straightforward enough but he later received the news that he was to attend the ceremony to receive his MBE on the Friday afternoon before the game in Warrington.

The question for him was how to get to the Warrington game in time to play for the Broncos. 'I like challenges, and the idea certainly captured the attention of the media. Television crews and journalists were planning to follow my every move.' News of Offiah's gong even generated excitement in Nigeria where his father was a respected judge.

How did he sort out his logistical nightmare? It was a lucky coincidence that the Broncos main sponsor was Virgin, whose head was the flamboyant entrepreneur Richard Branson. Branson never missed a trick where publicity for his company was concerned and came up with the idea of getting a Virgin helicopter to fly Offiah from London to Manchester Airport from where he would join the Broncos in time for the game. Unsurprisingly, he had a low-keyed game but the Broncos still won 38-18.

The next day, he got a friend to drive him to Rotherham and despite feeling somewhat shattered he was able to score a try in a very intense game.

> 'The events of the last 24 hours almost caught up with me while I was running down the wing but I just managed to make the line

> for the try. I remember thinking: "I won't be doing this again." But it was nice to sign the whole thing off with something a bit special otherwise it would have been an anti-climax. And both teams I played for won, so I was on double winning pay.'

But, at the end of the season, he was more than happy to reconsider his options at Bedford.

> 'The thought of getting up and going to Bedford to train was something that was beginning to make me physically ill. It wasn't because of any individual but more due to the whole set up. The thought of playing at Bedford for the next three years was just too much.'

Offiah got his wish and there was a mutual agreement that his contract would end that summer. Not long after leaving Bedford, London glamour club Harlequins offered Offiah a chance to join their squad. However, he was still smarting from his Bedford experience and politely declined their offer.

In 2000, Offiah joined the Salford Reds. The move to Salford was of course seen in some quarters as motivated by money but he denies this. 'I wanted to score 500 tries. I wasn't feeling (ready) to retire then, union wasn't an option and the opportunity came to join Salford or Warrington.'

In fact, Offiah would have preferred to join Warrington and still regrets that it couldn't happen. However it was something he had no control over, as Warrington simply ran out of money after splashing out on some big name players earlier that summer. He chose Salford because he wanted to stay in the Super League.

Like most rugby league players, he has never been ashamed of looking out for his own interests. He always expected to be well paid for what he did. To him, money was important not because he was greedy but because he was very aware that a bad injury could end his career suddenly or that he could be shown the door by a club after a bad season. Offiah's thinking was influenced by Ellery Hanley who always said that rugby was not a charity but a professional sport.

Shaun Edwards also shared that view. 'While sport was a passion for us all, it is also a business, and you should get the money you're worth while not just going for money. Happiness and money is better than just money and money and happiness is just better than happiness.'

Salford was nowhere as successful as Wigan, Widnes or even the Broncos. It was the first time that Offiah had been in a team that was staring at relegation. That experience showed him a side of rugby league he never previously understood:

> 'When we did beat Wigan and big sides, it reminded me of when I was playing at Wigan and Widnes because if we got beaten by a lower side, we always used to wonder why are they celebrating as if they just won a big competition? I actually saw that for what it was and I was in the dressing room of the side celebrating because they had won a League game.'

Offiah ended his rugby league career with two seasons at Salford and in his last season, he only scored seven tries and was blighted by hamstring, shoulder and ankle injuries and the team's patchy form. His last appearance for Salford was against the Halifax Blue Sox at a sparsely populated Willows in August 2001, and he scored the last of his 501 tries at home to Wakefield on 3 August 2001. The Reds finished in tenth place, one spot lower than the previous season. It was probably an anti-climax for Offiah.

On his departure from Salford, Leigh expressed the desire to sign him but as a proud and ambitious man, he didn't want to leave the sport anywhere but in the top division.

> 'I wouldn't have even considered doing it and I said to Leigh, "thanks but no thanks". And a lot of people were saying, "Martin, you don't want to harm your legacy for the sake of playing for an extra year or two." I think when you know someone is great; you remember them in the prime of their lives, competing against the top people. No one wants to see me playing for a second division club.'

And for many, Offiah in his prime was when he wore a Great Britain jersey. In the eight years that he was an international, he made 34 appearances and scored 27 tries. His debut came in January 1988 against France at Avignon. He had an impressive debut, scoring a try in Great Britain's 28-14 win. It was a dream come true for the young Offiah who made his rugby league debut only a few months earlier. He had some cause for worry when he wasn't picked for the return fixture at Headingley, but barring injury, his form in the League more or less assured a place in the Great Britain squad over the next eight years.

He would score a try in a very memorable 26-12 win over Australia in the Third Test in Sydney. It was Great Britain's first win against the Aussies in ten years. He described it as a 'watershed for rugby league tests between Great Britain and Australia'.

Like most other British athletes, Offiah knew that it was special to beat the Aussies especially on their own patch. The victory always seems sweeter if the British team is the underdog, as is usually the case.

> 'There have been quite a few times when playing against Australian sides when we didn't think we had a hope in hell of winning. But the fear of embarrassment makes you try harder, and when you've got that backs-to-the-wall attitude, you never know what can happen.'

One sweet win came for Great Britain in the Second Test in Melbourne in 1992. Offiah scored a try in a 33-10 win that equalled the highest ever score by a Great Britain side against Australia. Shaun Edwards, who also played in the game, has fond memories of that win.

> 'Martin was at the corner flag and I was in the catching position at kick-off, we both went to the scoreboard and burst out laughing. We looked at it and said, "Is that not the wrong way around?" Because no one expected us to win, especially not with that kind of score.'

Despite those two great wins against the Aussies, Offiah was disappointed that he has never been in a team that beat them in an international series. He feels particularly aggrieved about the 1990 Ashes series. In the second match, Great Britain had the chance to win the game and take the series and just after the second half, Offiah picked up a knee injury that forced him out of the game. He feels if he hadn't been injured, Great Britain would have been victorious.

> 'I was 30 seconds away from winning the Ashes at Old Trafford in 1990 when Mal Meninga scored a try. I was sitting on the treatment table in the dressing room with a damaged medial

ligament thinking if I was out there there's no way Mal would have run 80 metres down my side and scored that try.'

This disappointment aside, Offiah is proud of his international achievements. He scored the series winning try for Great Britain in their 1990 tour of New Zealand and in February 1991, he crossed the line a record breaking five times against the French. Above all, he loved the challenge of testing himself at international level. 'I enjoyed playing international football because I relished the challenge of taking a step up from club rugby and it was interesting to meet different players and coaches and working with them.'

Some have pointed to Offiah's ruthlessness in scoring tries, his pace and his footballing intelligence as qualities that marked him out from the rest. And by 2001 when he left Salford, he might have been down on pace but he certainly made up for it with his great finishing and his ability to read the game. He knew he still had a few more tries left in him and so did Shaun Edwards, who was now part of the London Wasps coaching staff. He convinced Wasps manager Nigel Melville to give Offiah a trial, and Wasps eventually gave him a one-year contract.

But, after an enjoyable season at Wasps, Offiah decided to put down the oval ball for good. He took a breath and turned his attentions to new challenges. 'When I retired, I did some bits of commentary for the BBC but rugby league isn't the biggest vehicle… I made the most of it and I needed to spread my wings.'

Having previously made two appearances as an actor on daytime soap operas, he decided to return to acting. This time, he took his career a step further by treading the boards in London's West End. His debut came in September 2002 when he starred in the role of Benny in the Courttia Newland play *Mother's Day* at the Lyric Theatre, Hammersmith. He fell into the part by accident, because the actor who was originally cast dropped out. His drama teacher heard about it and encouraged him to go for an audition.

Offiah gave *Mother's Day* his best shot and got favourable reviews from theatre critics in the national papers. The best compliments came from the director Riggs O'Hara. 'You throw Martin the part like you throw him the ball – he picks it up and runs with it,' said O'Hara. 'I think one of the reasons he is so good is his rugby background. He just gets on with the job and doesn't mess about. He has a wonderful speaking voice, incredible presence and he works really hard.'

Even though he was accustomed to performing in front of thousands, the more intimate setting of the theatre gave him a new and different kind of excitement. 'It takes time and slowly but surely I'll be successful. I've got passion now, I really enjoy the acting.' To those who've seen Offiah play in front of thousands of people and communicate his passion for his sport to the crowds, it's no surprise he got off on the right foot in his acting career.

For such a high profile athlete, Offiah has done well to keep his private life private. He has never been fodder for the tabloids and his clean image has been an inspiration for many young people from the UK to Nigeria. But despite his links with Nigeria, and the excitement his achievements have generated in Nigeria, Offiah's relationship has always been a love-hate relationship. It has become much worse since his father was murdered there in March 1999.

'I've had a lot of bad experiences there. Obviously my dad's death, and before that, seeing the gruesome things I've seen,' he said. 'If I see people in the street being burnt with tyres and petrol, I can't get that out of my head and I don't want to be in a place where that happens. Maybe because I haven't grown up there that's why I have a love-hate relationship with my mother country,' he said pensively.

Rodney Hinds, sports editor of the Black newspaper *The Voice* felt that Offiah's impact touched the black British community, which has not traditionally been attracted to rugby of either code:

> 'In his time, he made rugby sexy for the Black community. His long legs, his hairstyles, his nickname and his achievements made the sport very attractive to Blacks. As a community we like winners and his achievements are well noted.'

Offiah recognises that he is a black icon, and says that he likes the way that so many Black people approach him with positive comments. 'In our (black) community, we give people the props (respect). When you've done something, and you deserve your props, people will give you the props. Like people come up to me and say, "Hey, well done!".'

Hinds believes that Offiah was one of the few Black British athletes to break ground in the mainstream media, because he didn't fit a stereotype:

> 'Martin has the personality that people can relate to, he isn't a

> man of the streets, like a Nigel Benn but he has a clean-cut image. He's something of a "Steady Eddie". He's one of the black athletes who made it beyond the back pages and made it into the lifestyle pages of the broadsheets.'

He might be retired from the sport, but Martin Offiah still has the cachet to appeal to readers of those lifestyle pages. In the absence of players who will bring charisma, ability and flair to the sport of rugby league he remains the sport's icon. But he knows the way he did things might not have met everyone's approval, but that does not bother him:

> 'I enjoyed the beauty of rugby league in the same way that people who aren't rugby league fans could appreciate the way I played the game. It probably didn't endear me to the rugby league purists, but people outside the game will come up to me and say, "Man you're the greatest player of all time," and I say "No I'm not mate, I'm just a product of my time." '

When you sit and listen to Offiah speak about his achievements, you can't help but think that even though he's done so much, there is no way he could just sit back and take life easy. Still driven and extremely positive about life, he is attacking the next phase as vigorously as he did his rugby career. He knows that at 37, he's young enough to successfully pursue acting or any other goals he wants to.

And it's not likely that you'll ever see him on reality TV shows like *Celebrity Big Brother* or *I'm A Celebrity, Get Me Out Of Here* with a bunch of washed up has-beens trying to reclaim their glory days.

> 'At the end of the day, I have something the people on reality TV don't have and that's credibility. You can have 15 minutes of fame on *Big Brother*, but until I die I will always be Martin Offiah MBE, highest English try scorer of all times. It might not mean much to a lot of people but it gives me the confidence to say I've achieved something. That's why I owe a lot to rugby league and I will never bash it because it's made me what I am.'

13

IKRAM BUTT

Karl Spracklen

It's the day of the Challenge Cup Final in 2003 and this year it's the big Yorkshire local derby between Bradford Bulls and Leeds Rhinos. Although the road no longer leads to Wembley, thousands of northerners are making the traditional trek to the cup final, leaving the confines of the M62 to congregate in their usual good-humoured way in the pubs and cafes of a city where league, if it is played, has a small role in the daily lives of most of the city's inhabitants. This year we, the north, rugby league, have descended on Cardiff, in the heart of Welsh rugby union territory, and we have taken over the city. The colours of every professional league club are here, worn on the backs of men and women of all ages, and amongst them are many amateur teams with names that tell of the role league has played in our northern lives: Wath Brow Hornets, Underbank Rangers, Oldham St Anne's.

The colours that dominate the streets and pubs are, however, those of the two Yorkshire Super League clubs that will be contesting the day's final. Bradford fans are arrayed mainly in white, with flashes of amber, red and black; the Leeds faithful in blue and amber. Both of these sides represent large cities, rivals for hundreds of years from the beginnings of the Industrial Revolution to this new century of gratuitous displays of wealth and soul-destroying poverty. The two clubs have been tagged with the stereotypes other northerners have about those cities, and both seem to revel in these caricatures – the no-nonsense, gritty Bulls and their flash, debonair neighbours who never quite seem to have the determination to add the finishing touch. For the fans of Leeds and Bradford, this is more than a match between two teams of thirteen men, this is about settling scores, about proving which city is cock of the north, but most of all about celebrating and reaffirming their loyalties and identities in a changing world. Not all the fans who are here are from the north, of course – league has expanded beyond the M62 and today there are league loyalists from all over the country and the world – but the majority of the fans here are either from the old three counties of the Northern Union or have some sense of loyalty to those places.

And although the crowd is predominantly white, there are a few exceptions.

Asif Khan and a small number of other British Asians, all Muslims, are in the middle of the crowd. They have come down on the day and Asif is trying to contact someone who has promised them some tickets. Unlike many of the other league fans milling around outside Cardiff's Millennium Stadium, Asif and his mates haven't been drinking – instead, when they arrived in town, they went to a local mosque to say their prayers. This proved to be a lucky move, because they can leave their minibus parked up securely at the mosque while they go to the match, unlike many of the others here today who have had to park out of town and struggle in on public transport. Most of Asif's mates, like Asif himself, are league players and Leeds supporters, though there's at least one Bradford fan who has been ribbed in the usual manner.

Asif gets the tickets and they get to their seats in time for the kick-off. The match, as usual, reminds everyone in the stadium why they follow rugby league, though for the Leeds fans there is the heartbreaking missed opportunity when Kevin Sinfield chooses not to go for goal in the final minutes to tie the game. For Asif and his mates the disappointment at the hooter is tempered by the wry smile of their Bradford supporting companion, but by and large they are happy to have watched a close, tense match that did both teams proud. They file out of the stadium amongst the dejected Leeds fans to make an early start back to Yorkshire. It has been a good day.

Then, in front of them, oblivious of their presence, three white Leeds fans start up a drunken chant aimed at Bradford, one that has bounced around Valley Parade, the home of Bradford City Football Club, on a number of occasions whenever a visiting side has been struggling: 'You're just a town full of Pakis…'

The meaning is clear – Bradford might win, at football or rugby league, but the teams and their fans and their city belong to the demonised, racialised 'other'. Asif and the amateur rugby league players with him walk up to the white men chanting the racist abuse, but as they do so they are aware that a clutch of police officers are watching. The white men stop their taunt when confronted with the Asian rugby league players; the police look as if they are about to intervene and, rather than be arrested for assault, Asif and his mates leave the three white men, now silenced, and return to find their transport.

Overt racism is not unique to rugby league, nor to sport. Yet the assumption by one group of fans, the white Leeds supporters, that people from another ethnic group did not properly belong, either in rugby league or in British society, undermines the image of our game as one that welcomes and accepts people of all backgrounds. Rugby league, the family game, still has fans who think the word 'paki' is acceptable and not racially offensive, even when football fans are finally being sent to prison for chanting the word.

The example I have recounted is a real example, told to me by one of Asif's friends. Just because the fans Asif and his friends heard were Leeds fans should not be taken to be proof that Loiners are a particular problem. Ironically, Asif and most of his friends are Leeds fans, too, and support the team with the same passion as any Southstander. But the casual racism they heard at the Challenge Cup was a powerful reminder that the game's strength, the tightly-knit community of rugby league, can often be a fatal weakness that allows prejudice, discrimination and racism to take the place of pride and loyalty.

Of course, Asif and his friends, as rugby league players, represent a new trend in the game, the slow trickle of British Asians who are learning to enjoy league and take it up at a number of levels. It is a slow trickle, and for many years British Asians have not been able or in a position to take up rugby league because of the game's closely guarded, inward-looking symbolic boundaries. A 1995 survey of the professional game by Leeds Metropolitan University found there was only one professional rugby league player from the British Asian community, and, sadly, no supporters from the British Asian community at all at the games surveyed. When asked whether it was acceptable to use racial abuse when shouting at players on the pitch, thirteen percent of the rugby league fans surveyed said yes, it was sometimes ok to racially abuse players.

But things have changed since the first British Asian professional rugby league player, Gurdup Singh, turned out for Huddersfield and Hunslet in the 1970s. Most famously, Ikram Butt carved out a professional career in the 1990s at a number of top clubs and earned a cap for England, becoming in the process one of the first British Asians to represent the country at any professional team sport. But there have been others who have made their mark in the game: Issy Sadiq, a consistent winger for Eastmoor in the National Conference in the early 1990s; Junaid Malik, who became at the turn of the century the first British Asian to be selected for a BARLA national representative side, after winning rave reviews for his play-making role for Elland in the Pennine League; and in the women's game Saima Hussein from Keighley, selected to play for Great Britain in 2001.

It is a trickle, but British Asians are making their mark in rugby league. Half a year or so before the Challenge Cup Final between Leeds and Bradford, Ikram Butt, the first Asian rugby league player to represent England launched the South Asia Bulls team at the 2002 York Nines. The South Asia Bulls, a team drawing on the small but growing number of British Asians in West Yorkshire playing the game for other amateur clubs, made their first appearance at the Fairfax Nines at York after Ikram got together with Junaid Malik and a few other league-playing British Asians and decided they had a role to play to tackle racism, promote racial equality and promote rugby league to their own communities – to give something back to the game and to society. It was no coincidence that Ikram chose to use the Bulls to publicise the work of the Commission for Racial Equality's Sporting Equals project, which works with national governing bodies of sport, including the Rugby Football League, to help them tackle racism and promote racial equality in – and through – sport.

The Bulls are deliberately inclusive of people from this country's South Asian communities, cutting across religious boundaries by having Hindus, Sikhs and Muslims in the side. This isn't segregation, but a celebration of British Asian identity, British Asian involvement in the game and British Asian ownership of rugby league's traditions. Some supporters of rugby league in England had objected to the Maori team's inclusion in the 2000 World Cup, but that was because the Cup was supposedly a contest between nations, and teams based on ethnic groups playing against nations just didn't make sense. The South Asia Bulls could eventually evolve into a representative side like Lebanon, with players using their family origins to represent Pakistan, Bangladesh or India. But that is not the main aim of the team. The purpose of the team is to highlight the issue of racial equality, promote the game to British Asians and publicise the work being done in Bradford to increase the numbers of young British Asians taking up the game. This should then help attract more British Asians into the game as players, supporters and sponsors – and perhaps maybe then, racism of the sort Asif came across at the Challenge Cup, and that thirteen per cent of fans who thought it was sometimes acceptable to racially abuse a player, will really have no place in the game. And perhaps rugby league will finally be in a position to truly represent the communities in which it has traditionally been played, because over the last fifty years many of those communities have changed their demographic profile, and yet the profile of the fans hasn't.

Ikram Butt himself is a powerful role model for young British Asians, not just as a rugby league player, but as a successful athlete who has represented England and carved out a career in professional sport and, for the past few years, in sports development in the public sector. Ikram is also proof enough that British Asians can get involved in rugby league, and make an impact, if there's the right mix of development work by clubs, passion for the game amongst schools and teachers, and, significantly, the support of parents and family.

At the launch of the Bulls, Ikram could be found in the corridors of the Commission for Racial Equality's offices, speaking to a journalist on his phone while others waited in the conference room along with Junaid Malik and other British Asian rugby league players from amateur clubs in West Yorkshire. Because of his high profile, Ikram is in demand, not just at the launch of the Bulls but every day of the week. Officials at Red Hall and BARLA are keen to speak to him to get his opinion and advice on development schemes; British Asian businessmen want him to attend dinners as a speaker, or as a potential winner of some achievement award or another; journalists looking to write features on Asians in British sport queue up to ring him; and even rugby union officials are keen to talk, to try to get Ikram to replicate some of the success he has had with rugby league in Bradford in their sport.

It all began a couple of miles down Burley Road in Leeds, in the tightly-packed terraced streets of Hyde Park, at the Royal Park school. It was there, as a nine-year old boy, that Ikram had his first taste of rugby league when development officers from Leeds RLFC and the local council came down to treat the kids to a taster session. 'That was my first taste of the game, and I was hooked,' explained Ikram. Rugby league was new to the school, and to half of the kids there, even though they were only a mile or so away from Headingley. But the teachers at the school and the development officers saw the potential in Ikram. 'My PE teacher definitely encouraged me to continue playing, and that was that.'

For Ikram, taking part in rugby league, while new to him as a nine-year old, was not something completely alien to his upbringing. His older brother Tony had in fact also taken up the game through a similar route at school, and was soon signed up to Leeds, where he made a number of first-team appearances. Ikram and Tony were encouraged to play rugby league by their father, who saw the value in sport for his boys and wanted them to achieve success in whatever sport they played. 'My dad always encouraged us, he was very supportive,' said Ikram. 'He was a sportsman himself. In Pakistan he had been a champion boxer, and had boxed for the Air Force, so he was keen to get us into sport. He was happy for us to take part in any sport, so when me and my brother got into rugby league through school he wanted us to do the best we could.'

At the time, there were few opportunities to play at junior level on the west side of Leeds, and so Ikram's dad took him to Apperley Bridge in Bradford, on the border with Leeds. The club there had been quite successful in attracting a number of black players, and for a time was one of the better organised clubs in the area. Ikram's dad wanted him to play for a good club with reputable coaches, and this served Ikram in good stead because he was soon being watched by talent scouts for his strong running on the wing. When Leeds made an offer in 1987 Ikram accepted, and followed his brother Tony back down the valley to Headingley. However, once he was there, he realised there would be difficulties convincing the senior coaching staff of his ability to become a first-team player, even though he made four appearances for England Colts.

'I was getting frustrated, it was three years of being overlooked,' said Ikram diplomatically, when I asked him about the barriers he had faced. 'Tony had played twenty first-team games but still some people were saying we weren't mentally tough enough.'

After his frustrations at Leeds, Ikram was close to giving up the professional game and even rugby league altogether, but he managed to secure a stint in Australia with the Chinchilla Bulldogs, a team out in the middle of the Bush. There he got his taste for the game back, supported by ex-international Jackie Gleason, one of the club's leading lights. Rave reviews down under soon brought Ikram back in the frame in Yorkshire, and the man who threw Ikram the lifeline was then Featherstone coach Peter Fox. Despite his reputation as a straight-talking, old-fashioned rugby league coach, Peter Fox seemed to be able to see beyond the colour of Ikram's skin and concentrate on the one important factor – whether or not Ikram was good enough.

'Peter sent me a contract by fax, he was that keen,' said Ikram. 'He had faith in my ability, and judged me on that.'

Ikram's spell at Featherstone wasn't without its hitches – soon after he signed, for instance, Peter Fox, his mentor, was sacked and replaced by David Ward, who had been on the coaching staff at Leeds – but his strong defence and, ironically, mental toughness, was soon earning him recognition. As a stand-out British winger, Ikram soon came to the attention of ambitious London Broncos, then he followed his return to form with one of the highlights of his career: playing for England against Wales in 1995. After a spell in the top-flight with the Broncos, Ikram turned out for Huddersfield, then ended his professional career at Hunslet. Like many ex-professionals, Ikram continued playing in the amateur ranks at Victoria Rangers in Bradford, combining his work for Bradford Council as a rugby league development officer with his work promoting the game amongst Bradford's Asian communities.

Now, with the launch of the Bulls, Ikram is attracting the attention of important movers and shakers in the world of rugby union, as well as rugby league. At the end of September 2003, Ikram took Junaid Malik and a few of the Bulls to the Bombay Games in India, to take part in an invitation team playing in a rugby union tournament affiliated to the official event. But even though Ikram is happy to play both codes of rugby, given the opportunity, his heart is still in the game he grew up on. And he has an ambition for rugby league that extends beyond getting more British Asians into the game. 'I would like to use the South Asia Bulls as a first step to getting rugby league established in India and Pakistan,' Ikram revealed to me when I spoke to him just before he caught the flight out to Bombay. 'We want to go all the way, just like the Australian–Italians and Lebanese have done.'

How successful Ikram and the South Asia Bulls are ultimately depends on how ready rugby league is to support and nurture British

Asian involvement in the game. As Asif's friend said to me:

> 'Look at all the places where there are rugby league clubs. There are whole communities of Asians who have grown up there, but they haven't come through into the game. That's says a lot about the barriers that have to be torn down, but at the same time there's a massive opportunity. Rugby league's always had black players, and Polynesians and Aborigines. Now we need to open the doors to British Asians, because if we do, you'll soon find the next Ellery Hanley.'

England has always been a nation of immigrants, from the Arab and African Roman soldiers who settled in the country at the end of the fourth century onwards through the years of Saxon and Danish migration. Successive waves of refugees such as Flemings, Jews, Huguenots have added to England's (and Britain's) culture and brought new things to our lives such as hops in bitter beer that today we think of as peculiarly British. By the end of the eighteenth century, there were about 20,000 black people in London alone: freed slaves, servants, entrepreneurs and famous men of letters such as Olaudah Equiano. The growth of the British Empire, which by the end of the nineteenth century covered large parts of the globe, owed much of its success to over two million Indian and Chinese labourers working on plantations, mines, docks, ships and railways, abroad and in England where significant communities emerged in Liverpool and London. As British subjects, people from the Empire not only worked for the Empire but were expected to fight in all Britain's wars, even wars of colonial expansion, and the part they played in both World Wars made a crucial difference to Britain's prospects.

But it wasn't until the years following the Second World War that the numbers of immigrants and refugees from the Empire and beyond significantly increased. Faced with the massive task of reconstruction after the Second World War, and acute labour shortages, the British Government encouraged immigration, first from among European refugees displaced by the war, and then from Ireland and the new Commonwealth countries of South Asia and the West Indies. Before long, in some factories, mills and plants, the overwhelming majority of workers were Asian or black. And the invitation was soon withdrawn as successive Governments increased anti-immigration legislation, under pressure from racist campaigns and inflammatory rhetoric about the nation being 'swamped', much like the rhetoric used today to describe the new wave of immigrants seeking asylum in this country.

The significant thing about the growth of Britain's Asian and black communities in the last fifty years for rugby league is the concentration of many of those communities in traditional rugby league towns and cities. On the west side of the Pennines – Salford, Oldham and Rochdale; in Yorkshire – Leeds, Bradford, Keighley, Batley, Dewsbury and Huddersfield. The black community in rugby league towns and cities is quite dispersed except for a few places in the bigger cities, but the Asian community, and in particular the working-class British Pakistani and Kashmiri communities, is heavily concentrated in urban areas around rugby league grounds and in streets from where rugby league clubs once drew thousands of fans and hundreds of players. The figures for the 2001 Census show that British Pakistanis alone make up 14.5% of the population of Bradford (including Keighley), 7.7% of the population of Rochdale and 6.8% of the population of Kirklees (Huddersfield, Batley and Dewsbury, concentrated in the latter two) – factor in the British Asians from the Indian and Bangladeshi communities and you start to see there are thousands of British children from the Asian community growing up a drop-kick away from rugby league with little knowledge of the game and a fear of prejudice, exclusion and racism.

Post-war migration has changed the demographic profile of many rugby league towns, but not all. Traditional mining areas around Wigan and Castleford, and the rugby league hotbed of the Cumbrian coast, remain places where ethnic minorities are few in number. But in the larger towns and cities many of the rugby league streets and areas have changed, with white families moving to the suburbs but retaining some sense of association with the old club and locality, and newer communities of ethnic minorities establishing themselves and having their own sense of place and identity. A close analysis of towns where rugby league is played will show that the divisions between different communities of class or ethnicity often map on to the divisions between rugby league streets and estates and other localities where there is no rugby league tradition.

Rugby league has always been, and continues to be in many places, a game of close-knit localities. And in areas where people from the black community have settled, new traditions and networks have developed over the last thirty years that allow black people to become involved in rugby league: black players and supporters have become associated with certain clubs such as Queen's in the Burley district of Leeds, or Huddersfield St Joseph's, or Queensbury where the Pryce family has become a well-known source of rugby league talent. The other chapters in this book tell of the progress made in encouraging and welcoming black people into the game. But what about people from the British Asian community? Those journalists and commentators who have bothered themselves with trying to answer this question have often relied on lazy stereotypes: Asians prefer cricket, they're not built for rugby league, Muslims can't drink or they can't wear a turban in a scrum. These stereotypes are the symptoms of internalised, institutionalised racism in rugby league: they say that black people are all right because they're like us white people, but Asians are too foreign, too unknown, for us white people to feel comfortable around.

Ikram Butt's very presence should counter such stereotypes and prejudices. Ikram is a fairly devout Muslim, but not having a drink and not eating certain snacks at the after-match did not stop him going on to represent England, even though a few of his coaches tried to make his faith into a potential barrier. Any one of the British Asians currently playing rugby league will speak about the game with as much passion as anyone else, and only the most stupid right-wing fanatic would challenge Ikram and the South Asia Bulls to a fair fight. So how come there aren't more British Asians in the game at junior and open-age amateur level in places where there are significant and sizeable British Asian communities? Why haven't we seen British Asians playing at the top level of rugby league in numbers that would fairly reflect their numbers in the population?

Sport can be a medium for racial discrimination, either through institutionalised racism, where people from ethnic minorities are discriminated against through assumptions and structures in sport, or through a racist culture which attaches itself to that sport, as in football in England. It can be argued that sports themselves are part of a racist hegemony, where perceived racial differences are presented as norms through unequal representation. For instance, rugby league shows an unequal distribution of black athletes to non-central playing positions through what is termed stacking. But clearly there is more to the problem of racial discrimination and ethnicity and belonging in rugby league than stacking. In rugby league the problems identified by Leeds Metropolitan University in the *What's the Difference?* research of 1995 included abuse from crowds and players, a lack of support and a lack of access to the social networks that helped white players from an early age. Researchers into racism in football have described the double burden of black football players, who not only receive abuse about their colour, but also the general abuse directed at players, simply because of their 'otherness'. Sport can be a medium of expressing and exploring ethnicity and celebrating identity, as the South Asia Bulls show, but at the same time the structure of sport in this country lends itself to white culture: and in rugby league, concepts of 'northern-ness' are implicitly (and sometimes explicitly) read as white, male and working class, and this reading lends itself to a process that excludes others who don't fit that identity – people from ethnic minorities, Muslims who do not drink alcohol, women, southerners.

Racism is an issue that pervades all of this country's contemporary culture: sport is no exception to the rule. And at the same time, those who do wish to be involved in 'the game' of rugby league find racism and prejudice built into the boundaries of the imaginary community in the form of shared history and meanings which they do not share, and stereotypes and assumptions. So for British Asians, there are still a number of boundaries and barriers they have to surmount to become accepted in the game. Even where those boundaries and barriers allow in Polynesians as examples of the exotic, and when black players can find belonging and a sense of identity in amateur clubs where racism is not tolerated and support networks exist, Ikram Butt has a lot of work to do – the question is, what are the Rugby Football League doing?

The Rugby Football League (RFL) was one of the first governing bodies of sport to take racism seriously, when it commissioned the *What's the Difference?* report in the mid-nineties. Since then rugby league has signed the Sporting Equals' Racial Equality *Charter for Sport*, an initiative supported by Sport England and the Commission for Racial Equality and has launched the *Tackle It* campaign tackling racism and promoting league in the Asian community in Bradford. The League's work has led it to being awarded the Preliminary Level of the Sporting Equals Standard, one of the first four organisations to achieve it.

But of course there are still problems in rugby league. The *Difference* report showed that there were still plenty of people in the game who thought racist abuse was sometimes acceptable. There are still too few Asian and black people involved off the pitch as fans, administrators, coaches and board members. Asian and black players are still stereotyped about their ability or lack of it to play in certain positions. There is only one professional player in the whole of the game with a British Asian background. Professional clubs are still being found guilty of failing to investigate allegations of racism. Players are still being charged off the pitch for various offences involving racial abuse. And despite genuine commitment at BARLA HQ to tackle racism and promote racial equality, numbers of Asian and black players below the professional level are low, and instances of racism, both visible and indirect, continue to occur. For many Asian and black people, rugby league is a game they cannot identify with – they see it as a game only for white, working-class northerners.

So it is very encouraging to see that Ikram Butt has not given up on the game, but has remained committed to introducing league to the Asian community in a big way. With the support of BARLA and the RFL (in varying amounts), and the backing of the Bradford Bulls, Bradford Council employs Ikram to develop the game in Bradford's predominantly Muslim, predominantly socially-excluded Asian community. As part of the *Tackle It* campaign, Ikram's job is to work with the local ethnic minority communities to get children to take up the game and progress through into playing at an open-age level. Local amateur clubs in Bradford have received support and resources to help them ensure they provide a welcoming environment to people from the Asian community, including promotional material in different community languages and guidance on matters such as halal food (no ham in the after-match buffet!) and religious festivals. For a city divided by the riots of last year, rugby league's attempt to reach out across all communities is a beacon of hope.

And Ikram's work is beginning to show signs of making a difference, not just in bringing Bradford's different communities closer together, but on the rugby league pitch, too. It would be great to see British Muslim children from Bradford following in Ikram Butt and Saima Hussein's footsteps and representing Great Britain on a world stage. Only by getting as many children as possible from all our communities playing the game will we be able to find the talent we need to find if we are to maintain the Super League and beat the Australians on a regular basis. This can only be good for the future of rugby league.

Rugby league does have a long history of being open to all, and we have much to be proud of. But we could do so much more to attract people from more communities into our game. When we struggle to attract youngsters, supporters, volunteers and sponsors, isn't it in all our interests to make sure racism has no place in rugby league?

14

Ellery Hanley

Tony Collins

In May 1989 the BBC journalist Michael Peschardt flew in to Sydney to take up a new post as the BBC's Australia correspondent. As he walked into the arrivals lounge after his flight, he was amazed to be confronted by dozens of journalists, TV cameras and radio microphones, not to mention hordes of enthusiastic onlookers. Who could they be waiting for, he wondered? And how could he, a trained journalist, not have noticed that he had been on the same plane as a major celebrity?

The superstar the Sydney press were waiting for was Ellery Hanley. Peschardt, despite having been a cricket reporter, barely knew who he was and was incredulous that a rugby league player, of all people, could be the focus of so much attention. It was not a little ironic that the BBC, so long guilty of marginalising league in Britain, found itself marginalised in Australia because of its failure to appreciate the greatest British rugby league player of his generation.

Ellery was at the peak of his powers when Peschardt became aware of his stature. But for those in rugby league who had followed his career, Ellery had seemed destined to go far even before he came on as a Bradford substitute against Rochdale to make his professional debut on 26 November 1978. He had been spotted by scout Eric Hawley playing as a teenager for the amateur Corpus Christi club in his native Leeds. Born in March 1961, soccer had been his original sport of choice but he began playing rugby league at his secondary school and found that it matched his talents and personality perfectly.

He first seriously attracted the attention of league fans in the 1983 Challenge Cup semi-final between Bradford and Featherstone. In a tight game which was to see underdogs Featherstone unexpectedly progress to the final, where they eventually defeated Hull, Ellery scored the try of tournament. Bradford's Alan Redfearn picked up a loose Featherstone ball ten yards from his own line, fed it to Ellery who set off. With three defenders covering him nothing seemed to be on, but one by one, he simply powered through them and outpaced the last defender to score, eighty-five yards after getting the ball. Although Featherstone eventually won 11-6, Ellery was the talk of the match.

The try embodied everything that he came to symbolise. It was based on strength and speed. It highlighted his self-confidence. But most of all it demonstrated his unquenchable determination to succeed. And it was this that not only made Ellery Hanley one of world rugby league's great players but also helped to make him the symbol of British rugby league's revival in the 1980s.

From the moment he scored against Featherstone his career seemed similarly unstoppable. The following season he made his Great Britain debut against France and later in the year was selected for the 1984 Lions tour down under. In a young and vastly inexperienced side he and Garry Schofield were the outstanding names. He scored one of the three tries that Britain managed against the Australians and two of the four scored against New Zealand, as both series ended in 3-0 whitewashes. He was maturing rapidly as a player, but no-one expected what was to happen the following season.

It is difficult now to convey what Ellery's scoring of fifty-five tries in a season meant to the game in the 1984–85 season. The last time anyone had passed the fifty tries in a season mark was Billy Boston in 1961–62. In the decades that followed it became accepted that it would never happen again. Not only had the game changed, especially through the innovation of limited tackle football in 1966, but the introduction of two divisions in 1973 meant that the top sides no longer had fixtures against the weakest sides, which would always guarantee a pot full of tries. As the 1984–85 season progressed, however, a sense of expectancy grew whenever Ellery played. Eventually the peak was scaled with room to spare, despite his missing three games against weaker opposition against whom, it is safe to assume, he would have scored more tries. Displaying a quality which was to come to the fore many times in the future, an aura of inevitability came to surround his quest to top the magic number and no-one was surprised when he reached fifty tries. What made the achievement even more amazing was the fact this was the first time that a non-winger had ever scored more than fifty tries in a season. He had played all of his games at stand-off, apart from two at centre. Such was his ability that Bradford coach Peter Fox allegedly told the rest of the team that if Ellery called for the ball, they had to pass to him, no matter where he was or whether they were playing a set move. Alongside the 1982 Kangaroo tour and the growth in crowds in the early 1980s, Ellery's feat seemed to signify that rugby league had recovered from its seemingly terminal decline of the late 1960s and early 1970s.

From that point on, Ellery became almost a talisman of the game's recovery. He also realised that his immense talent entitled him to equivalent reward. Pay negotiations with Bradford reached a deadlock and Ellery said he would not play for the club. Consequently in September 1985 he moved to Wigan in the game's first-ever £100,000 breaking deal. Maurice Lindsay gave Bradford £85,000 plus Phil Ford and Steve Donlan, who were valued at £65,000. Lindsay's boundless ambition for his club was to see him bring in New Zealand coach Graham Lowe in 1986 and open the chequebook to bring Joe Lydon and Andy Gregory, among others, to Central Park. And, of course, he simply had to have the man who had become acknowledged as the game's best player. Ellery's arrival in Wigan signified the beginnings of a new attitude at the club. The early years of their mid-1980s revival had seen them adopt an almost swashbuckling approach to the game; their short-term Australian imports such as Brett Kenny, John Ferguson and Steve Ella appeared to play the game by instinct and intuition alone. But Ellery brought steel to the club, putting a premium on personal commitment and team organisation.

In his first season at Wigan he scored 38 tries in 40 games. The following season of 1986–87 he achieved the almost unbelievable feat of scoring 63 tries, despite playing in one game less than the previous season. Wigan won everything that season apart from the Challenge Cup, capturing the first division title with records for the most points scored and least points conceded. As a player, Ellery was now in territory that no-one had occupied since the heyday of Brian Bevan, Billy Boston and Lionel Cooper in the 1950s. There was even speculation on the terraces that he might challenge Albert Rosenfeld's all-time record of 80 tries in a season. Off the field however, there were obvious signs of tension under Graham Lowe's coaching regime. Indeed, in December 1986 Ellery submitted a transfer request to the club, although this was never acted upon. Such cracks were partially due to the inevitable frictions that arose in the assembling of a team of stars. But it is also likely that Lowe's more personal, emotionally-based approach to coaching conflicted with the highly focused work ethic that Ellery had developed. Under John Monie, who became Wigan coach in 1989, these tensions eased, not least because Monie shared the same understanding that playing rugby league at the highest level was about discipline, organisation and having thirteen players who would, to use one of Ellery's stock phrases, 'put their bodies on the line' for each other.

Ellery's relationship with Monie mirrored the one he had with Great Britain coach Malcolm Reilly. Reilly was appointed to the national coaching role in January 1987 following yet another Ashes whitewash and almost his first decision in the job was to make Ellery captain. Perhaps the most remarkable thing about the appointment was how unremarkable it was. One can imagine the reaction if the England soccer or cricket team had appointed a black captain at the time. But not a single comment was made in rugby league. This was partially because Ellery was unchallenged as the best player in the game at the time, but it was also a reflection of how racially-integrated league had become on the pitch. The prominence of black players in the game over the previous fifty years meant that the skin colour of the captain, or of anyone else in the side, was simply not an issue.

The captain and the coach shared a similar approach and an uncompromising attitude to the game and their occasionally uneasy alliance was to last until Reilly was poached by the Newcastle Knights in 1994 and Ellery took over his job as British coach. But in 1987 the focus of both was on the 1988 Lions tour of Australia. A combative performance in the last test of the 1986 series and the emergence of young players like Schofield, Gregory, Lydon and later Martin Offiah had renewed hope that the Ashes might be winnable. Many of these hopes faded as the Lions started the tour with a string of weak performances. But the first test in Sydney produced a memorable match that at half-time appeared to be within Britain's grasp. And it was Ellery that made the difference, thanks to a classic Hanley try just before the break when a step and a dummy to his right confused Peter Jackson and Peter Sterling and off he went into the corner. The euphoria didn't last as the Wally Lewis-led Australians stepped up a gear and pulled away 17-6. An ill-disciplined and injury-weakened side lost the series with a 34-14 loss in the second test, and by the time of the third test, the injury list was longer than a kangaroo's tail. Yet marshalled by Ellery, the injury-decimated team pulled off one of the great test victories that ranked with the 1914 Rorke's Drift test and 1958's Prescott's Match at Brisbane. It was the first time that Britain had defeated the Australians for ten long years. The 26-12 victory highlighted yet another aspect of Ellery's game, his unflinching commitment in defence. Unusually for the time he did not score himself but was instead the rock around which the British defence was built – his dedication to the team effort was supreme.

The 1988 Lions tour led directly to what was probably Ellery's greatest triumph: his conquest of Australia. Allegedly, Balmain's Keith Barnes had signed a deal with Ellery for $5,000 per match in the street outside the Lions' team hotel, but whatever the truth his impact was enormous. The excitement among Balmain fans that his signing generated was equal to that of Sterling at Hull, Lewis at Trinity and Mal Meninga at St Helens. The Sydney league at that time had a top five play-off system and Ellery joined the Tigers when they were outside of the five with at best an evens chance of making the play-off. Playing at centre, he made his debut against Manly and from his first touch of the ball, it was clear that he was not there for a holiday. He picked up the ball at dummy-half twenty-five yards from the Manly line, burst through the markers and was eventually hauled down a couple of yards from the try-line by what appeared to be half the Sea Eagles' side. From then on there was no stopping him. Although they narrowly lost that match, the Tigers did not lose another, finishing equal fifth and becoming the first side to reach the Grand Final from fifth spot. And Ellery was the catalyst for this. 'He had such a great psychological effect on our players… everyone looked up to him,' remembered Tigers and Kangaroo hooker Benny Elias. Even in a team featuring Elias, Wayne Pearce, Garry Jack, Paul Sironen and Steve Roach, Ellery looked a class apart, scoring five critical tries in his eight games.

'Gee, this fellow Hanley's hard to put down,' exclaimed TV commentator Rex Mossop during one game, a sentiment that was echoed by each of the sides the Tigers dispatched on their march to the 'Big One'. Unfortunately for Ellery and the Tigers, one team did find a way to put him down. The team was Canterbury Bulldogs and the match was the Grand Final. Late in a tight first-half which neither side had dominated, Ellery was caught in a tackle turning round trying to offload. Bulldogs' stand-off Terry Lamb came over the top and Ellery hit the ground hard with his head. Video replays – which are still played to this day by disgruntled Tigers' fans – show Lamb's arm coming up but are inconclusive whether it came into contact with Ellery's head. Whatever happened, he was knocked out cold: 'all I remember is being in the changing room and I thought I was in the Wigan dressing room,' he recalled, 'I don't blame anybody. I think that's football'. He was so badly concussed that he couldn't return to the match and from 8-8, Canterbury pulled away in the second half to win 24-12.

Sadly for Balmain, and probably in hindsight for Ellery too, negotiations to bring him back the following year stalled over money. Despite a fund-raising campaign by Tigers' supporters led by Olympic swimming triple gold medallist Dawn Fraser, Ellery was offered a better deal by Western Suburbs. Balmain once again reached the Grand Final, only to lose in extra time to Canberra, while Ellery was left to provide inspiration to a lacklustre Wests side. Even in a mediocre side, he made a difference, boosting the club's average crowd by 1,500 and leading them to five victories in his thirteen matches, three more than they had managed before his arrival. Eventually however Ellery did return to Balmain to play out his career in 1996 and 1997, when he opted to sign for the Australian rugby league side during the Super League war. In a period of terrible angst and torment for the game, Ellery's return to Leichardt Oval was one of the few things that happened at that time which made sense.

The 1988–89 season became the year of Ellery. He had led Great Britain to their first test win over Australia in ten years. He had steered Balmain to their first Grand Final in two decades. He picked up the Man of Steel award for an unprecedented third time. He won the Lance Todd Trophy, the Man of the Match in the Regal Trophy Final and, perhaps most tellingly of all, he became the first British player to win *Open Rugby's* 'Golden Boot' award for the world's best player.

His powering of Balmain to the Grand Final in 1988 demonstrated to the rugby league world that he was indeed a great player. No Englishman since Malcolm Reilly had made such an impact on Australia, and given the low esteem with which the British game was held down under at that time, Ellery's achievement was even more remarkable. This, and his performances on tour for the Lions, also underlined that he was a big match player, someone who could be relied upon to excel when it counted most. Like Wally Lewis, Ellery had the knack of being able to insert himself into a match at a crucial moment and turn the tide for his side. He scored the crucial tries in Balmain's narrow play-off wins against Canberra and Cronulla and he brought this almost supernatural ability back with him when he returned home.

In the 1989 Challenge Cup final, his amazing forty-five yard run through five St Helens' defenders seemed to knock the wind out of Saints, who eventually surrendered to a 27-0 defeat. In the following year's semi-final at Old Trafford, Saints were drawing 14-14 just seventy-five seconds from time, and looking the side most likely to win against a mediocre-looking Wigan team, when Ellery popped up from nowhere, beat four men and slipped the ball out to Andy Goodway who scored at the side of the posts to take Wigan back to Wembley. Four years later, playing now for Leeds, he scored the two crucial tries in a Cup semi-final to deny St Helens another Wembley final.

Perhaps the most memorable of his big match triumphs was the first test in the 1990 Ashes series in which he and Garry Schofield engineered a classic 19-12 win. Once again, his ability to do something extraordinary when the moment required it came to the fore. He broke a 2-2 half-time deadlock by breaking through the Australian line and, face to face with Gary Belcher, chip-kicked the full-back to set up the play that led to Paul Eastwood going over in the corner. Fifteen minutes later he once again demonstrated his rarely seen kicking skills when, trapped by defenders with seemingly nowhere to go, he hoisted a bomb near the Kangaroo line and then raced to recover it, putting Belcher under so much pressure that his normally safe hands failed him, and the ball fell meekly to Martin Offiah who gleefully plonked it down over the line. The Aussies had been out-played and, for once, out-thought.

Genius often has its price and footballing geniuses often appear to extract a higher price than others. In the mid-1980s Ellery began a policy of not speaking to the press. This followed tabloid reports that 'revealed' that he had spent time in a young offenders' institution as a teenager and various attempts to dig up dirt about his private life. Although many rugby league journalists were quick to complain that they had nothing in common with the reporters who used underhand methods to 'expose' stars, the reality was not so simple. Many of them worked for the same tabloids that were so keen to dredge the gutters for dirt; and some had been occasionally confronted about this fact by players who had felt the lash of the tabloids. Indeed a small stream of players and officials found themselves in the Sunday newspapers for alleged sexual or other misconduct in the 1980s and 1990s, and it was a reasonable assumption to make that these stories had been fed to the gutter press by people within the game.

Certainly in soccer, as was most graphically shown by the case of Paul Gascoigne in the early 1990s, it was often the very same sports reporters who were telling players that they could trust them who were also tipping off their colleagues in the newsrooms about players' marital difficulties, drink problems and other details of their private lives. Indeed, soccer in the 1980s had developed an unedifying cycle of dependency and denunciation between players and the tabloids, whereby players such as Gascoigne could be found writing ghosted columns for a period, followed by front page exposés of their supposed moral failings. The cruel treatment of Frank Bruno by the tabloids in 2003 following his nervous breakdown amply demonstrated that being popular among sports writers was no defence against a ravenous press pack. Ellery himself was highly aware of the danger of the reporter's dual loyalties. Speaking to Australian TV in 1994 he alluded to this when he justified his refusal to deal with the press: 'I never trust journalists now because if somebody invades your privacy, and he wants to speak to you about football matters and then he tries to twist the situation I think that's pretty rude and pretty deceitful'.

His decision undoubtedly caused difficulties for the RFL when it came to promoting the Great Britain side. But these were by no means insurmountable, not least because there was always a large number of leading players only too keen to talk to the press, from the garrulous Andy Gregory to the telegenic Joe Lydon. The issue came to a head in March 1991 when the newly formed London Monarchs gridiron team, one of the founding sides in the NFL's World League of American Football, announced that they had signed Ellery as a running back and proceeded to tour him around the media, including an appearance on Channel Four's prime time Jonathan Ross show. Despite the outcry in league circles, these appearances did little to enhance Ellery's image or damage rugby league's. In front of the camera, Ellery came across as somewhat shy and uncomfortable and it was clear that the NFL wanted him because he was already a high profile name. Indeed, the fact that he alone had been chosen by the NFL to spearhead their PR drive for the Monarchs undermined the claim that he had damaged his public profile by not speaking to the press. He could hardly have been more famous if he had been on speaking terms with the press, leading some to ask if his attitude to the rugby league press might have been different had he been confident of the RFL's press and marketing abilities. And, in general, it does appear that the core of many of the disputes in which he was involved was the clash between his unremitting professionalism and the ham-fisted incompetence of many of the officials he encountered in the game.

But there was also another reason for Ellery's reticence towards the press. Quite simply, he was not interested in looking back. He did not want to be forever locked into the stereotype of 'problem youth redeemed by sport' so beloved by lazy or prejudiced reporters. Why should he constantly be reminded of the mistakes of his youth? Here he was, one of the great British athletes of the age, a man who had got to the top of the toughest sport in the world through his own dedication and commitment, yet much of the press was only interested in his past or his private life. Why should he talk to them? He didn't need the press. To use one of the oldest clichés in the journalist's lexicon, he did his talking on the pitch.

Wigan rugby league writer and jazz lover Bill Lythgoe once remarked that if one could draw parallels between league and jazz, Billy Boston would be Louis Armstrong and Ellery most resembled Miles Davis. It is an intriguing likeness. Like Ellery, Miles marched to his own drum and refused to listen to his critics, self-confident in his own talent and the route he wanted to travel. And while Miles was universally respected and admired, he had an often abrasive relationship with jazz fans, especially after he switched direction to use electric instruments in the late 1960s. But for those who played with him, he was regarded as a master of his art and held in the highest esteem, something that could equally be said of Ellery.

But maybe we don't have travel so far to understand Ellery. Because his single-mindedness and desire to cash in on his footballing talent, for which the Australians nicknamed him 'Salary' Hanley, belonged to a tradition as old as rugby league itself. Many of the game's greatest figures had public fallings-out with their clubs over their worth on the field and off it. We only have to look at just four of the original nine members of the Rugby League Hall of Fame. Billy Batten refused to play in a trial match to select the 1920 Lions touring side because he felt it was an insult to a player of his stature. Jonty Parkin fell out with

Wakefield over wages and ended up paying his own transfer and signing with Hull KR. Jim Sullivan had a grievous row over money with Wigan during the Second World War and signed for Dewsbury. And Alex Murphy's capacity to fall out with clubs both as a player and a coach was rivalled only by his supreme playing skills.

Even before the 1895 split, the same processes were at work. Dicky Lockwood, the greatest northern rugby player of the late 1880s and early 1890s, abandoned Dewsbury in pursuit of more money, even though such payments were illegal under rugby union rules. It was, and is, part of the league player's natural psyche to want to ensure they get as much as they can from their clubs. This was not greed but simple self-preservation – the knowledge that the next tackle you take could be your last is never too far away from a professional player's mind. Ellery was very much part of this rugby league culture, a culture that was often highlighted during his time with Wigan, which was also punctuated regularly by similar disputes between the club and Andy Gregory and Shaun Edwards.

The comparison between Ellery and Billy Boston is also revealing when we look at the crowd's attitude to them. Whereas as Billy was universally loved across the game, no-one would make the same claim for Ellery. Opposing crowds thought he was greedy, self-centred and constantly seeking to undermine the referee's authority, yet everyone knew he was a winner. But behind the abuse from spectators was a fear of his ability and a respect for his fearsome commitment to winning. In many respects his relationship with the crowd was similar to that of Alex Murphy: everyone hated to see him line up against their own team but each would have welcomed him with open arms into their side. And this was exactly what happened when he joined Leeds at the start of the 1991–92 season. From being the object of the crowd's vitriol, he became their inspiration. A similar transformation occurred at St Helens, where he became coach in August 1998. Formerly public enemy number one, his popularity with Saints' fans was such that their pressure initially stopped the club from sacking him in 1999 after he had, in his own inimitable fashion, publicly criticised the board of directors.

There were other controversies too. His sending-off by Robin Whitfield in September 1990 for disputing decisions and the subsequent halving of his ban to one match only heightened the suspicion of him among opposing supporters. In fact, it was actually more remarkable that this was the only time he was ever sent off in a match. His selection as captain for the 1992 Lions tour, despite an injury, which meant that he only played nine minutes of football on the entire tour, was again portrayed as an example of supposed RFL favouritism to him, rather than a desperate attempt to field the strongest possible side against the Australians.

But too many people have focused on the controversies surrounding Ellery and that has detracted from the enormity of his achievements. His 428 career tries make him the seventh highest try-scorer in the history of the game. He holds the season try-scoring record not only for a non-winger, but also for a forward, after having scored 41 for Leeds in the 1994–95 season. He was the first player ever to be transferred for more than £100,000 when he moved to Wigan from Bradford Northern and then £200,000 when he joined Leeds from Wigan. He captained Great Britain 18 times and only he, Harold Wagstaff and Jonty Parkin have ever captained two Lions' teams to Australia. And as a coach he guided Great Britain to a win against the Australians in 1994 and St Helens to the Super League title in 1999.

In the 1980s, British rugby league produced four great players, each one a master of his art: Andy Gregory was the classic scrum-half, trickier than a bag of cats and meaner than a junkyard dog. Garry Schofield was born to be a stand-off, all craft and guile, and with the ability to pass, kick and sidestep with the precision of a diamond cutter. And Martin Offiah was a speed king who belonged with the immortal wingers, itching to get his motor running and head off down the highway to the try-line.

But Ellery was more. In his ferocious determination to succeed, his commitment to give everything for his team and refusal to take a single backward step on the field and off it, Ellery Hanley *was* rugby league. It therefore seemed especially fitting that in the February 2004 poll of the 100 greatest black Britons, the top-ranked sportsman was Ellery. His position? Thirteen.

15

JASON ROBINSON
Huw Richards

Jason Robinson always did have a genius for changing direction. So much so that the best prepared, most committed defender was more often than not powerless to stop him.

So there's something appropriate about the role for which he is likeliest to be remembered in the history of the two rugby codes – the man who represents the moment at which the terms of trade shifted and a century-long migration of sporting talent acquired a reverse gear.

Of course, he was not the first former league player to make it big in union. Karl Ifwersen played for New Zealand in the first series of league internationals after the First World War, then returned to union to become an All Black, widely regarded as tactically the most astute player in a nation never short of rugby nous. The remarkable full-back Bob Scott, who also had an exceptionally tough childhood in common with Jason, played senior league before joining the New Zealand forces in the Second World War, won reinstatement to union and went on to be regarded as one of the greatest of All Blacks. Wales offers the strange story of Glyn John, who signed and played for Leigh when only 17, was reinstated on the grounds that he was both under age and had repaid the signing-on fee, and played two internationals at centre in 1954.

Jason – he is one of those players who inspires affection and invites description by first name only – was not even the first to change codes under the post-1995 dispensation when union, in a volte face as complete if not as stylish as the Vatican II Roman Catholic church dispensing with Latin and turning the priest to face his congregation, shrugged off more than a century of loathing of professionalism in all its real and imagined forms.

Five years had passed, and a clutch of Welshmen had returned whence they came, to relatively little fuss. This was not because they were poor players – Scott Gibbs, Jonathan Davies, Jon Devereux and Allan Bateman in particular could point to successful, fulfilling league careers. Scott Gibbs has left little doubt that, as a game, he much prefers league. Jonathan Davies proclaimed after his last game of league – a World Cup semi-final – that he was returning to union because it was 'f****** easier', although this was before he discovered that he was expected single-handed to revive the decaying fortunes of a once-vibrant sporting culture.

But as Dave Hadfield once put it, 'Unless you don't have much depth of feeling for either code, you're either League or Union. You can't just change your emotional allegiances like you change your socks.' There are nuances and qualifications. To grow up Welsh in an era when few players 'went north', making the league scout's demon king role more a matter of tradition than current relevance, was to be someone of undoubted union origins who still feels more at home at Headingley than Twickenham. Such quibbles apart, Dave Hadfield is pretty much spot on. We know whether we are league or union, and think we have a pretty good idea what everybody else is as well.

Nobody imagined that the Welsh players would have played league had union allowed them to make a living from their skills. Now it did, and they were returning home, literally and culturally. It was the equivalent of Bev Risman returning to his natural location in league after playing union as a student with such success that he was chosen for England and the British Lions.

Jason was different. Nobody doubted that he was league. And he wasn't just any rugby league player, but the most popular and exciting performer in the entire game. Wigan, and by extension the whole of league, suddenly found out what it had been like to be the Welsh communities who had lost a stream of folk-heroes over the previous century. All such losses hurt, but it is the departure of the players who tested and extended the limits of the possible and the credible – the darters, improvisers and deceivers – that really hits hard. A good case can be made that the greatest loss to Welsh union in the final crop of players who went North from the mid 1980s onwards was the prop forward Stuart Evans, who could have given substance and stability to a scrummage that instead bent, buckled and eroded like an old mineworking. But the one that hurt was Jonathan Davies, heir to cherished traditions of darting diminutive deceptionism.

You could argue about whether Jason was the best British player of the Super League era. There are strong countercases for his clubmate and contemporary Andy Farrell – consummate straight man to Jason's irrepressible joker, leader, goalkicker and fulcrum of every team he has played in since arriving at Central Park as a teenager with the presence and perception of a gnarled veteran – and for St Helens and Wales hooker Keiron Cunningham. Farrell was rated fourth, one place higher than Jason, when *Open Rugby* magazine celebrated 21 years of publication by ranking the best players of that era. The top three were Ellery Hanley, Garry Schofield and Roger Millward, incontestable giants rated on the whole of their careers, while the Wigan duo were both still in their early 20s.

They too were courted by union and Cunningham in particular came close to succumbing. As well that he did not, for even if Welsh union had been in much better shape than the shambles which greeted another cross-code transfer Iestyn Harris, there is no position in union that he could have played half as well as hooker in league, a position for which he appears to have been specifically designed by nature.

To lose either would have been a shock, but would either have occasioned quite the sense of loss that accompanied Jason? One factor undoubtedly was timing. It came during a period of deep unease for the game, when old campaigners for the free gangway, noble cause that it was, were left wondering whether this was quite what they had had in mind. The flow from league into union was much more trickle than flood – Henry Paul, Iestyn Harris, Mat Rogers and Wendell Sailor hardly constitute a mass migration. It was admittedly accompanied by something of a brain drain, with coaches like Clive Griffiths and Phil Larder appointed to defence specialist roles with national teams and the undoubted marketing genius of Peter Deakin lost to Saracens.

There was a brief fear, largely stilled by Cunningham's last-minute drawing back, that union might be capable of reaching out and taking anybody it wanted. It certainly occasioned a flow of comment showing how far rugby still divided into the sporting equivalent of CP Snow's two cultures – parallel worlds existing in a state of mutual ignorance and incomprehension. Rugby union voices, conveniently ignoring the fact that their own game had survived infinitely larger migrations of talent over the best part of a century, proclaimed the impending doom of league. Their league counterparts expressed shocked horror that anybody should sink so low as to offer players money to change codes.

Jason became a lightning conductor for the cultural and class conflicts between the two codes. His change of codes, and the debates that surrounded it, exposed both the strengths and the limitations of league at the end of the twentieth century.

He was frank about the reasons for going. Not for the money (although even if it were, could league fans honestly have objected?). Wigan had made him an offer reported at £750,000 over four years and he would shortly have been due a testimonial that, given his immense popularity in the game, should have been highly lucrative. The sensible financial option would have been to stay in the game of which he was a proven master, with no risks to his standing save those of injury and loss-of-form common to any sport.

The problem was league's besetting competitive weakness – the absence of a serious international dimension. Union offered him the possibility of playing annually in the Six Nations championship – which fills the biggest stadia in Britain – regular matches home and away against New Zealand, Australia and South Africa, a quadrennial World Cup and British Lions tours. None of this was guaranteed. He had to prove himself in a new, different game in which his high-profile recruitment would make him as much a marked man as former union recruits have been in league.

League had no way of matching it. It had a World Cup 33 years before union, but has failed to establish it as a regular competition. There was always the possibility of intermittent Ashes series, but that was dependent on both pulling the Australians out of the long spell of self-preoccupation which followed the enormously destructive Super League-provoked civil war and persuading them that there was anybody else in the world worth playing. Jason had achieved everything he possibly could in domestic league – every trophy, just about every individual award possible. All that was left was beating the Australians, the quest that has thwarted generations of league players and coaches since 1970 (It is instructive that while the rest of the English union coaching team were most excited by beating New Zealand in the summer of 2003 Phil Larder's roots in league meant that he instinctively found beating Australia the greater thrill.) The move to a summer season, coinciding with Australia's winter season, and Australian introspection have made Ashes tours, even when they do occur, a brief shadow of the season-defining events they once were.

If his move was in part the product of league's off-field weakness, the fact that he was in demand demonstrated on-field strength. To be able to move as if you have ball-bearings where the rest of us have joints is, Jason of all people would doubtless assure us, God-given. But the extent to which those natural talents were cherished and developed says something about league. Dave Hadfield has told the story of All Black Va'aiga Tuigamala, soon to play a still more significant role in Jason's personal development, remarking soon after joining Wigan on his ability to beat defenders on either side 'as if it were a concept entirely new to him'.

The skill that the best league players develop in beating a man one on one has been evident in less successful code-changers than Jason. Neither Henry Paul nor Iestyn Harris has been an unqualified success in union, both having to wrestle with the greater complexity of decision-making in union midfield roles, while Harris carried the additional weight of being Wales's latest version of King Arthur – the mythic hero sent to save a suffering nation. Both, though, have consistently demonstrated an ability to beat an opponent and open up a defence far in advance of players who grew up playing union.

Jason's skills in this respect were never more evident than on perhaps the most memorable night of his union career. This was the first British Lions test against Australia at Brisbane in the summer of 2001. It was Jason's first start in a union test – his appearances so far for England, still less than a year since switching codes, had been as a substitute.

Within the first few minutes Jason, playing on the left, received a pass in a good attacking position. You would have backed most quality international wings in either code to have scored, even with a highly-ranked full-back like Chris Latham as the one obstacle between him and the line. What, one strongly suspects, nobody else could have done was to make Latham look like a traffic island. The photograph in Jason's autobiography shows that Latham did, just, manage to lay a hand on him – grabbing at the elbow of his shirt as he shot past on the outside – but to zero effect. He might just as well not have been there.

That early score set up a memorable victory, although like their league counterparts a few months later, the Australians recovered from the initial setback to take the series by two matches to one. It was a union triumph with deep league roots – the defence that blunted Australia's assaults was organised by Larder – in a league town. Far more local press coverage, and a larger crowd, attended the following night's State of Origin decider when Allan Langer – acclaimed as though he were Dally Messenger's long-lost elder brother – returned to scheme a memorable Queensland victory.

It was a moment that equally epitomised much of Jason's league career. There was that capacity for the cartoonishly improbable that made the 'Billy Whizz' nickname acquired early in his career so appropriate, combining the extraordinary speed off the mark that made him such a terrifyingly effective runner from dummy-half – instant death to inattentive defences – with that pinball-like ability to switch direction without any loss of pace.

He also had the born star's instinctive sense of moment. Harry Edgar saw him playing as a primary schoolboy, and recalls him as having evident star quality even then:

> 'He was playing for Hunslet Boys Club when I first saw him; he'd be aged about 9 or 10. Later he moved on to Parkside when he got a bit older. When I saw him play for Hunslet Parkside he'd be about 12 or 13. What made him stand out were his pace, elusiveness and overall sharpness when he got the ball. The other kids couldn't pin him down, you could see it was almost effortless for him to beat defenders even in the tightest space. Jason was just like so many other kids you see at that age in Rugby League. But sadly, so many of them don't go on with the game and fulfil their potential. Jason was one who did, and of course he just got better the older he grew.'

Well under a decade later, as an 18 year old spotted by the same scout – Eric Hawley – who had discovered Ellery Hanley (Hawley's feeling of being the man who found a four-leaf clover twice may be one of the understatements of league history) and signed by Wigan on his seventeenth birthday, he scored on his senior debut against Hull. A few months later he was scoring in his first Cup Final, slicing past three defenders to the corner in a 15-8 Regal Trophy win over Bradford Northern.

A few months more, and he was in the Great Britain team, making his debut against the 1993 New Zealanders at Wembley. It was not an especially memorable match, with the opposition below normal Kiwi standards and a 36,000 crowd rather lost in the cavernous old stadium. The one imperishable memory from a 17-0 win is of Britain's debutant wing, still only 19, bemusing New Zealand's incontestably world class wing Sean Hoppe on his way to two tries in the first half-hour.

By the end of his second season his status was unquestionable. He displaced Willie Carne from the World XIII chosen by an international panel of journalists for *Open Rugby*, and his twentieth birthday was listed among the events of the day in the *Times* Court and Circular section. When he played his first Ashes series in the autumn of 1994 Laurie Daley reckoned him by far Great Britain's most dangerous player, saying: 'He's quick, and difficult to put down'.

There were two tries in the 1995 Challenge Cup final against Leeds, by now extremely aware that they should have taken more notice of the kid who used to be a ball boy at Headingley, and the Lance Todd trophy to go with them. Then came a score in the opening match of the 1995 World Cup, crashing past Tim Brasher to the corner in a 20-14 win that raised hopes that would be dashed, as so often, in the match that really mattered when England and Australia returned to Wembley for the final.

Following that he scored in each of the three Super League tests against Australia in 1997, the last charging past four tacklers, and won Great Britain's Man of the Series award. He was Britain's best a year later again against New Zealand, when Kiwi coach Frank Endacott recorded:

> 'We actually simulated training sessions for 20 or 25 minutes just on Jason Robinson. We knew exactly what he would do, but he still scored the first time he touched the ball… he would be the fastest player that I've ever seen in my lifetime over a short distance, agility wise and acceleration wise I've never seen anyone better.'

A few weeks earlier he had scored, and claimed the Harry Sunderland Trophy for Man of the Match, when Wigan beat Leeds 10-4 in the first Grand Final.

Greater even than this were his contributions to two of Wigan's most memorable days. There was the extraordinary night, in front of 54,000 fans at ANZ Stadium come to see the routine execution of the Poms, when Wigan – with a makeshift front row – beat Brisbane Broncos to take the 1994 World Club championship. He scored the vital first try and, Paul Wilson has recorded 'The overriding image everyone took home was of Robinson's incredible energy and elusiveness. The winger began the game as one of the smallest men on the pitch, in reputation as well as physique, but finished a colossus in both respects.'

Just as illustrative of his capacity to rise to the occasion was a more local event, Wigan's final match at Central Park, against St Helens, when he scored two tries and appeared at times to be ensuring single-handedly that they would not depart their historic home with a defeat against their greatest enemy.

And given his big game record, it was totally unsurprising that he should have scored England's only try in the Rugby Union World Cup Final (in which, it should be pointed out, Australia's score also came from a league convert, Lote Tuqiri).

In recalling this litany of brilliance it is easy to forget other qualities not always associated with genius – consistency and all-round competence. His scoring totals for the five Super League seasons he played for Wigan are striking – 26, 20, 17, 20 and 23. He lacks the hunger evident in the totals run up by Offiah and Hanley, but those figures point to a remarkable consistency in form and physical resilience. Those qualities were evident when all-star teams were being chosen – he was the constant factor in Super League selects during its first five seasons and invariably there or thereabouts when New Zealand and Australian writers joined with their British counterparts to pick World XIIIs.

There is little doubt that he was a better all-round winger than Offiah, who was wholly unrepentant about his somewhat perfunctory defence, arguing with some justice that his concentration on try-scoring brought his teams benefits far outweighing the occasional try that went past him. There have been few complaints about Jason – Endacott has spoken of his taking front-row forwards head on, while test coaches in both codes have been happy to play him at full-back. His only, marginal, weakness is an occasional vulnerability to the high cross-kick – as John Monie pointed out there is little he can do about being 5ft 7in – exploited by Sheffield Eagles in their 1999 Challenge Cup Final defeat of Wigan.

There is also much more to his game than remarkable physical gifts. We are so accustomed to him as a winger or full-back that it is easy to forget that he played his junior representative rugby – and came to Wigan – as a half-back who was widely expected to follow the pathway trailed by Shaun Edwards and Hanley back into the midfield decisions after serving an apprenticeship on the outsides. Anthony Sullivan, son of Clive, and one of the few wings to score as consistently as Jason in Super League, has called him 'A half-back on the wing, always doing the unexpected.'

A sharp rugby brain doubtless benefited from his early days at Wigan, where he lodged with coach John Monie and still has fond memories of sitting up watching rugby videos. Clive Woodward, who demands thinking and decision-making skills before almost any other attribute in his players, is prepared to play him at centre for the England union team.

It is tempting to ascribe some of this to Jason's evident seriousness of mind and purpose. The American magazine *Sports Illustrated* must regret that neither code of rugby matters very much to its readership, since his story is the sort of thing they do best, or at least most frequently. Scarcely a weekly issue goes by without some tale of personal redemption – a coach still trying to prove something to a tyrannically demanding father or a player doing his best to overcome a horrendously deprived childhood, more often than not held together only by the sacrifices of his mother or grandmother.

Jason's own story – the mixed-race child who grew up on a Hunslet council estate, his adolescence blighted by the violence of his step-father towards his resilient, steadfast mother, only to grow up to be a sports star, find God and attain serenity, is a natural for them. He talks in an autobiography lifted above by the norm by those descriptions of a tough childhood of going with his cousin Vinnell to the Chapeltown carnivals: 'Not once has my colour been an issue in my family,' he writes (his mother and his elder brothers are white) 'but I wanted to understand a little of my Caribbean side.' He enjoyed the spectacle, the music and the food: 'There was no other chance to get a taste of my Jamaican heritage. Perhaps I was searching for my identity. All children do that, I suppose, it was just that I didn't have a place to start from.'

There is a sense of his looking for something, but not being quite sure what, in his stories of his early days as a young star with Wigan. He fell predictably to the temptations on ready offer to a fit, good-looking young man in a glamorous job and with plenty of money in his pocket – particularly, it would appear, in the months after he signed a lucrative contract with the Australian Rugby League in 1995. This meant he had even more money, but soon realised that he really did not want to go to Australia.

Redemption, not inappropriately given that he tackled like the wrath of God, came via Tuigamala. Jason was struck by the big Samoan's calm serenity, and followed him into Christianity. The story of how he found God, renounced alcohol and clubbing and settled down as a family man who spent evenings working with deprived kids on the streets of Manchester is perhaps even better known than his on-field feats. Journalists, trapped in an endless cycle of interviews with players who are as bored by the process as they are, inevitably seize on the player with even a hint of hinterland and a different story to tell. It gives you something to talk about other than rugby, even if British journalists are less accustomed to and less comfortable with overt religiosity than their American counterparts. Jason's God would appear to be among the less merciful ones – his comments on homosexuality inspire the hope that somebody introduces him to Ian Roberts – but has served him very well.

There was also an irony in his coming to God via Tuigamala. They were initially competitors – Tuigamala beat him out of a place in the 1994 Challenge Cup Final, causing Jason to rage, uncharacteristically, that coach John Dorahy had misled him when he asked him to prove his fitness in the Alliance team – but Wigan soon resolved that conflict, albeit at the cost of an appealing nickname, by turning Inga the Winger into a centre. Inga's move from the New Zealand All Blacks rugby union squad to Wigan was seen at the time as a symbolic defeat for union, still wrestling glumly with the final vestiges of amateurism, in the same way that losing Jason would be seen as epitomising a shift in the balance of power in the opposite direction.

But then most of Jason's career has been evocative of change and conflict in league. His senior debut in 1992 coincided, more or less, with David Oxley's departure after a long spell as chief executive of the RFL, Sky Television's launch of its *Boots n'All* magazine programme and the appointment of Roger Draper, little more than a decade later the chief executive of Sport England, to the slightly less exalted post of Rugby League Development Officer for London.

In retrospect, though this may have something to do with living in London rather than Lancashire, the second half of Wigan's long hegemony is something of a blur. They were a wonderful team and we were privileged to see them. They did magnificent things, like beating Brisbane in that World Club Challenge. They were so absurdly good that they could win four trophies in a season when most players fell out with the coach. You might make the case, as Neil Tunnicliffe – later to be yet another example of league's unparalleled capacity for wasting its own talent – once did, that to be tired of Wigan was to be tired of excellence. It wasn't their fault that the rest could not match up to their standards. There was nothing objectionable about them. But nevertheless, like a people subjected to a benign and enlightened, but nevertheless unwanted, occupying army, we just wished they'd go away and give somebody else a chance.

Jason gave this trophy-eating machine some humanity. No matter how fed up you were with Wigan and just about everything about them, you couldn't dislike or be bored with him. Part of his charm was to do with his size. The appeal of the little man making fools of bigger ones is as old as Chaplin – or David and Goliath.

More than that though was a sense of joy in his play. It has always been there, whether he was the wild youngster with two pregnant girlfriends or a god-fearing family man. It is what Eric Hawley saw in the teenager playing for Hunslet Parkside: 'Here was this little lad, his legs going like pistons, big guys not knowing where to turn or how to bring him down and the crowd going potty every time he had the ball.' You can still see the child who found a refuge from the grimness of everyday life within the confines of a rugby field, a place where he could exalt in remarkable god-given gifts. That sense of delight communicates itself to the spectator, and is hard to resist. You could admire and respect Ellery Hanley, and you'd always have wanted him in your team, but there was never that sense of having fun inseparable from every time Jason played.

There were, he confirms, a few racist jibes from the terraces, but it was never clear whether it was the colour of his skin or his shirt that upset the more primitive minds. He should have been one of the major beneficiaries of the revolution of 1995. Summer rugby was designed for the open, running style in which the game is most exciting. A player hailed by *Open Rugby* as 'the new face of rugby league' as early as 1993 was a natural for greater prominence once the rest of the game caught up with *OR*'s belief in marketing.

Instead, in spite of winning the largest contract offered to any of the players signed by the ARL – who knew a good thing where they saw it – you could make the case that his league career was blighted, and ultimately ended, by the Super League revolution. His international career was put on hold – the ARL refused him permission to play in the

Super League tests of 1996 and he only played at the last moment in 1997, after Wigan had bought out his contract.

Super League was supposed to be part of an interlinked international game. Instead the game was shorn of much of its international dimension. Traditional tours were made impossible by simultaneous seasons on opposite sides of the world. Civil warfare turned Australia in on itself, and British league's choice of Super League over the ARL linked it to an organisation, which, as Dave Hadfield was to write, 'gained such a reputation for backstabbing and bullshit that it became an unsaleable brand'.

The rest of league finally caught up with Wigan. It was partly due to the improvement by Bradford, who seized the new era as nobody else did, and St Helens – who never seemed to catch on to what they were supposed to be doing off the field but developed the useful habit of invariably winning big games. It was futile to hope that Wigan could maintain the standards of the 1988–95 period, which stand with those of any team in any sport at any time, but they could certainly have been a happier, better-run and more solvent club than they were.

None of this was Jason's fault. He went on being the best and most exciting wing in rugby league. But the game, partly because of the consequences of the 1995 revolution, had few fresh worlds to conquer.

Union had known about him since 1996, when he pinballed unstoppably across, around, through, past and quite possibly under and over the Bath defence in Wigan's 82-6 victory in the cross-code match at Maine Road. It saw more of him as a key member of Wigan's winners in that summers Middlesex Sevens – given the rules of union sevens, perhaps the most predictable victory in the history of that competition.

He spent the following winter with Bath – this during the strange early years after union had gone pro and league had moved to summer, when it was theoretically possible to play all year round in the two codes, although it rapidly dawned that this was no way to a long career on either side of the divide. He did not do that badly – as he points out, he managed to keep Jon Sleightholme, a current England player out of the Bath team. Nor was he the roaring success that some had hoped, discovering that the instinctive responses that come from playing one game from childhood do not automatically transfer to the other.

That might have been that, had league had more to offer him. Or if the Rugby Football Union had not appointed a coach, Clive Woodward, in 1997 who had spent several formative years in Australia and learned to enjoy and appreciate rugby league. That spell at Bath instead became a useful apprenticeship, meaning that he went into his second spell in union knowing what to expect.

How you regard Jason's union career depends on how you regard the relationship between league and union. For those who wish to conduct a jihad, he is damned. But they'll have given up this chapter some time ago, or possibly not even started it. For the rest of us, the model was provided by Welsh union fans (perhaps the only way nowadays in which one would look to Welsh union for an example) and the way they reacted to the loss of players to league over many years. While those losses were mourned, making the league scout a demon king figure and league an unfriendly predator, opprobrium did not in general attach itself to the individual. It was understood that he had compelling reasons for going, and pride was taken in his achievements in the new game.

To identify with Jason, to want him to succeed, is in no way to genuflect to union. His remarkable talents reflect league's virtues as well as his own. He is, as the advert almost used to put it, one of our guys doing very well over there.

16

CEC THOMPSON

Cec Thompson

I am blessed with two rather posh Christian names, Theodore Cecil, and a white man's surname, Thompson, which is from the slave days. My father was a jet-black Afro-Caribbean from Trinidad who died when my mother was pregnant with me. This was in the 1926 depression and I was the fourth child in the family. We all had an orphanage upbringing: hence we were reared without a mother's love. These circumstances are mentioned in order to stress the additional problems of being coloured in a white society, plus not having an adequate education. Hence the huge debt I owe to the game of rugby league and its players, supporters, managers, directors and journalists. The relationship I have with the game is very precious. Whenever I am asked to help in any way I try my best.

Little did I know that rugby league would bail me out of a bottomless pit. The orphanage life was a nightmare. It made me dull and lifeless. Even when I became a member of the labour force life had its problems. In my first job as a moulder's labourer I was humiliated by some young men who forcibly took my trousers down to see if I was brown all over. I had no friends. Life was a matter of drifting from day to day. Imagine my feelings when a youth called out: 'Hi nigger, did you come out of your mother's backside.' Pleasantness seemed an unattainable dream.

My mother remarried in Leeds and as a consequence of this I experienced some frightful events in my life. I heard the word 'nigger' for the first time and did not know what it meant. Everyone stared and pointed at me. I never saw another black face in a city of 500,000. I walked the back streets seeking some sort of semi-escape and when I couldn't find it I ran back to the orphanage. Another important problem came to the surface when I attended school. Books and sports equipment were beyond the basic budget of my orphanage. These circumstances resulted in a mammoth handicap in my day-to-day living.

As well as having coloured skin and being void of social skills, I was an outcast in other ways. When it came to employment I was labelled an unskilled labourer. When I was evacuated along with other children to Sprotbrough from Leeds, I was the only person to be returned. My instinct told me that the host family had rejected me because of my colour. When I was playing rugby I had these memories of being treated like a second-class citizen and I would say to myself, I must prove that I am as good, or even better than white people. No one would sit next to me on public transport or in the cinema.

A chronic inferiority complex developed within me. I was bullied and tormented. I heard mothers say to their children: 'a black man will gobble you up if you don't behave.' I had so little confidence during my time as a serviceman I felt like a social outcast, as though I belonged more to the third world than the Royal Navy. Servicemen who went to countries where the population was naturally black saw serious poverty. Food, which they threw away, was collected and eaten by the destitute. These servicemen had an image of the natives as inferior to them and adopted a superior attitude, classing them as lower social creatures. Sometimes I felt they were referring to me.

During my navy days a very muscular member of the crew, a mess mate, pestered me for a few bouts of boxing. Our ship was berthed in Singapore harbour. I reluctantly obliged, even though I am a pacifist I hate such sports and he battered me all over the place. I pretended that I wasn't hurt. Years later, in 1958, when Workington were playing their twenty-third game without defeat in the semi-final of the championship, we played Saints at Knowsley Road. I let it be known if Saints were beating us easily we should let them win and save ourselves for the following week and the Wembley final. Saints took the lead when Alex Murphy dropped a goal. They were in the lead by one point with five minutes to go and I could hear Murphy instructing his team to keep us down in our defensive half. This was before the six tackle law was introduced. Two minutes from the final whistle, Norman Herbert, our tourist prop, broke the Saints defence line and passed to our winger, Ike Southward, and he scored. We had made it to two finals. Back in the dressing room there was a note for me from a Mr Mathews asking to see me. It was the same chunky guy who had pummelled me in Singapore. He was a St Helens supporter and he congratulated me.

After beating his team so dramatically, I really appreciated this fine gesture and enjoyed our meeting. What was truly amazing was the great change that had taken place within me. I was a different person: cheerful, confident and articulate. I had become very sophisticated compared to the person he once knew. I had come a long way since the time I played in the first works competition way back in 1948. Every time I see Alex Murphy I remind him of that semi-final. Self-assurance and a sense of humour have finally replaced doubt and indifference.

Due to my orphanage upbringing, I had little chance of becoming a professional person. My long-term prospect was to be a manual worker, but rugby league allowed me to escape from such a morbid ordeal. I could avoid the fate of coloured people who are trapped for life due to poor school results, uneducated parents and those with menial occupations. I was a lorry driver's mate in one of the factories in Hunslet, an industrial area of south Leeds. The selectors must have been desperate because I was chosen for the works rugby league team in a local competition. I did not want to take part in this rough sport. However, my pride was greater than my fear, so I played. My instructions were: don't kick the ball and don't pass forward. I must have done something right because within two games I was a professional rugby player. One of Hunslet's scouts had watched me play and thought that I had some talent. In no time at all I was paid £250 to sign a contract. It was 1948 when I signed – I thought I had become a millionaire. I was six foot tall, I weighed fourteen stone, had bags of energy and a dead keen attitude to succeed.

The game of rugby league changed everything for me. It brought joy and companionship. I had never experienced such precious emotion. Supporters desired my autograph; this was an embarrassment and I printed my name. To score a try once in a while brought great applause from the crowd. Young females were taking an interest in me but I was tremendously shy. The players were friendly enough. I looked forward to training sessions and match days were a big part of my social life.

During my first five seasons at Hunslet no player ever made a remark about the colour of my skin. We were like siblings, I felt honoured to be amongst them. The first season in the 'A' team we won the Yorkshire 'A' Cup. Shortly after this I suffered a fractured leg and for a time things did not go too well. But then they picked up. The players helped. Most of them were manual workers with broad Leeds accents, who wore heavy working boots, boiler suits and enjoyed drinking beer. I really enjoyed being with them.

I was now staying in Shaftsbury House, a bed and breakfast establishment. I mention this because Alf Burnell, the Hunslet captain at the time, invited me to stay at the house the night before my first international match, Great Britain v New Zealand, on 10 November 1951. Alf and Mary, his delightful wife, were extremely kind to me. Their food and accommodation were first class, but most important they were most benevolent. Friendship of this nature undermines any form of racism. I will always be indebted to rugby league and my Hunslet team-mates for the camaraderie and self-confidence they instilled into me when I was inexperienced. When I first signed to play for Hunslet for £250 I was lost for words. A regular player, Frank Watson, became my mouthpiece. I never said thank you to him until June 2001 at the annual Hunslet reunion. As I stood alone and surveyed the room, watching all the ex-players, the incident of the £250 came to mind and I immediately wrote a cheque for the same amount. Frank was astonished and refused to accept the cheque, but I insisted and he reluctantly accepted. A host of similar stories could be told. I have always tried to reciprocate, whenever possible, with those who have behaved decently toward me. I believe that such experiences have made me a better person.

Once I became an international my employing company in Hunslet invited me to the boardroom, and after congratulations and a cup of tea and biscuits I was informed of the reason for the meeting. I was told I had been promoted to inspector in order to maintain quality control at work. My income increased by fifty per cent and a white boiler suit was provided. My world gradually became larger and I moved away from unskilled work. I hailed from very humble beginnings and rugby league allowed me to climb further up the social ladder. I was now positioned between the directors and the players. I had authority and direct responsibility. The pattern of my life was changing and with it came prestige. When I was promoted to a supervisor new possibilities opened up. I now mixed with staff that were polite and well spoken, dignified and well dressed.

Following a plane trip to the South of France with the England team we were welcomed by a brass band and stayed in a delightful hotel. A new world opened up for me. The better I played the more enthusiastic I became. Success in one area lead to success in another. This developed into a regular pattern as I became older. It wasn't always easy. The evacuee situation and other wounding experiences had scarred me for life. I still have the symptoms of humility that other coloured people must feel. But, similarly, I was motivated by a continual desire to improve my social situation and lifestyle. This driving force is probably what has urged on lots of coloured players and given them a unique record of success in the game of rugby league.

It hasn't been easy. The Caribbean blood in me used to reduce my enthusiasm to play in adverse weather conditions. When mud is icy cold you lose all sense of feeling in the fingers and have to put your head in between two pairs of dirty wet shorts at sub-zero temperatures. Sometimes I was singled out and people used to misunderstand my intentions. Some teams have an aggressive – bordering on violent – player who aims at cancelling out a member of the opposition with a stiff-arm tackle. At one un-named ground I had a blinder of a game. Walking off the pitch a woman ran towards me with an umbrella and tried to hit me. The players stopped her but she spat in my face and yelled out: 'Get back to the jungle you f****** black bastard.' I went to the toilet, shed a few tears and took the stoical approach by keeping silent.

Rarely did a rugby game rouse my anger. At work it was different, now and again an employee would be deceitful and maybe steal something from the company. If it was someone to whom I had shown kindness and generosity, this would infuriate me. I am a complex character who likes his escape routes, I have developed a taste for walking the Lakeland fells, visiting the theatre, reading classical books – things I never did as a child.

You can never predict the sort of game you will have before running onto the field. We played home and away games against Workington Town Rugby League Club and I played brilliantly in both matches. Workington were in the top quarter of the league and we beat them narrowly on our own ground. I scored a try and made one and generally played well. With five minutes to go in Cumbria, we were two points behind. I broke clean away with only the full-back (Gus Risman) to beat. A team-mate was following me and as I drew Gus I passed the ball. Before passing I realised that we had done the double. A mediocre team had slaughtered a class outfit. Gus tackled me as I made the pass, smiling; sadly, the supporting player dropped the ball. I felt terrible.

When I went on the transfer list Gus snapped me up immediately at £2500. I thought I would get some bonus from the increase in my value, but the Hunslet board took advantage of my quiet nature. On reflection, the Hunslet club was rather mean, considering the tenfold increase, by not allowing me a share of the transfer fee. I was compelled to be quiet when I found myself in the company of educated people. I realise now how intellectually backward I was. This applies to several other coloured players who have remarkable talent and yet are scared of standing up for themselves. It is interesting to note what Jeremy Guscott has achieved in the other code. The financial advice he has received from his agent has allowed him to rise in the social rankings from bricklayer to male model.

Gus Risman was an icon in the rugby league world. I observed him carefully. To me he was like a god, a mercurial player: modest, dignified, quietly spoken and tastefully groomed. I wish he had been my father to guide me. I was now among stars, nearly all of whom had played representative rugby. Gus's delightful wife Ethel always made me welcome in the home. I was treated as one of the family. I learnt a host of things about being an excellent human being. I was improving in behaviour, grooming and modesty. I was delighted when I scored within five minutes of my first game. This seemed a good omen for my future.

For long-distance away matches we stayed in hotels, two to a bedroom to cut costs. Andy Key was my room-mate. We had a remarkable relationship and never encountered racial issues. Our friendship was that of blood brothers. Gus encouraged it. There was a mutual admiration between Gus and myself. I held him in awe. He gave me a great deal of credit for playing well. As a former Great Britain captain and press correspondent he thought I was playing well enough to at least have a tour trial. Here is what he wrote:

> 'Forget the colour bar, with two grand players in Boston and Thompson, our selectors should have no prejudice about colour. The playing ability of these two men would be welcome down under.'

The year I became a Hunslet player was the year my mother died of cancer and my stepfather disappeared. Within three years I had played twice against New Zealand, once against the British Empire and travelled to France with the England team. My selection came about after favourable press coverage of my play, particularly from Gus and

Eddie Waring. They were mesmerized by my vitality. Eddie was the national voice of rugby league at the time and he wrote the following:

> 'Some people scoff at the suggestion that there has ever been a colour bar so far as British test team players have been concerned. Against this I would cite the case of George Bennett, former Wigan half-back, a brilliant coloured player who was never chosen. The league's attitude may soon be put to the test however for, Cecil Theodore Thompson, the coloured Hunslet second row forward will have to be considered for international football.'

In my first game for Great Britain, the national anthem was played and our names were called out. I shed a tear and disciplined my body not to shake. My thoughts were with my mother. If only she could see me now, I thought, we could cry unashamedly. I was thinking: well mum, people can make fun of me all they want, but I've done something I am proud about.

It was unbelievable, what was to come. All of those interested in the game of rugby league, the players, supporters, officials, press, were right behind me. Moving from a large city to a remote rural town on the north west of the Lake District the celebrity status zoomed larger. Workington had a remarkable history for a young club and I was rather apprehensive about joining such an illustrious outfit. Even today the county of Cumbria has only one per cent of coloured citizens and they are mostly medics. However, I had no need to fear anything on the racial question. The club bought me a window cleaning business to supplement my rugby earnings. This opened a whole new world to me. I could now begin to understand the British class system as I gazed through working and middle class house windows. Each day became a sociological study. As a local celebrity I was also invited to the local golf and tennis clubs as well as the fell walking association. The latter led me to being involved in rock climbing. Most of the clubbable types I met were educated to sixth form and university level. Furthermore, I was asked to write a weekly article on the activities of the three clubs in the northwest: Workington, Whitehaven and Barrow. These different activities activated my mind. It was fascinating how, through rugby league, a whole new world was opening up to me. I was intuitively aware when a friendship developed with another person who was devoid of prejudice. My mind would pick this message up and I would be totally relaxed in their company.

The Risman family were of that calibre. The day that Gus passed away, his sons visited my Cockermouth home and asked me if I would say a few words from the pulpit at his funeral. I was astonished and honoured by their request. Whilst preparing this article for publication the thought crossed my mind as to why had they asked me. Later, in conversation with Bev, I asked him this question and without a moment's hesitation he replied: 'because you are one of the family.' It was a joy to hear such precious words from Bev. My talk, entitled Gentleman Gus, was published in full by the local press. The day after Gus's funeral, at a test match at Wembley, there was a minute's silence. Both teams bowed their heads in memory of Gus's outstanding contribution to rugby league. In addition to this, a postage stamp was issued in his memory. This is the side of rugby that is noble – like the way we have named a road in Hull after Clive Sullivan.

As I have progressed through my life, I am astonished at the degree to which the game of rugby league has influenced vital decisions: signing for Hunslet, moving to Workington and then going to Barrow. I enjoyed myself enormously at Workington and hold a unique place in my old club. I am the only Town player to have scored four tries in a match and two hat-tricks in a season. My forte was backing up. I had a career total of over 74 from over 300 games. In the final match of 1957–58, the Championship Final at Odsal Stadium, I damaged my left knee. This injury was to finish my playing career. I was immediately offered a coaching contract with Barrow. Feeling somewhat untrained for the post, I contacted Roy Francis, who was going great guns at Hull as their coach. I wanted his advice and some coaching tips. Roy was a fantastic person. He had great charm and an attractive personality, and was a first class after-dinner speaker, oozing with dignity and intelligence. Roy's company was mesmerizing. It was a worthwhile journey I made from the west coast to the east coast and back. He was extremely helpful, inviting me to visit his home in Beverley. I stayed overnight and he could not have been more forthcoming with his advice. His last words to me as I was leaving were: 'Call any time and don't keep your problems to yourself. We're in this together.' This unexpected invitation was good because I was entering uncharted water. What of my business, which I had expanded considerably? I was also engaged to be married. Another complication was that I had begun to think of venturing into full-time adult education. If I took the Barrow coaching post, was I heading into a cul-de-sac? After much thought and consultation I signed a two-year contract, having negotiated the broad terms that allowed me Wednesdays off to attend to my business in Workington.

On the Barrow board there was a broad mixture of drinkers, church people, egotists, social climbers, businessmen who wanted to use the club as a marketing device and dedicated directors who gave one hundred per cent, eager for their town to get some glory. I was a tennis player, as was a director on the board, and he got me enrolled in his club. The position of coach gave me authority, especially with the players. What a turn around from my first entry into the labour force as a member of the underclass and an unskilled labourer. The question was, could I cope? There were over forty players and some youngsters who lived on every word they heard from the coach's lips. But could they be moulded to my desired standard? Ready-made players were no problem but the veterans had to be watched and controlled. They are past their best and try to hoodwink you. They are required in special situations as a back-up in case of illness and when there are heavy casualties due to injuries. I even had to turn out twice myself, despite my damaged knee. Those two years at Barrow made me psychologically strong. I was involved in perusing the transfer list and trying to persuade the players on it to join Barrow Rugby league team. I would go to a player's home town and if they were married or had a girl friend I would take them out for an evening. If convenient, my fiancée, Anne, would make up a foursome. A couple of the directors had the cloth cap image and I frequently had to circumvent them, in a diplomatic manner.

Barrow is a famous shipbuilding town, accustomed to all types of foreign people. My colour did not matter. My authority was respected. I never told people what to do, I asked them and only rarely did anyone not oblige. This was a brilliant period from a social point of view. I was now becoming experienced in controlling people and using authority. It was also a period of expansion in my business. It virtually doubled in size over this period. As my contractual period drew to an end I became a different person and was much more self-assured. Players were willing to heed my advice and the whole scenario boosted my self assurance. Anne and I were given a splendid farewell dinner in the town's finest hotel. Once again, I was so very appreciative of the opportunities given to me due to my involvement in rugby league.

On my days off in Barrow I travelled to Workington early each Wednesday morning to cover business matters. I also enrolled on a one-year 'O' level English course. I was the only male on the course, the rest were young nurses. I was motivated to take this English course after I became friendly with one of my young players who was a teacher. He would talk about matters I did not understand. I asked him how he knew things I had never encountered. Here was my Achilles heel and it had come to the fore when I had first joined the labour force in 1940. Books, books, books and more books – this was what I lacked, an education. I confided in the guy how ignorant I was. He told me how I could not do anything in education without 'O' level English. This was the stimulus that took me to Workington College and set me on a course of further education, something that would dramatically change the pattern of my life for years to come.

At the end of the year I got a grade A in English 'O' level and I felt like a real-life professor. From this small but significant step forward in educational progress I developed an ambition to join the teaching profession and use this qualification to help others. This led me into seven years' full-time education, taking 'O' and 'A' levels and then a BA degree in economics, a diploma in education followed by a career change in mid-life and twenty-three years in the teaching profession. It was there I developed a profound interest in the British class structure. I was experiencing upward social mobility and, after reading Anthony Sampson's *The Anatomy of Britain*, I became an avid reader of any book on the subject of class. Sampson's book helped explain some of the simple yet very profound class differences that exist between rugby union and rugby league. These differences are less precise than they used to be but they are still useful as a way of explaining the tensions and conflicts that exist in our sport.

I am a working-class lad and however well I have done for myself in the ranks of the middle class, I am not a defector and I never wish to forget my roots. During the years I spent teaching, I never allowed the profession to obliterate the spark which the game of rugby league had ignited in me. In the period from 1948–2003 there have only been three years when I was not involved in rugby. Those years were tougher than anything I did on the rugby field. This relates to when I was taking 'O' and 'A' levels. I sat German three times and maths twice before I finally obtained the required qualifications for entry to Leeds

University. Incidentally, this is where my involvement in student rugby league began. Jack Straw, the present Foreign Secretary, was the president of the student union and he helped to get us our first grant to cover our initial expenses. Andrew Cudbertson was the principal administrator and I was president and coach from 1968 to 1969. Jack Abernathy and I spent a great deal of time developing openings to launch the game. In this period there were no coloured students playing, however most of the present teams have players of all nationalities, most notably in the Oxford v Cambridge match.

Not only was I a founder member of student rugby league whilst studying at Leeds University. On completion of my degree, I was also invited to be on the BBC advisory committee for sport and society. Whenever possible, I immediately give of myself, not for any reward but from a feeling of duty. A few years later I was awarded an honorary degree from the Duchess of Kent for services to the community. More recently I have been honoured with the Freedom of the Borough of Allerdale. These activities led people to make other requests on my time. I have given a series of lectures in Chapeltown, the black area of Leeds, advising coloured people on how to fit into British society. I have been asked to award prizes, give talks and after-dinner speeches, speak in churches and annual school speech days. In north-west Cumbria, every village has a carnival. A queen has to be selected and yours truly has obliged with these events. I also became involved in supporters' clubs and, whenever possible, have taken on an ambassadorial role beyond the game of rugby league. Through being involved in these activities, I have found that my status in the community has been held in high esteem and it has given me great personal satisfaction.

I am always happy to give help when anyone is urgently in need of assistance. On the other hand, I am also very conscious of my colour, particularly when I meet people for the first time. Friends and relatives forget that I am coloured. Somehow there is always within me a feeling that I must excel, especially before an audience. There is a degree of narcissism in most people, but in sport one can easily become narcissistic because of your achievements on the field. Crowd adulation feeds the narcissistic player even more and celebrity status is often conferred when tries are scored. The coloured player often walks tall. His unique place in rugby league gives the game a special richness.

I became a professional rugby league player by accident and had no skills. I could not have been a soccer player, where there is a necessity for particular skills. Rugby league lifted me from my miserable situation and the future for me became much more enjoyable. My new situation changed my life style in a remarkable manner. Years later, Michael Parkinson visited my Chesterfield home. He had been recommended to read my book and spent three hours discussing my life. The following week's coverage in *The Daily Telegraph* was headlined: 'Theodore Cecil Thompson, From Zero to Hero: This is Your Life'. One extract reads, 'Cec Thompson's enthusiasm for life enabled him to survive and succeed after a childhood of deprivation. If they made a film about Cec Thompson's life people would not believe it.'

Rugby league played its part in giving encouragement to lads like me, who were poor and black and thought of themselves as no-hopers. I also like to think that black players, while being only a small proportion of the total number that play rugby league, have been significant in the number of tries they have scored and the way they have scored them. I believe there is something unique about their contribution to the overall development of the game.

Black celebrities like Billy Boston, Roy Francis, Clive Sullivan, Ellery Hanley, and Jason Robinson have paved the way for hordes of black youngsters to come into the game, both amateur and professional. I played against Billy at Wembley in 1958 but had very little social contact with him, possibly due to my under-developed social skills at that time, or maybe the sheer exhaustion at the end of such a match and the disappointment of losing to Wigan.

When Ellery was at Leeds, my son was a student at the university and he worked part-time at Headingley. Several times I met him and he was always an amiable gentleman with a cheerful disposition. It was a pleasure to be in his company. On one occasion, when Ellery was playing at Wembley, my manageress's daughter was with us and asked if I could arrange for her to be photographed with him. She had travelled by coach from Workington and the bus was leaving in thirty minutes. He had sustained an injury and was having treatment on his thigh. I was never one to shun a challenge from an attractive young lady. So, holding my VIP card aloft we manoeuvred our way through numerous security personnel and arrived at the masseur's table where he was receiving treatment. I insisted he get off the table and put a towel around his middle and come outside, which he did. That young lady can now tell a few stories about that photograph.

Ellery also came to our home in Chesterfield to learn about the best and worst in rugby league. I was a director of Mansfield Marksman trying to spread the game to the Midlands area of Nottinghamshire. I was amazed at how dignified he was and the way he was handling himself among the hierarchy. I admired his self-discipline. After one Wembley final we found ourselves on the terrace of the VIP hospitality bar. We are both teetotallers. I asked him outright if he ever got any hassle regarding his colour. 'No,' he replied, 'definitely not.'

At Christmas 2000 I took my family on a ski-ing holiday to Zermatt, Switzerland. Whilst walking through the main street on Christmas Eve we saw a church with a notice outside which read *Christmas Eve Service in English*. We entered the very crowded hillside church. The vicar had been a missionary worker in Africa and half-way through his service he remarked about Jason Robinson, the Wigan rugby league wonder and how he had led a life of late-night drinking and wild women and how he had thought this was the style of living for a rugby player. Then Jason began to notice that the Samoan player, Tuigamala, went home after training and was very much a loner. Jason had a word with him and Tuigamala introduced him to the Bible, converting him to a more disciplined and worthwhile lifestyle. How incredible it was to hear this story in the middle of Europe on Christmas Eve. Rugby league gets everywhere!

If opportunities are taken, rugby league can alter a player's life. It opened the door for me to become a writer, a teacher and an entrepreneur. The game enriched my life and gave me amazing chances to meet people I would never otherwise have met. Black players in a predominately white society have, in recent years, experienced a dilution in the problem of racism. It is interesting to note the government's plan for a new anti-racist curriculum in schools. The newsreader Sir Trevor McDonald, the comedian Lenny Henry, and our own Jason Robinson are among prominent black people whose careers will be discussed in the classrooms. This initiative is entitled *Respect For All* and is aimed at preventing school children from developing racist views and encouraging them to develop a pride in multicultural Britain. The above people have become role models for racial harmony as well as making remarkable contributions to good will and understanding.

People talk about racism in sport but we have to keep the problem in context. Racism is not something I associate with rugby league and I speak as a black person. Some might say I don't know what I am talking about and that I'm out of touch. I would answer them by saying that I know the people who played the game when I was around. And those who would call them racist because of the way they expressed themselves do not understand what we thought of each other.

I will finish my story with one example. As a rugby player I was very energetic and I would chase people all day long and tackle them hard if I had to. I remember tackling Alan Prescott, the Saints prop and really flooring him. Prescott looked up at me and said: 'You black bastard, Thompson, I'll have you for that.' I don't remember the rest of the game, but I'm sure he didn't catch me.

Afterwards, as I was about to get in the bath, Prescott came up. Remember, this was Alan Prescott, the hard man of rugby league who played against Australia with a broken arm. I looked at him and there were tears in his eyes. 'I'm sorry', he said, 'I'm really sorry.' He walked away and got in the bath.

I followed him in.

About the Contributors

Phil Melling

Phil Melling is a reader in American Studies at the University of Wales, Swansea. Author of plays and biographies on rugby league, including *The Day of the African* and *Man of Amman*. Since 1978 he has been at the heart of the development of the game, particularly in the Universities and Colleges. He is the current chairman of Swansea Valley Miners RLFC and vice-chairman of the Wales Conference.

Tony Collins

Tony Collins works at the International Centre for Sports History and Culture at Leicester's De Montfort University and is the archivist of the Rugby Football League. He is the author of *Rugby's Great Split* and *Mud, Sweat and Beers* (with Wray Vamplew). He is coming to terms with the fact that it is unlikely he will fulfil his life's ambition and be selected to play at stand-off for Great Britain against Australia.

Michael Turner

Michael Turner will be 50 at the end of 2004 and for well over 40 of those years he has followed Oldham RLFC avidly. His history of the club published in 1997 was very well received by the Oldham public and RL media alike. He still lives in the town with his wife and two daughters.

Peter Lush

Peter Lush first watched rugby league in 1980 at Fulham. With Dave Farrar he founded London League Publications in 1995, and since then has written or edited books on the history of the game in London, a history of Welsh rugby league and two rugby league grounds guides.

He co-ordinated the publication of a new and extended edition of

George Nepia's autobiography in 2002, and with Dave Farrar has published 11 other rugby league books. He works as a freelance housing consultant.

Trevor Gibbons

Trevor Gibbons grew up in the Boulevard's Threepenny stand where his real first sporting hero was Clive Sullivan. He worked for the trail-blazing *Open Rugby* magazine and he now works for the BBC in Leeds.

Robert Gate

Robert Gate was the RFL's first ever archivist and is the author of many acclaimed books on the history of rugby league, included *Gone North*, *The Struggle for the Ashes*, *The Great Bev* and *The Rugby League Hall of Fame*.

Mike Rylance

The founding editor of *League Express*, Mike Rylance writes extensively for both British and French publications. His most recent book, *The Forbidden Game*, the story of rugby league's fate under the Vichy regime was a groundbreaking study of the untold history of rugby league in France.

Harry Edgar

Harry Edgar has been writing about rugby league for over 40 years after publishing his first 'fanzines' whilst still a schoolboy. He produced the ground-breaking *Open Rugby* magazine for 22 years and has had four books on rugby league published as well as contributing to numerous others.

He has had a lifetime's involvement organising and promoting (and, on more than one occasion, rescuing) the game, at both professional and amateur levels and in various parts of the world. A stand-out among his list of successful projects was creating the original Golden Boot award in 1985 for the world's leading player. He now publishes the *Rugby League Journal*, a magazine dedicated to preserving the original spirit of *Open Rugby* and keeping the game's history alive.

Dave Hadfield

Dave Hadfield has been writing about rugby league since joining the *Evening Gazette* in Blackpool in 1977. Since 1990, he has been the rugby league correspondent of the *Independent*. He also works extensively for the magazine *Rugby League World* and for *Radio 5 Live*. He has written and/or edited four books about the game, including *Up and Over: A Trek Through Rugby League Land*, which is being published by Mainstream in 2004.

Bev Risman

Bev Risman has spent a lifetime in rugby as a player, coach, administrator and 'writer'. He is a dual code international having played for England and the British Lions rugby union and captaining Great Britain rugby league. He was one of the prime movers in the growth of Student Rugby League and, more recently, the rapidly expanding Rugby League Conference.

After five years as a director of London Broncos, he has now moved from London to Cumbria and works as a consultant with the Rugby Football League on development and expansion.

Clive Griffiths

Clive Griffiths cites the biggest influences on his career as his father and his wife. His best moments the birth of his two sons. And his most memorable achievements in rugby he lists as gaining his first Welsh Rugby Union cap and becoming a Triple Crown winner. Then joining the rugby league family, coaching Wales to two World Cup semi-finals and Great Britain on the 1996 Lions Tour.

Franka Philip

This Trinidadian journalist list sport as one of her main interests. She has been living in the United Kingdom since 1999 and after seeing her first rugby league game on television in 2000 became a fan of the 13-man code.

She was totally intrigued that so many black players – especially those of Caribbean origin – have made their mark in rugby league. It was no surprise that she jumped at the opportunity to contribute a chapter to this ground-breaking publication.

About her subject Martin Offiah, she said: 'He is one of the most positive people I have ever met, and his impact on the sport will be felt for a long time to come.

Karl Spracklen

Karl Spracklen has had a stint as designer and editor of *TGG*, the magazine of the Rugby League Supporters Association, and has written for *Open Rugby, Rugby Leaguer* and the *League Express*. He has a PhD on social identity, community and the two codes of rugby, and co-authored the Leeds Metropolitan University research into the nature and extent of racism in rugby league. He currently works for *Sporting Equals*, a project within the Commission for Racial Equality.

Huw Richards

Huw Richards is the Rugby Correspondent of the *Financial Times* and Visiting Researcher at the International Centre for Sports History and Culture, De Montfort University. He has been watching and reporting league in London since 1983 and has contributed to eight earlier league books, including Dave Hadfield's *XIII Winters*.

Cec Thompson

Cec Thompson played for Hunslet and Workington and was capped for Great Britain against New Zealand in 1951. After a difficult childhood, Cec achieved great success as both a student and teacher gaining an honours degree from Leeds University and a diploma in education. After teaching in South Yorkshire, he was appointed head of economics at Chesterfield Grammar School. Since then he has received honorary degrees and numerous civic awards in recognition of his services to the community.